AF657616

EMPOWERMENT OF WOMEN IN INDIA

Myth and Reality

EMPOWERMENT OF WOMEN IN INDIA

Myth and Reality

Dr. Rahul Rai

JNANADA PRAKASHAN (P&D)
NEW DELHI

Published by :
JNANADA PRAKASHAN (P&D)
4837/2, 24, Ansari Road, Daryaganj
New Delhi-110002
Phone : 011-23272047
Mobile : 9212137080

Assisted by :
TEXT BOOK PROMOTION SOCIETY OF INDIA
4837/2, 24, Ansari Road, Daryaganj
New Delhi-110002
Phone : 011-23272047
Mobile : 9212137080

© The Global Open University, Nagaland (India)

Edition: 2009

Empowerment of Women in India: Myth and Reality

ISBN : 978-81-7139-337-4

No part of this book can be reproduced, stored in a retrieval system, or transmitted in any form, by any means, including mechanical, electronic, photocopying, recording, or otherwise, without prior written permission of the publisher.

The views expressed in this book are those of the author and not necessarily that of the publisher. The publisher is not responsible for the views of the author and authenticity of the data, in any way whatsoever.

Typesetting by :
Vardhman Computers
New Delhi-110017

Published by Mrs. S. Chowdhary for M/s. Jnanada Prakashan (P&D) Daryaganj, Ansari Road, New Delhi-110 002 and printed at Balaji Offset, Navin Shahdara, Delhi-110032.

PREFACE

Empowerment of Women in India: Myth and Reality is an outcome of our involvement in social issues since thirty years. Both of us belong to the different discipline, different profession, but working for same cause though with different ideologies and open mind.

We believe that empowerment issues require vigorous study and deep research in the era of Liberalisation, Privatisation, and Globalisation. Gender gap is increasing and other types of problems are arising out of application of modern and sophisticated technology in all fields. A large number of women empowerment issues continue to determine the nature and shape of Indian society, like most traditional societies where women are treated unequally and do not/can not enjoy, on average equality of life equal to that of men in terms of life expectancy, health, morality, access to education, access to employment, access to lawful freedoms, and the meaningful exercise of civil and political rights. Developing countries like India is doubly difficult. They have to break loose from the bonds imposed upon them by their traditional societies, and at the same time avoid the trap presented by development and modernising process in which new forms of exploitation and new problems are embedded.

Even after six decades of the post independence era have seen us struggling to find ways and means to wriggle out the acute problems entangling the process of development.

Yet, the fact remains that the country is facing acute problems of human development and the fact also remains that the women participation and consumption is exceeding low in the entire dynamics of the development process. Neglect of women, particularly girls, continues to be an issue of serious concern in India, as India and South Asia as a whole remains the only region in the world where men outnumber women in the total population. A detailed comparison of mortality rates, morbidity rates, hospital care and nutrition intake would reveal a fairly clear picture of the systematic deprivation of women in large parts of the country, especially rural India.

The processes of liberalisation, privatisation and globalisation have accentuated empowerment of women. Experiences of countries which have experimented with structural adjustment policies during 1980s clearly show that market forces unleashed by such policies without built—in safeguards result in adverse consequences for women as manifested in the increased physical violence against women on a global scale. In the Indian context, it has been found that due to the New Economic Policy and the Structural Adjustment Programmes, women have been marginalised not only economically but politically and socially too. They are in the thick of the global crisis and have to fight desperately for their survival. The thrust of new economic policy has been more on specialisation and high technology, which means that women are bound to be thrown out of their jobs. As a result the income and economic position of the women is bound to suffer.

Consequently, women's quest for equality becomes global phenomenon. Twentieth century has brought a significant change in the life of women all over the world, influencing their attitudes, values, inspirations, ways of feeling, standards of behaviour and effective participation in all walks of life. It is participation in all walks of life. It is particularly relevant in the societies, which have deep roots of patriarchy and subjugation of women. Gender division is found in all walks of life. This division influences family, division of labour, class structure and nation-states.

It was thought that if women enter the legislative/ decision- making numbers, inhibitions, that result from their minority status in these institutions, may disappear faster and giving them greater freedom to articulate their views. It may also increase the legislators' concern for the problems affecting women. A system of reservation would also help increase the degree of political modernisation of women both among the electorate and within the parties. For that political education and training in gender sensitivity is required so as to establish and lobby for women's agenda, and to sensitize both women and men to women's issues and the role of women.

CONTENTS

1

WOMEN EMPOWERMENT: AN ANALYSIS

Introduction

Women constitute nearly half of the world's population. As per as their social status is concerned, they are not treated as equal to men in all the places, through in the western countries women are treated on par with men in most of the fields, their counterpart in the East suffers from many disabilities.

The disabilities on the one hand and the inequalities between men and women on the other, have given rise to what is known "Gender problem". All one the world and particularly in South and East Asia and Africa the gender problem has assumed importance during the recent years the gender issue has become virtually a crucial point of argument. It is now widely accepted that empowerment of women *i.e.,* providing equal rights, opportunities and responsibilities to women, will go a long way in removing the existing gender discrimination. Women empowerment in contemporary Indian society in forms of their work, education, health and media images in the context of lineage, rule of residence and household chores, their participation in social and political activities, their legal status in terms of marriage, divorce and inheritance of property, seeking wealth care should be taken into consideration. Empowerment in terms of knowledge and awareness of ones own life and society including legal raise their status with regarded to the lives.

Empowerment: Conceptual Analysis

Before thinking about the empowerment of women, one needs to understand the exact meaning of the word empowerment. According to Cambridge English Dictionary empowerment means "to authorise". In the context of the people, they have to be authorised to have control over their lives. When applied in the context of development, the particular segment of population, the poor, the women, the vulnerable, the weak, the oppressed and the discriminated have to be "empowered" to have control over their lives to better their socio-economic and political conditions,. But the questions raised are, who empowers them and how to empower them? Ideally speaking no one empowers any one, the best way us 'self-empowerment', by the segments of population mentioned above are handicapped both structurally and culturally to empower themselves without any outside help and affirmative action by the State and others. But still as long as these segments of population does not make any effort at self-employment. It would be long and arduous task and process for the outsiders to empower them.

Empowering may be understood as enabling people, especially women to acquire and possess power resources, in order to make decision on their own or resist decisions that are made by others that affect them. A person may said to be powerful when he/she has control over a large portion of power resources in society. The extent of possession of various resources such as personal wealth, such as land skills, education, information, knowledge, social status, position held, leadership trains, capabilities of mobilisation.

The National Policy on Education (1986) suggested certain strategies to empower women. Accordingly, women become empowered through collective reflections and decision-making enable them to become agency of social change. The global conference on Women Empowerment (1988), highlighted empowerment as the best way of making own partners in development the Development of Women and Children in Rural Areas (DWCRA) programme was initiated as a sub scheme of the national wide poverty alleviation programme *i.e.*, the Integrated Rural Development Programme (IRDP). It aims at imparting self-reliance to rural areas through income generating skills along with group organisation skills. Keeping this in view the year 2001 was celebrated as *"The Women's Empowerment Year"*. Human resource development and empowerment of women unlock the door for modernisation of society,. Instated of remaining as passive beneficiaries, women must become active partner. Participation and control over resources of power are considered as the critical indicators in the process of development discharged women especially in rural areas, possess the least proportion of these resources and as a result they are powerless and dependent on the powerful and wealthy.

Role and Empowerment

We will now realise the vital importance of the terms such as role, empowerment and function for an understanding of society. These terms tell us how individual and groups organise themselves as well as relate to each other. Very simple, role tells us about what is expected from individuals in a particular situation. While empowerment deals with her or his expectation arising out of the situation. Similarly, a role deals with duties and obligations wile empowerment deals with rights. For instance, it is commonly assumed that the most is a women, a wife a cook, a teacher of her children and daughter-in-law all rolled in one. What happens when the mother is also the principal of the local village school? Not only does she have to deal with a range of roles and empowerments, but also with he tensions that may raise out of her roles mother and her role as an administrator.

"Woman reposes more closely on the central surface of life, while man hunts it in the boundaries of existence, always concerned to overcome, and in the last analysis, to kill. A woman has a secret alliance with eternal life and man with the principle of death. Woman wants to embrace the contradiction of life and to reconcile them in the act of degree so. Man on the other hand release the tension between opposites by annihilating one of the sides, the one he finds unpleasant. He seeks the solution not in love and reconciliation, but in overcoming and annihilation. He has a militant and not an erotic manner.

The male principle borne of isolation, makes solitude thermal, seeks being in itself and disturbs life as a wholes his being is battle and self service, his will-to-life is concerned with ascertaining his own person or overthrowing that of the stranger until the motive of salvation kindles with in him. Woman with her sustaining constitutions is at one and is harmony with the basis of the world. But man wants to change the world to bring it forward to overcome it".

Women's Empowerment in Contemporary India

Contemporary Indian society has been exposed to the broad processes of social transformation, agricultural modernisation and economic development, urbanisation and globalisation. However, these processes have generated regional imbalances, sharpened class inequalities and augmented the gender disparities. Hence, women have become critical symbols of these growing imbalances. All these have affected adversely the various aspects of women's empowerment in the contemporary Indian society.

The family and women's work is not enough to say that any society consists of men and women. It is equally important to look at how the two groups of people interact, as well as at the role and exceptions each group has of the other. Such roles and exceptions are a product of the stereotypes of each gender. By gender stereotype, we mean attributes and qualities commonly associated with a gender.

Thus, the first idea on gender role differences, which a child acquires, is that of women of one's family marrying and leaving their homes to leave with different groups of people. Secondly, men appear to exercise far greater influence in decision making and are far more visible and audible than their wives. Third most of the tasks within the home are done by the mother, grand mother, sisters and so on. At meal times they carry food to the fields for the men. All these tasks, which consume time and energy, are not counted as work and there is no payment involved.

In western countries, women's groups, politicians and other concerned individuals have been arguing for payment for housework and childcare. In India, the question of payment for household jobs has not really been an important issue or demand. As we shall see, there are many other issues, which require urgent attention. At the same time, it is important for us to remember that non-payment should not also mean non-recognition. The fact that women are expected to perform all these tasks as a part of their conventional roles and on special merit is awarded to them for these tiring and tedious jobs.

As per to 1981 figures 19.7 per cent Indian women were recorded as paid workers. Of whom over 87 per cent were in the unrecognised or informal sector of the economy. The work participation rate woman in 1991 and 2001 was 22.3 and 25.7 per cent respectively. The increase in the work participation of women during the decade 1991-2001 is mainly due to the increase in the proportion of marginal workers (6.3 per cent to 11 per cent) in total female workforce. It is held by many observation of Indian economy that without women's paid or unpaid labour the Indian agricultural economy would not be able to function. In the informal sector, there is no legal redressal for problems; no maternity or other leave benefits and little security of service. Working long hours as domestic servants, stitching clothes for the garment export industry, working on the assembly line of small electronics manufacturing units or the *beedi*, tobacco, cashew nut factories. A woman lives in fear of retrenchment, exploitation and low wages.

According to Maithreyi Krishna Raj, though women were concerned about continuing their jobs, they were not looking for better prospects nor have they begun with a long-range carrier strategy. Once in a job, women rarely attempted to acquire further qualifications was by no means clear-cut. T.S. Papola's study of working women, which covered a range from those in supervisory post in industrial establishments to unskilled workers, showed that women were more different than men in respect of their promotion prospects.

Papol's study showed that women were discriminated against at the time of promotions tended to be crowded into lower status electrical and primary school jobs. They were rarely promoted to executive and supervisory posts. As regards employment and promotion to supervisory category, male employers defend themselves by pointing out that women did not come forth to be recruited or promoted.

In the urban areas, the working class, and men in particular have a wide range of job options available to them. The study by Leela Kasturi reveals that when unemployed weavers from Tamil Nadu migrant to Delhi, the women folk found jobs only as domestic servants. While men become mechanics, cooks or drivers. The shift in residence meant a severance with an established way of life and the support of the extended family.

For the majority of working class women, a job is essential. In relation to the limited chances for occupational mobility, when men and women work in the same occupation, female tasks are often the more arduous and time consuming. For instance, in paddy cultivation they spend long hours in sowing, weeding transplanting. In Kerala, the extraction of the cashew seed from a corrosive liquid is women's work. Again when both sexes do identical jobs, women often get paid less than man. Protests are rare, apart from ignorance of legal and other rights; there is a fear of exploitation and sexual harassment by the landlord or contractor.

Irrespective of social class there is at the level of belief, widespread commitment to the nation that a women's job just not interfere or compete with her primary role of wife and mother. There is also concern with her physical safety and the respectability of the occupation. Clearly, working class familiar are far less able to ensure circumstances.

The principle of gender equality has been basic to Indian thinking for over a century; *i.e.*, even in the pre-Independence period a thought was given to this principle through various social reformers like Rajaram Mohan Roy, Vidhyasagar, Pandita Ramabai, Mahatma Phule, Agarkar, Ranade, Veeresalingam Pantalu, Sri Narayana Guru, etc. It was in 1931 that the Indian National Congress (INS) adopted gender equality as a guiding principle in the Fundamental Rights Resolution. The Constitution of India adopted in 1950, not only grants equality to women, but also empowers the State to adopt measures of affirmative discrimination in favor of women and it also imposes a fundamental duty on every citizen to uphold the dignity of women, which, in reality is still an illusion.

Despite the above provision within the Constitution, it was not until 1971 that the Indian Government gave much thought in actuality towards the principle of gender equality and even this, only after the request from the U.N. The Govt.

of India appointed a Committee on the Status of Women in India (CSWI) to examine the position of women in the changing socio-economic context. The Committee in its report (1975) entitled "Towards Equality" recommended and stressed the need for special temporary measures to transform the de-jure equality guaranteed by India's Constitution into de-fact equality. As a consequence one could see that the shift in recognition to women and the welfare measures regarding women were reflected in the VI Five Year Plan (1980-85). In 1985, under the Human Resource Development (HRD) Ministry, a separate Department of Women and Child Welfare was set up.

The year 1993 witnessed two constitutional amendments *i.e.,* 73rd and 74th, which guaranteed one-third representation to women at Local Self-Government (Rural as well as Urban). Despite the efforts of the Government in leading the women into the national development process, there are still many problems like marginal employment, low level of skill, problem of being excluded from decision making, poverty, lack of education, training and information, patriarchal impact etc. With such challenges the women's movement has been asking for more space in the decision-making process at all levels: economic, social as well as political. In this context, it is important to highlight three important issues undertaken by the Government of India, *i.e.,* (1) The new economic policy, highlighting the impact on women. (Economic status), (2) The Uniform Civil Code, discussing what is it that is being asked for? (Social status), (3) The proposal of one-third reservation for women in the House of People and State Legislative Assemblies, (Political status).

New Economic Policy

The New Economic Policy (N.E.P) was introduced primarily due to the 1990s fiscal position of the Central Government which came under severe strain because of sustained borrowing over several years. The worsening fiscal deficits of 1980s had weakened the micro-economic situation, and the Gulf War of 1990 precipitated the balance of payment crisis. The growing political instability at the turn of the decade into the 1990s further contributed towards the collapse of international confidence in the ability of Government to manage the economy. This led to a drying up of the market for external commercial loans in 1990/1991 and capital outflow of Non-Resident Indian (NRI) deposits.

Despite emergency borrowing from Reserve Tranche and the compensatory contingency financing facility of the International Monetary Fund (IMF), the level of foreign exchange reserves dropped precipitously to a little over $4 billion in June 1991, barely sufficient to finance imports for a fortnight. All these factors compelled the Congress Ministry to formulate a new economic policy on 1st June 1991. With the introduction of new economic reforms, the Government of India accepted liberalisation, privatisation and globalisation. Basically, in the reformed economic system, liberalisation broadly meant reducing import duties, giving more scope for foreign investment, lessening the control, reducing the 'Quantitative' restrictions on the imports, privatisation, lessening state intervention and making the economic system more free.

Taking into consideration, the period prior to the entry of the new economic policy, the State played an important role concerning the problems of women. Most of the gender issues pertained 'to oppression within the family or outside to which redress was sought through the intervention of the State. Legal reforms in criminal law, particularly against dowry, rape, domestic violence and of recent regarding the property rights along with laws for equal wages, maternity protection, etc. led to considerable progress. Although the progress achieved was not up to the expectations of the women's movement, the very actual existence of the rights and guarantees meant that an appeal could be made to an enforcing authority. Thus prior to 1990, state intervention led to much progress in the status of women although not as anticipated. The pre-reform model of development, although supported by a number of policies, was too half-heartedly established, e.g., subsidies took care of the poorer but not always all the poor; eradication of poverty was never achieved, despite wide network of schools and Public Health Centres; basic health services remained unattended and complete literacy is miles away.

With the process of liberalisation and privatisation of the economy, it is argued by the feminist that the new policies will further marginalise the majority of women through reduction in their employment, reduction in their family resources, withdrawal of subsidised food, and abandonment of preferential and affirmative policies like lower interest rates for the unorganised sectors and poor women. Besides, with privatisation of educational and health institutions, the high cost would deprive a large number of women and poor of education and health facilities. Female labour would be exploited by the free market economy in areas where women are at a disadvantageous position. With such an economy, can a women avail herself of and afford education with the tremendous cost that goes along with it? Although the old policy was not so good either, from the point of view of the poor and women, it did achieve a few things for both of these categories.

Securities and guarantees are given in the organised sectors where one can find only 6 per cent of women working. The organised sector has done much to draw women out of the family and household circumstances. It has also given a sort of independence to women under this sector but they meet with problems regarding their future career advancement. Further rapid changes in technology, automation and curtailment of employment has immensely reduced the opportunities of women to work in an organised sector. Transportation, communication and financial services are areas, besides insurance, post-telegraph, tourism, industries, and banks, where women find opportunities. But here it seems to be open only to women with education. Women are also concentrating on information handling, secretarial and clerical jobs. This being a small group they do not enjoy the same status with their male counterparts in the trade unions or associations. Most of the union or association movements have systematically neglected the women's interest e.g., the insensitivity of trade unions towards women problems has forced some of the activists to move and establish their own organisations like SEWA (Self-Employed Women's Association) split from the textile labour association of Ahmedabad (Gujarat).

Taking into consideration the above two areas, women had a ray of hope in the organised sector under the public enterprises with a definite scope for educated women to enter into the work force and be a part of national development in the economic front. In the unorganised sector, with a large number of women toiling in traditional roles, women are going to face acute insecurity in the era of privatisation. The 6 per cent women workforce in the organised public sector under the old economic policy is going to face a sharp decrease under the New Economic Policy. With the free trade, particularly in the agricultural field as construed in the GATT, denial of freedom to small farmers follows as a natural concomitant, but it will also hit the women hard. The GATT policies are aimed at further marginalising the household and domestic food economies in which women play a significant role. It also leads to setting up multilateral trade organisations with which World Bank and IMF (International Monetary Fund) will form the centre of world governance.

The GATT is the platform where the capitalist patriarchy's notion of freedom as the unrestrained right of men with economic power to own, control, and destroy life is articulated as 'free-trade.' But for the Third World, and for women, freedom has different meanings. In what seems the remote domain of international trade, these different meanings of freedom are a focus of contest and conflict. Free trade in food and agriculture is the concrete location of the most fundamental ethical and economic issues of human existence of the present times. It is here that Third World women have a unique contribution to make because in their daily lives they embody the three colonisations on which modern patriarchy is based, the colonisation of nature, of women and of the Third World?

Reservation Policy for Women in Lok Sabha and Legislative Assemblies

The most important question raised is regarding women empowerment by political participation which is expected to come through reservations, where opinions diverge. The delay in the acceptance of the proposal of 33.33 per cent reservation for women in Lok Sabha, first presented in September 1966, is caused by various factors. The basic fears raised are (i) only elite women will get in, (ii) the proxy women *i.e.,* wife, daughter, daughter-in-law, sister, sister-in-law, etc. would be put up as candidates. But some believe positively that 33.33 per cent of women's presence would definitely improve the state of affairs in the Government.

While such fears are raised and debated in the context of reservation for women in the Lok Sabha, why was there no such outcry over the 73rd and 74th Amendments to the Constitution, providing reservation at the level of Local Self-Government—both rural and urban? As the study points out most of the women elected at local levels *i.e.,* urban and rural, could be easily dominated and handled by their male counterparts, which it is felt, may not be so easily done at the national level. Moreover, one third means nearly 163 men losing their power position to women in the Lok Sabha considerable enough to effect the decisions made in the House. This points towards the patrilineal tendency of providing space to women in politics at the lower rungs of the ladder without any debate. The politics of reservation could be read in between the lines of the provision of Reserved Constituency by rotation. There has been an optimistic approach of many feminist analysts that reservation has helped at least to bring up a woman who never dreamt of contesting election. The fears raised today, in the case of Lok Sabha reservation, are true for Local Self-Government level, too. The 'daughter, wife, sister, phenomena' has been working even in the third round of election of Panchayats (elected body for village administration) or Corporation due to the rotation proviso. A survey showed that only one per cent of women were elected for the second time without reservation. The Woman Sarpanch (Head Woman of village by election) again, to the extent of 99 per cent were proxy, governed by the male members within the family, caste and community. This raises a question as to whether women elected in such a manner really represent women issues and achieve the objectives of the reservation policy? The feminists are confident of having a qualitative change in the system with the introduction of women in large numbers. This is a basis for them to argue that there would be less corruption, less criminalisation and less of all those negative tendencies in the system. In doing so they neglect/ contradict themselves on account of accepting the gynocentric thesis of equality and equal human traits.

Further, the fear of elite women upper caste/class getting in political positions is also not unrealistic. This could be supported with the small survey that was conducted which showed that as large as 80 per cent of working women in organised sector belonged to upper caste/class. This is associated with the opportunity of education for women. It indicates that the 33 per cent of reservation for women in job is carried away by the upper caste/class category. Hence the fear of female elite class domination cannot be ruled out. This leads to another question as to whether the women we elect under reservation really represent the middle class and the grassroot rural women. The argument regarding representation of women on caste basis particularly to Other Backward Community (OBC) women being denied by the set of women politicians ticks the mind of an unbiased—nonpartisan analyst. Although political parties by themselves are naturally not making any effort to increase the number of women membership or women candidates for election, it has been astonishing to see the very little effort expended by women members of almost all the parties to increase the women membership of their respective parties as well as to influence the party to allow women members contest. The 1998 election had just 292 women contesting, which was half of 1996 election where 547 women had contested. Reservation will definitely make a lot of difference but, again, as at the Local Self-Government level, even if caste lines are accepted, there is still a doubt that the representatives really represent their women community from all strata.

Hence, it is obvious that reservation is necessary for women as an opportunity to achieve equal status by entering into the decision/policy making arena. But the above said discrepancies cannot be ruled out. This is once again a major issue before the women's movement, which needs to be sorted out taking into consideration the socio-religious cultural implications on one hand, as well as the objective to be achieved, *i.e.*, empowerment of women on the other. It is rather a delicate issue to be dealt with without providing fundamentalists/communalists as well as patriarchs the opportunity to divide women along caste/class lines. The caste-class factor, the traditional social hierarchical system which dominated the male politics, is bound to influence the set up of politics.

The women's movements today have to formulate a strategy within the sociocultural framework without disintegrating the women community. It becomes necessary to create conditions so that women would be able to forge alliances and platforms cutting across party/caste/class barriers on issues concerning women. Unfortunately, although all political parties, despite being positively unanimous regarding the reservation positively, are not supporting it when it comes to the floor of the House in the Parliament. It is being opposed and delayed—delay means denial.

The above three areas that have been discussed show that the New Economic Policy, particularly the process of privatisation and liberalisation, has had a very negative impact on the developmental process of women, especially in agriculture and in the unorganised sector. The Government of India needs to bridge up the lacunas that are bound to widen if no conditions in private sector are laid down. The reservation policy needs to be extended to the private sectors to equal the facilities that women in public sector enjoy.

The Uniform Civil Code, too, has become a political issue and since all personal laws are discriminatory against women it is doubtful as to whether changes within personal laws to the extent as expected by women, will be made.

This speaks of the inability to breakout of the caste-community bondage that has been playing havoc in the society, and is reflected even in the case of political reservation for women in the Lok Sabha and State Legislative Assemblies. There has been a demand of Other Backward Communities reservation for women, which needs separate amendment to the Constitution. But then there seems a point in the political parties' (Male counterparts) argument that Other Backward Communities would not be adequately represented just by General or Scheduled Tribe/Scheduled Caste women. As there is a need for Scheduled Tribe/Scheduled Caste women, there is a demand for OBC women reservation, too. This is a new trend emerging within women's movement, reflecting the need to address women's identity as members of their community, class, caste or religious group with a growing sensitiveness to India's diversities within her unity.

WOMEN EMPOWERMENT IN INDIA

The concept of gender equality is a common concern all over the world. The same has now acquired new dimensions with the advent of Information and Communication Technology (ICT). The ICT has a potential to bring development for a nation. It can reduce trade distortions, eliminate poverty, empower weaker segments including women, etc. The same is, however, possible only if a nation follows sound ICT strategies and policies. We have to set our priorities to those areas where we are lagging far behind. One such area is the unequal access of ICT to women.

Information and Communication Technologies comprise a complex and heterogeneous set of goods, applications and services used to produce, process, distribute and transform information. Traditional technologies continue to be important for large numbers of people around the world, particularly in rural areas. However, new technologies have a vast potential for empowerment which needs to be fully exploited. Over the past decade, there has been a growing understanding that these technologies can be powerful instruments for advancing economic and social development through the creation of new types of economic activity, employment opportunities, improvements in health-care delivery and other services, and the enhancement of networking, participation and advocacy within society. ICT also have the potential to improve interaction between Governments and citizens, fostering transparency and accountability in governance.

While the potential of ICT for stimulating economic growth, socioeconomic development and effective governance is well recognised, the benefits of ICT have been unevenly distributed within and between countries. The term "digital divide" refers to the differences in resources and capabilities to access and effectively utilise ICT for development that exist within and between countries, regions, sectors and socio-economic groups. The digital divide is often characterised by low levels of access to technologies. Poverty, illiteracy, lack of computer literacy and language barriers are among the factors impeding access to ICT infrastructure, especially in developing countries. Another hindrance pertains to ICT is lack of its access to women.

Gender Equality and ICT

While there is recognition of the potential of ICT as a tool for the promotion of gender equality and the empowerment of women, a "gender divide" has also been identified, reflected in the lower numbers of women accessing and using ICT compared with men. Unless this gender divide is specifically addressed, there is a risk that ICT may exacerbate existing inequalities between women and men and create new forms of inequality. If, however, the gender dimensions of ICT—in terms of access and use, capacity-building opportunities, employment and potential for empowerment—are explicitly identified and addressed, ICT can be a powerful catalyst for political and social empowerment of women, and the promotion of gender equality.

In the past few years, the global community has seen the "gender issue" come onto the agenda. Despite economic and socio-cultural barriers to women's use of Information and Communication Technology (ICT), when women are able to use them productively, they can substantially improve their lives and increase their income. They have proved useful in: health care delivery; distance education; enhancing rural productivity through access to market information and access to finance; promoting empowerment and participation in national and international policy processes; improving service delivery by governments; improving environmental monitoring and response systems; and facilitating environmental activism. In general, women make up a small percentage of internet and computer users. This is changing in some countries, generally those which have greater levels of development and gender equality. ICTs are potentially an important knowledge resource for women, but a focus on access is insufficient. We need also to consider what kind of information is being accessed? Who produced it? Who can use it? What is it used for? In sum, we need to view women not as passive recipients of information, but active knowledge and technology developers.

To orient ICT projects so that they address these areas, ICT project planning and implementation for social development and gender equality must take place in a context which consists of five main components:

(a) Creating an enabling environment which supports and encourages strategies to promote women's equal access to and opportunity to benefit from ICT projects, as well as creating a regulation and policy environment which supports women's use of ICTs;

(b) Developing content which speaks to women's concerns and reflects their local knowledge, and which is of value for their daily lives, business enterprises, and family responsibilities;

(c) Supporting increased representation of women and girls in scientific and technical education, and using ICTs to promote their increased participation in education at all levels;

(d) Promoting increased employment in the IT sector for women and the use of ICTs for women's SMEs.

(e) Implementing e-governance strategies which are accessible to women; and promoting women's lobbying and advocacy activities.

International Treaties and Conventions

The 20th century has witnessed the upsurge of women empowerment movement universally. The Universal Declaration of Human Rights (1948) reaffirming faith in the fundamental Human Rights, in the dignity and worth of the human person, and in the equal rights of men and women, contemplated the entitlement of all cherished freedoms to all human beings without any distinction of any kind, including discrimination based on sex. The World Conference on Human Rights at Vienna in 1993 had declared the human rights of women and the girl child to be "inalienable, integral and indivisible part of universal human rights" and eradication of any form of discrimination on the basis of sex, is the priority objective of the international community. The Convocation on the Elimination of All Forms of Discrimination Against Women (CEDAW), 1979 is the United Nations' landmark treaty marking the struggle for women's rights. Described as the Bill of Rights for women, it spells out what constitutes discrimination against women and propagates strategies based on "non-discriminatory" model, so that women's rights are seen to be violated, if women are denied the same rights as men.

For centuries, women in this country have been socially and economically handicapped. They have been deprived of equal participation in the socioeconomic activities of the nation. The Constitution of any country is supreme law of the land and is followed absolutely, subject to the limits provided in the solemn document itself. So much is the importance of the Constitution that if a statutory law is in conflict with it, the same would be "unconstitutional" and void in nature. The Constitution is organic and living in nature. It is also well settled that the interpretation of the Constitution of India or statutes would change from time to time. Being a living organ, it is ongoing and with passage of time, law must change. New rights may have to be found out within the constitutional scheme. It is established that Fundamental Rights themselves have no fixed content; most of them are empty vessels into which each generation must pour its contents in the light of its experience.

The attempt of the court should be to expand the reach and ambit of the Fundamental Rights by process of judicial interpretation. There cannot be any distinction between the Fundamental Rights mentioned in Chapter III of the Constitution and the declaration of such rights on the basis of the judgments rendered by the Supreme Court. Thus, horizons of Constitutional law are expanding. Further, it is presumed that the Parliament intends the court to apply to an ongoing Act a construction that continuously updates its wordings to allow for changes since the Act was initially framed. While it remains law, it has to be treated as always speaking. This means that in its application on any day, the language of the Act though necessarily embedded in its own time, is nevertheless to be construed in accordance with the need to treat it as a current law.

Thus, we cannot allow the dead hand of the past to stifle the growth of the living present. Law cannot stand still; it must change with the changing social concepts and values. If the bark that protects the tree fails to grow and expand along with the tree, it will either choke the tree or if it is a living tree it will shed that bark and grow a living bark for itself. Similarly, if the law fails to respond to the needs of changing society, then either it will stifle the growth of the society and choke its progress or if the society is vigorous enough, it will cast away the law, which stands in the way of its growth. Law must therefore constantly be on the move adapting itself to the fast-changing society and not lag behind. Thus, for conferring the strongest protection and to emancipate women, the provisions of the Constitution should be interpreted liberally and in a purposive manner.

The Constitution of India recognises women as a class by itself and permits enactment of laws and reservations favouring them. Several articles in our Constitution make express provision for affirmative action in favour of women. It prohibits all types of discrimination against women and lays a carpet for securing equal opportunity to women in all walks of life, including education, employment and participation. Article 51 of the Constitution obligates the State to honour international law and treaty obligations. Our natural obligation to renounce practices derogatory to the dignity of women has been elevated to the status of fundamental duty by Article 51-A.

The Constitution of India recognises equality of the sexes and in fact provides for certain provisions under the Chapter on Fundamental Rights more favourable to women but in actual practice they are observed more in breach than in compliance. In our society the freedom of women to seek employment outside the family is a major issue. This freedom is denied in many cultures and this attitude in itself is a serious violation of women's liberty and gender equality. The absence of this freedom militates against the economic empowerment of women, with many other deleterious consequences.

Thus, these Constitutional ideal have by and large remained unaccomplished and we have to cover a long distance before the benefits of ICT can be reaped by women effectively. One of the ignored ICT issues in India is the "gender sensitisation" that must be adopted while formulating and implementing the ICT policies in India. It is commonly understood that men and women understand and use computers and internet differently. Thus, the policy decisions must make sufficient provision for adopting itself with this aspect. Within India also we must understand that the training, use and adoption of ICT must be "gender neutral". For a gender neutral technology we have to first place the women on an equal platform. They cannot be put on an equal platform till they have equal capacity and opportunity to use ICT. They cannot also effectively use ICT till their "feedbacks and concerns" are incorporated in the National Policies including the E-governance plans.

The position is worst when it comes to women that also rural women. In our society, whether they belong to the majority or the minority group, what is apparent is that there exists a great disparity in the matter of economic resourcefulness between a man and a woman. Our society is male-dominated both economically and socially and women are assigned, invariably, a dependant role, irrespective of the class of society to which she belongs. It must be appreciated that a nation that does not respect its women cannot be described as a civilised nation at all. Such a nation cannot grow and develop and will ultimately perish due to its own rudimentary and tyrannical dogma. Thus, the national consensus should concentrate on betterment of women by suitably empowering them. The plight of the women, however, cannot be improved till they are duly represented in the "power structure" of the nation. In a democratic country, the voice of women can be heard only to the extent they are sharing the power structure in the supreme governance of the country. Thus, ICT can play a major role in women empowerment if they are provided employment opportunities at the village level after providing them suitable training. We have to open more village kiosks so that greater women participation can be there. This cannot happen till we first make the e-governance and ICT strategies and policies transparent and accountable. Mere computerisation is not e-governance.

The advent of ICT has changed the global scenario and many unexplored areas are now open for encashment. It is for us to utilise the benefits to the maximum possible extent. The best part about ICT is that it is capable of various adjustments as per the requirements of the segment using the same. The same can also be adjusted as per the needs and requirement of women in India. So much so that it can be operated from every home irrespective of its location. This means that even the traditional and orthodox families can allow the women to participate and use ICT from their respective homes. In India, there is an abundance of "women entrepreneurs" who are capable of making their mark at the global level. However, the awareness and facilities are missing drastically. The national policies and strategies have not yet considered this unexplored potential pool of intellectual inputs. With simple training and awareness programmes we can make a big difference. Further, we can also encourage the establishment of "Small and Medium Enterprises" (SMEs), Small Scale Industries (SSIs), etc. The need of the hour is to show a positive will to achieve that much needed purpose.

REFERENCES

Chiranjeevulu, T. (2003). *Empowering Women through Self-Help Groups-Experiences in Experiment*, Kurukshetra, March.

Gopalan, Sarala (2002). Towards Equality—The Unfinished Agenda. *Status of Women in India*, National Commission for Women, New Delhi.

Kapadia, Karin (2002). The Violence of Development: The Politics of Identity, Gender and Social Inequalities in India. *Kali for Women*, New Delhi.

Krishnaraj, Maithreyi (2002). Growth and Rural Poverty. *Economic and Political Weekly*, September 21.

Manohar, Sujatha (2002). Women's Empowerment—Law and Gender Justice. Paper Presented in the International Women's Day, 8th March 2001. Department of Women and Child Development, New Delhi.

Sarkar, C.R. (2004). *Poverty, Education and Economic Development.*

2

FREEDOM STRUGGLE AND EMPOWERMENT

The political role of women as a subject for research is of recent origin in India.[1] It is significant that there are so few studies of women's role in the nationalist movement or of the implications—social or political—of their momentous entry into the public sphere. Important works on the national movement mostly fail to examine the significance of women's participation in the struggles.[2] Analysis in this area so far has received insufficient attention in histories of India both before and after 1975 when the need to study women's role in history began to be acknowledged worldwide. One searches in vain for an adequate study of women's participation in nationalist historiography.[3]

Studies published between 1968 and 1988 do touch upon various aspects and dimensions of women's participation in the national struggle for freedom. There are some factual accounts: most standard histories of the national movement mention women's entry into the Civil Disobedience Movement.[4] Some historians have noted the emancipatory effects of such participation.[5] Women in revolutionary terrorism have also been described[6] and women have been occasionally discussed as a political nuisance.[7] Some accounts of contemporaries who participated in the movement refer to the strength and broad base acquired by it as a whole through women's participation.[8]

It is important to note that in general, information on women in the work of modern Indian historians writing in English prior to 1975 relates to women in elite sections of society. The lives and conditions of the large majority of women, or their response to changing historical forces have consistently been unexplored and thus marginalised in history.[9] Apart from a few autobiographies of women leaders, mostly from elite groups, we know little about the lives, the beliefs or the social background of the mass of women who entered the movement in the different regions, as virtually no work has been done in this area, except in the last few years.

Most of the accounts of women's role in the national movement are descriptive not critical or analytical. They do not examine either the reasons or the implications of this spontaneous upsurge of political activity by women of all classes. The dominance of elite perspectives is best demonstrated by the efforts of most historians to link women's participation in the struggles with women's education or the social reform movement, ignoring the large number of women from the peasantry and the working class, including prostitutes, who took part in the various struggles directly, or the thousands of housewives mostly mothers and wives who provided indirect support by shouldering family responsibilities when their men went to jail or got killed. It is surprising that the socioeconomic impact of colonialism on women's lives and beliefs, turning them into sources of radical inspiration for the youth of East Bengal recorded by a British administrator as early as 1907[10] and repeatedly mentioned by Gandhi-has received so little attention from historians so far.

There are some exceptions to the general pattern; for instance, Bipan Chandra,[11] who has discussed the women's movement, women's participation in peasant and trade union movements along with women's role in the freedom struggle. After Independence, state-sponsored directories of freedom fighters including women were compiled in Andhra Pradesh, Delhi, Karnataka, Gujarat, Punjab, Tamil Nadu and Uttar Pradesh. In general, the approach in these was laudatory and enumerative rather than analytical. Where analysis was attempted, it tended to be brief. Some references to women freedom fighters are scattered in miscellaneous sources all over India and in works on Gandhi.

Existing research on women and Indian nationalism can therefore be described as non-comprehensive, cursory in nature, and generally a "history from above".[12] Proper reconstruction of this period of Indian history, with a special focus on women's political participation and the women's movement which was a concomitant part of and yet separate from the national movement, is now essential for a reinterpretation of these movements which were entangled with one another. More local and regional studies are required to provide in-depth data, but macro-level analyses also need to be pushed forward to eliminate simplistic generalisations that continue to be prevalent. For example, better explanations are required for regional variations in the level and nature of women's participation than the single factor of female literacy.

The relevance of a study of women's role in the national movement cannot be over estimated for either the discipline of history or the study of women. But where do we start and what are our sources? There is a scarcity and unevenness of material in terms of region and time periods. Recent works on the women's movement and women's political participation have used a multiplicity of published and unpublished archival records but we cannot say that such sources have been fully utilised. Government documents form a major source of information. Including secret police and intelligence reports, not all of which have been analysed. Many private collections are still not open to scholars. Some sources of data are outside this country.

Records of some political groups were destroyed by police action or otherwise through riots or careless maintenances.[13] Some were ad hoc in nature or not systematic.[14] We maintain that adequate search for and use of even conventional sources still remains to be done systematically.[15]

Analysis of the records of women's organisations has already yielded valuable insights into the national movement, and the attitudes of the British Government, the bureaucracy and political elites as perceived by the leadership of the women's movement. It is to be expected that elite women's organisations would have maintained detailed records.[16] Many journals in India and Britain of this period (1857-1947) also contain highly useful material, with predictably more information for some regions than others. Other rewarding sources such as the journals of women's organisations which were mouthpieces and/or forums in which debates on women's issues were conducted; women's autobiographies: collections of speeches and essays by women leaders (e.g. Besant, Naidu, Cousins); regional literature, reflecting variations in social perception and the response of specific societies and communities to the movements; proceedings of local women's associations etc. would certainly need to be analysed in this massive effort.

Oral histories and reminiscences of women in the national movement are to some extent available on tape in some archives. Much more needs to be done in this respect. Interviews with family members of women who participated in the national as well as the women's movement, and in local women's associations could form a valuable source of data. If women who participated sponatoneously in the struggles refuse to or find it painful to talk about that period now,[17] what does that mean? Or when lower middle class women from small towns tell us that their mothers knew and encouraged or covered up their activities in revolutionary movements[18] how should we interpret that fact?

So many questions need satisfactory answers and some answers lead to further questions:

1. How did participation affect the women's families and the women as individuals? Did it affect their position in the family? If not, why?
2. What were the changes that were brought into their lives as a result? Did social values change? How did society react then and later?
3. What were the facilitating factors—were they common to all women participants in all regions? Why do most accounts mention male encouragement, and so few the attitude of other women, or children in the family?
4. What were the social strata of the women in each region to which the participants belonged? Who took care of their familial responsibilities (including earning) when women went to jail?
5. What was the relationship between nationalist ideology and women's issues in the minds of men and women? Did women participate only for the country's swaraj or also for women's freedom? Did political participation aid women's liberation?
6. What were the regional patterns in women's participation? For instance, in Bengal, many women expressed their nationalist feelings by joining terrorist organisations or supporting them in many ways, in addition to all the overt ways in which they were encouraged to participate.
7. What were the patterns of women's participation in other movements in different regions which fought

against exploitation, and ultimately against imperialism? Why have they been ignored so long?

8. What was the role of the media—newspapers, films, local journals etc. in all this during this period?
9. What were the perceptions of the leadership about women's participation? Why, and how did gender equality get incorporated in the Fundamental Rights Resolution of 1931? What connections, if any, did it have with contemporary events within and outside India (Geneva Conference on Women's Equality, 1931, Resolution of Chinese Communist Party on the 'same line'. 1931: Lahore Conference of Asian Women for Equality, 1931 preceding Geneva), or with internal political imperatives?
10. Why did the Indian National Congress (INS) fail to take any follow-up action on the Resolution for nearly a decade?

In its report, towards equality, the Committee on the Status of Women in India (CSWI) accused the government, the educational system, social analysts, the media, political parties, trade unions as well as women's organisations - *i.e.* most members of the intelligentsia of a failure to understand the implications of gender equality guaranteed by the Constitution. The Committee was especially struck by the total invisibility and neglect of the economic roles played by the "overwhelming majority" of women among the peasantry, in most rural industries and services, and among the urban poor in policies for agricultural, industrial and infrastructural development. Despite the growing evidence of a decline in poor women's economic opportunities and consequent distress available from Census and a few other sources, official planners, social scientists and others continued to view women as economically inactive and dependent consumers, whose basic needs were confined to "education, health and welfare" not employment.[19]

Seeking an explanation for the wide gap between the reality of poor women's lives and official and academic beliefs that women were at the most "supplementary earners" for the family, whose contribution to the family's survival or improvement was "dispensable",[20] the Committee attributed it to the class bias of the intelligentsia, which projected middle class experience as normal for all women.

The development of women's studies in the post-1975 period, however, added other dimensions to this explanation. The theory of 'sanskritisation'-explaining a long-established pattern of social behaviour among upwardly mobile social groups-offered a handy framework for the social status of a family being linked to 'non-worker' status of women. or their 'withdrawal' from the labour force, among families or groups (caste, community, class) seeking higher status within the social hierarchy.[21] A more outspoken point of view came from a senior demographer, who in his days as a development administrator had lost a battle to include better economic opportunities for women within the Community Development Programme that 'fuzzy' definitions and silence on the value of women's work was part of a deliberate effort to "keep women subjugated economically, socially and politically".[22]

Another scholar, examining the Interrelationship between the nineteenth century social reform movement, the debate on women's education, and the emergence of a new family ideology among the educated urban middle class, found that this 'dominant' social ideology bore considerable resemblance to the gender role ideology of the British middle class of the Victorian period. Interestingly, the propagators of the ideology took little cognizance of not only the reality of roles played by the majority of women, but even the 'voices from within' of women in their own homes whom they were seeking to educate and transform.[23]

The CSWI had criticised the educational system for its failure to inculcate the value of equality among the youth, to counter the influence of inherited traditions and socialisation practices. The Committee's report gave substantial evidence of the persistent 'ambivalence' among educationists and policy makers regarding women's expected or desired roles in Soefety.[24]

The absence of any serious examination of the political significance of the acceptance of gender equality as a basic principle of the Indian political system also suggests a critical lacuna in academic assessment. Why has this "radical departure from the inherited social system"[25] been treated so cursorily even dismissively, by scholars? A member of the CSWI has argued that this gap in critical analysis has strengthened a dominant tendency among the intelligentsia to view gender equality as the culmination of the nineteenth century social reform movements, which threw up women's status as a major issue for debate and change.[26]

In our opinion, this perception of a linear connection between the reform movements and gender equality ignores several critical issues and contradictions within the reform movements.[27] It has certainly prevented adequate analysis of the politically critical role of gender equality within Indian nationalism and the political system born out of it. Thirdly, it has altogether ignored women's own views, aspirations and needs that provided many additional dimensions to the multiple struggles that contributed to the anti-imperialist movement. We feel it therefore necessary to contextualise this collection within these new perspectives on the social reform movements.

Most of the nineteenth century social reformers were male and members of the learned elites. The majority were products of the new system of 'English' education, though some came from the indigenous traditional systems. All were scholars in their own right, who had mastered one or more of the major philosophico-cultural-religious systems that met in India, modified through centuries of acculturation in the Indian subcontinent. The amalgam of indigenous cultural pluralism-mediated by centuries of philosophical efforts to systematise or homogentse-for want of an alternative word came to be known as Hindu religion, philosophy and culture.

Reaction to the ecopolitical changes that were initiated or accelerated after the British emerged as the undisputed dominant power found many forms of expression. The cultural form, among the highly literate new middle class-pioneers as well as products and beneficiaries of the new social order-has overshadowed all others, because of (a) the prolific literature they produced; (b) the social debates that they stirred up: and (c) the consequent high profile which they acquired among the urban literature. There were many other mass stirrings, some of which even erupted into rebellions against British rule and its socio-economic consequences but they lacked the recording and publicising capacity of the literature. As a result, the link between these cultural movements as precursors of the growth of national consciousness and nationalism has received much greater attention from historians and contemporary commentators.[28]

It is interesting to note that while early twentieth century historians and analysts were effusive in acknowledging the contribution of the reform movements in improving women's status, some of the contemporary analysts[29] of the movements keep silent on this issue, not even mentioning why the status of women acquired such a centre-stage focus in all the reform debates. Especially when the critiques are set within the context of the discourses on 'modernisation', 'nationalism' or 'revivalism' this extraordinary omission appears to be doubly curious.

Of the three cultural systems absorbed by the nineteenth century reformers, the Hindu system perhaps retained or demonstrated the maximum ambivalence between patriarchy and matriarchy.[30] Unashamedly anti-women practices like child marriage, female infanticide, polygamy various forms of oppression of widows etc. existed simultaneously with wide-spread worship of female deities and well-developed literature and rituals on cults of the mother goddess, in both scriptural and popular versions.[31] By the last quarter of the nineteenth century, the extension of this mother-worship to the emerging consciousness of the nation visualised as Mother India, enslaved by alien rulers, was an easy transition for many. By the early twentieth century, the symbolism of Mother India became acceptable to nationalists of non-Hindu heritage also, possibly because of its popular appeal and potential for revolutionary mobilisation.

The nineteenth century reform however, were neither unanimous nor homogeneous in their inspiration and objectives. The common element was their preoccupation with problems that primarily affected women in their own social class and milieu, and made them vulnerable to humiliation. These 'social evils' brought charges of barbarity and uncivilised behaviour from the new rulers, the new teachers and the new dispensers of rewards and recognition. This preoccupation with the West, either to emulate, to assimilate, or to reject, was an inevitable consequence of the circumstances which made the cultural contact possible. Changing socioeconomic relations, the growth of urban living, new modes of communication and education, as well as the pressure to acknowledge the scientific, technological and political dominance of Europe over the inherited cultural identities unleashed several tendencies that brought about the many contradictions within the reform movements.

Most of the reform movements combined some elements of revivalism, to assert or reinforce a desired or perceived cultural identity, as distinct from that of the rulers, along with radical or reformist challenges to some facets of the inherited cultural systems. Intellectual acceptance of the need for modernisation and progress, for national resurgence, and eventual overthrow of imperalism became increasingly marked, throwing up the need for new social ideologies, including a transformed social construction of gender.

Accepting women's status within the family as an index of their own progress and modernity, the earlier reformers criticised particularly inhuman practices like widow self-immolation (*sati*), marriage of child brides to much older men, ban on remarriage of widows, and sought to promote some form of education for women. Orthodox criticism of such moves was countered by statements that such reforms would arrest conversions to Christianity or the drift of oppressed widows to prostitution, and strengthen the stability of the traditional (patriarchal) family. The changes that they sought to promote reflected fairly crudely the social, especially family ideology of the nineteenth century British middle class. They did so without examining its possible long-term impact on the gender role prescriptions-ideal or actual-within the indigenous cultures of the highly diverse Indian society. The CSWI pointed out that the projections of widows' oppression and the ban on divorce or remarriage as the greatest evils in Hindu society ignored the customs of the majority of the Hindu population. On the basis of ethnographic and Census data the Committee demonstrated that as late as 1931 only 13.9 per cent of the Hindu population, and less than 10 per cent of the total population of the sub-continent could be accused of such practices.[32]

The second group of social reformers, focussing on the same issues but far more outspoken in their rejection of western values, projected their attempts as those of 'revival' of pristine traditions of 'Indian' culture, to rescue women from the cultural degeneration of which they had become victims. Education of a controlled kind and positions of protected dignity within the family and the community were argued as necessary to enrol women as 'custodians of traditional cultural values', against the onslaught of Westernisation.[33] The role prescriptions for the aryaniahilas (noble or respectable women, or followers of the Arya Samaj, one of the reform movements) strangely enough, reiterated not only the ideals prescribed for high caste Hindu women—thus reasserting the traditional claim of higher caste groups to be leaders of culture within the hierarchical social systems-but also of the 'gentlewoman' of Victorian England.[34] Similar role prescriptions were made for upper class Muslim women.[35]

Some strands within the reform movements which rejected caste hierarchy using the slogan of human equality, did not extend the concept to women. Instead. they too followed the 'revivalists' in imposing the traditionally dominant, higher caste model of gender role ideology on women among their following.[36] The fact that such an ideology bore little relationship to the actual roles that the women played in their community was ignored deliberately or unconsciously.[37]

Barring a few exceptions, the 'modernists' or the 'revivalists' were not really concerned with gender equality, women's own desires or their perspectives on dignity and justice. Nor were they aware of the inter-relationship between patriarchal controls over women's freedom, roles and behaviour and the carefully preserved pluralist hierarchical Organisation of Indian society.[38] Issues such as the radical restructuring of the social order or of bridging the social gap between different classes/ castes/communities were very far from most reformers' aims. There were however some outstanding exceptions

Iswar Chandra Vidyasagar neither a product of western education nor inspired by the need to 'whitewash' Indian practices to earn the approval of the rulers—was pushed into his campaigns for widow remarriage, the education of women and against polygamy by his mother's influence. His attitude to women was not instrumental (as with the 'modernists' or the 'revivalists'), but humane. Nor did he nurse any illusions about women's status having been high in ancient India as projected by revivalists, or nationalist historians later.[39] On the other hand, he declared that Mother India had always been unkind to her daughters. He deliberately selected for his anthologies for school students extracts from classical Indian literature that brought out women's subordination sharply.[40] An agnostic who rejected religious rituals, the caste system, and the monopoly of education by elites, he attached enormous importance to educating women and men equally through a system of mass education half a century before the introduction of compulsory elementary education in Great Britain and nearly a hundred years before some nationalists began to propagate mass education in India.[41]

One generation later, Jyotiba Phule, from another corner of the sub-continent and from a very different social background pushed the analysis of the inter-relationship—between women's subordination and the maintenance of the caste hierarchy—far beyond the point that Vidyasagar—a doer rather than a theoretician-had managed to articulate. Phule identified women's subordination as an instrument to perpetuate existing models of hierarchy. Phule's and his wife, Savitri Bai's efforts for women's emancipation acquired a far greater radical stance.[42]

Pandita Ramabai, whose intellectual upbringing matched that of most nineteenth century reformers, remains distinct "in her status as a solitary woman leader of the women's cause, whose equal in stature is yet to emerge in Maharashtra."[43] A high caste Hindu, steeped in both Sanskrit and Western learning, she challenged patriarchy, both through her personal life and the causes that she adopted for her struggles-self reliance for women, motivating women for self-improvement, and women's participation in public including political life. In all these respects, she was far ahead of the rest of the nineteenth century reformers. Her personal independence, her marriage of her own choice to a man of a different linguistic community and caste, and her religious conversion marked her out as a rebel and a feminist. Her analysis of a clear and close connection between the condition of women and the degradation of the nation reads very much like Mahatma Gandhi's statements made four decades later.[44] She too advocated the critical necessity of educating women, but reconunended the need for women teachers, inspectresses of schools and women doctors as essential to break through the prevailing oppression of 'educated men of this country.'[45]

These contradictions within the reform movements were reflected, mirror-like, in the reformers' struggles to promote women's education. The new opportunities thrown up by the colonial administrative and legal systems (landed property, education-based jobs and professions—in law, medicine, clerical work, education, the press, publishing etc.) were utilised in the most part by members of the class to which the reformers belonged *i.e.* those sections of upper caste, upper class Indians who already possessed the requisite cultural skills and social roles enabling adaptations.[46] The rise of such elites created disparities between men and women of this class, and these, in turn, were sought to be bridged by a specific type of education for women.

This was a key issue in this period when new demands were being made on women. There was a need to modernise and Westernise women adequately through education to enhance the image of a modern and civilised India. They had to be presentable in colonial society, models of virtue and fit companions to men of the new bourgeoisie who would serve the colonial system. This could be achieved through education which would henceforth be an additional female embellishment. Women would be utilised housewives and useful partners in marriage to suit the needs of a changing society particularly the urban upper class segment.[17]

Contemporary debates on the content of women's education testify to the unanimity with which the subject was approached by all concerned: reformers, revivalists and the

Victorian British. The goals of education for women were limited and cautious. It was considered adequate for girls/ women to receive basic educational skills and training that would make them better wives and mothers. The nurturant and creative aspects of women's nature were consistently stressed, reinforcing the home and family oriented stereotype. The curriculum revalidated the family as the most important social influence. The educational system merely enabled women to undertake a wider range of activities within the traditional framework and ideology, leading to the paradox of a progressive step such as education contributing to the unquestioned acceptance of prescribed values.[48] Thus, the promotion of women's education was undertaken not to liberate women's minds or out of esteem for women's rights but to promote the welfare of homes and families and to enhance the prospects of upwardly mobile men.

Women's Education

Elite and reformist families were responsible for the substantial expansion of women's education. Private institutions for girls and women were established and *zenana* education encouraged. Proponents of women's education had to adapt to prevailing social norms, patterns of behaviour and attitudes. Prejudice, apathy and orthodoxy were major hindrances, but within these limits some communities and regions did better than others. Hindus generally did better than Muslims, not necessarily because *purdah* hindered the latter as high caste, Hindu women, too, observed seclusion, particularly in North India which lagged behind Madras and Bombay Presidencies in women's education.[49]

Muslim reformers arguing for women's education were not as successful as the Hindus[50] nor could they transcend the imperatives of their traditions, but they did establish major centres of education for women in Aligarh and Lahore. Indigenous. vernacular centres of learning attracted Muslim youth including girls, in Bengal, United Provinces and Bihar.[51] Unexpectedly, on the whole *purdah* was not as regressive a factor as it might have been in the case of women's education.

Despite limitations on girls' access to equal education, access per se was emancipatory in the long run, contributing to the formation of consciousness and its articulation, and had far-reaching implications for women. Education opened up and widened women's intellectual horizons, exposed them to new ideas and other processes of modernisation, altering their view of the world and themselves. While most reformers and British officials propagated a separate type of education for women, the newly-educated women's aspirations were developing on very different lines. Organised representations by women graduates of Calcutta to the Calcutta University Commission (1917) emphatically demanded the same curriculum for women as for men—a demand maintained by women's groups through the twentieth century, until its clear acceptance in the national education policy in 1986.

The Committee on the Status of Women in India (CSWI) highlighted this continued ambivalence regarding the content of women's education within the educational system through the decades after Independence.[52] The mandate that the national education system as a whole had to play "a positive Interventionist role" in changing social (not merely women's) attitudes to one of acceptance of gender equality and 'empowerment' of women entered the Education Policy only on the demands of the women's movements.[53]

The social reformers' attempts to alter social values relating to women's status through the education of women succeeded in creating a dominant social ideology of gender roles which bore no relation to the critically important roles that the mass of women played in the family and the national economy, and ignored many of the effects of subordination that crippled the growth of intellectual and moral freedom and social responsibility of many women in the growing middle class.

In the long run, the reform movements strengthened women's 'socialisation for inequality' within the middle class as a whole, and fostered the growth of institutions like dowry and the supremacy of the patriarchal family in women's lives.[54] The controls of caste, community and religious norms which already dominated most women's lives, became in fact stronger and more complex with the added dimension of class norms in the case of the educated middle class. Instead of its expected liberating influence, education became a powerful force in strengthening the sanskritisation process, which manifests the integral links and mutually supportive relationship between partiarchy and hierarchy.[55]

Participation in the anti-imperialist struggles however encouraged many middle class women to challenge and break out of these controls during the three decades before independence. They were also the first group of women to benefit from the gender equality clauses in the new Constitution of the Indian Republic.[56] Post-independence developments promoted the economic and socio-political dominance and expansion of the middle class. Instead of playing a vanguard role in eliminating socioeconomic inequalities and hierarchic power relations that needed the subordination of women to perpetuate itself, middle class women in the post-Independence period came increasingly under the influence of expanding class norms. While conceding some share of the material benefits to women in the middle class, thus blunting their desire for a change in power relations, patriarchy acquired new forms of ideological and institutional control. The legacies of cultural ambivalence bequeathed by the nineteenth century movements, and the disintegration of the women's movement by the mid-1950s contributed to the eclipse of the nascent radicalism that sought to integrate gender equality as a critical element in the restructuring of Indian society on democratic lines. There was, as the CSWI described it a "regression from the norms developed during the Freedom Movement.[57]

Although middle class women's involvement with the outside world was limited by the ideology that limited their education, formal education led to the emergence of a group of women with a desire for organised action to improve the lot of women.[58] The early associational activities of elite women played a role in the identity formation of the new regional elites of all the major religious communities who were eager to provide evidence of the advancement, progress and potential of Indian women—within the colonial frame of reference-hoping to establish thereby the readiness of their class for increased influence, social leadership and political ascendancy.[59]

Numerous local women's associations, organisations, clubs, societies, samitls and institutions (hostels, rescue homes, shelters, schools) were founded in both British India and the Princely States. Women's uplift, philanthropy, social work among poor and destitute women and social reform were central to their work. These later developed into public activities in support of women's democratic rights and contacts with women's groups and movements outside India. Concern for the economic uplift of women was not absent but was not an over-riding issue. The majority of members of these associations were from reformist, educated and privileged families.[60]

The earliest organisations in the first half of the nineteenth century faced much social opposition, until the intervention of the 'revivalists' whose attitude had mixed implications for women's participation in activities to 'uplift' women. During the latter half of the nineteenth century, the rediscovery of their past led a section of the Hindu elite to seek a religious foundation for reform. While spreading consciousness and pride in indigenous cultural traditions, institutions like the

Arya Samaj, Ramakrishna Mission, the Prarthana Samaj etc. encouraged social service, educational and reform activities to bring about social change favouring women's uplift. An enlarged definition of religious activities thus permitted the application of religious ideals to social problems. Models of women's social contributions going beyond the family, available within Hindu tradition, were utilised to demonstrate that Hinduism did not degrade women.

No attempt was made, however, to tamper with either tradition or the prevailing value system. Women's role was merely sought to be widened in order to serve the community and the family. Thus 'revivalist' ideology provided an alternative rationale for improving women's status. It was also stressed that women's uplift was in the interest of not only women but men.[61]

Consequently, there was less opposition than to earlier reformers' efforts for the same cause and a rudimentary women's movement was under way. By the turn of the century, there was little opposition to local women's associations engaged in self-help activities. In Western India, reformers from the elite of three communities (Parsi, Maharashtrian and Gujarati Brahmins) led the way in the mid-nineteenth century, by establishing girl's schools in the face of stiff opposition. Later, the Prarthana Samaj, founded in the late nineteenth century, organised the Arya Mahila Samaj, Pandita Ramabai set up a series of mahila samajs or women's associations, girls' schools, orphanages, and widows' homes. Ramabai Ranade, (another eminent social worker of the period) did much work for women and the poor and established the Seva Sadan. In Bengal, Swarnakumari Devi's Sakhi Samiti (1886), a women's association, was concerned with traditional women's handicrafts.[62]

There are several distinct points of view that seek to explain the impact of the growth of nationalism in the later part of the nineteenth century on the situation of women and the debate on women's status. Natarajan, primarily concerned with the fate of 'social reform' as defined by most nineteenth century reformers-argued that reform issues, and particularly the women's issue lost their appeal and favour by being subsumed within nationalism.[63] A similar viewpoint is put forward by Ghulam Murshid, who places the debates on the women's issue in the early nineteenth century as 'modernising' attempts in response to the 'penetration' of Western liberal ideas. The limited success of these efforts, in his view, declined perceptibly in the later part of the nineteenth century, with the "hardening of popular attitudes" towards them. The new politics of nationalism 'glorified India's past and tended to defend everything traditional" all attempts at change being viewed as aping Western manners and values. Nationalism in this phase, in his opinion, fostered conservatism in social beliefs and practice.[64]

Sumit Sarkar has argued that the early 'renaissance' reformers were in any case, not full-blooded liberals. Fundamental elements of social conservatism such as caste distinctions, the patriarchal family, the sanctity of ancient scriptures and a preference for symbolic rather than substantial change in social practices were conspicuous in the reform movements of the early and mid-nineteenth century. On the position of women especially, there was no autonomous struggle by women themselves to change relations within or outside the family. According to Sarkar, these early attempts at reform were not so much the outcome of Western liberal or rationalist values, but more an expression of some 'acute problems of interpersonal adjustments within the family among western educated men.' The "social ostracism and isolation" that they had to face drove them to "a limited and controlled emancipation of wives as a personal necessity for survival in a hostile social world."[65]

Accepting much of Sarkar's critique of the liberal content of the early reformers' ideology, Partha Chatterjee argues that "the relative unimportance of the women's question in the last decades of the nineteenth century is not to be explained by the fact that it had been censored out of the reform agenda or overtaken by the more pressing and emotive issues of political struggle." In his view, nationalism "resolved the women's question in complete accordance with its preferred goals."[66]

What were these 'preferred goals', and how was the 'resolution' achieved? According to Chatterjee, nationalism was not simply a political struggle for power. On the other hand, it related the issue of independence to every aspect of the material and spiritual life of the people. Nationalist, in fact, had to decide what to select from the West, and what to avoid or reject -because they were equally sensitive about their own 'self-identity'. This dilemma was finally resolved by accepting a dichotomous framework between the 'material' and the 'spiritual' world, between the 'outer' and 'inner' life. Applied to day-to-day living, this dichotomy separated social space into the home and the world.

The world is the external, the domain of the material the home represents our inner spiritual self, our true identity. The world is a treacherous terrain of the pursuit of material interests where practical considerations reign supreme. It is also typically the domain of the male. The home in its essence must remain unaffected by the profane activities of the material world-and woman is its representations.[67]

The material superiority of the West had to be matched by learning modern science and arts to overthrow colonial role. But "the inner core of the national culture, its spiritual essence" had to be preserved, protected and strengthened-allowing no encroachments into this "inner sanctum".

Matching this new meaning of the home-world dichotomy with the identification of gender roles, Chatterjee discovers "the ideological framework" within which nationalism resolved the women's question. Education, travel in public conveyances, watching public entertainment programmes, "in time even employment outside the home" could be permitted.

"But the 'spiritual' signs of her femininity were now clearly marked in her dress, her eating habits, her social demeanour, her religiosity." The new patriarchy of nationalism gave women "a new social responsibility" not to imitate men, but "to maintain the cohesiveness of family life and solidarity with the kin group to which men could not now devote much attention." In addition, by associating the task of 'female emancipation' with the goal of 'sovereign nationhood', nationalism "bound them to a new, and yet entirely legitimate subordination". Lastly, Chatterjee explains the 'disappearance' of the women's question from the political domain by the end of the nineteenth century as the result of nationalism's "refusal to make the women's question an issue of political negotiation with the colonial state."[68]

Tempting as these attempts at analysing nationalist ideology *vis-a-vis* the women's question are, they suffer from the basic problem pointed out in the earlier section viz. looking for a linear connection between the nineteenth century reform movements, the growth of nationalism on to the twentieth century and the roles prescribed for or played by women in Indian nationalism. Chatterjee's heroic effort to distinguish women's familial role ideology from their social responsibility (as defined by nationalism in his Interpretation) ignores several aspects of history, which we propose to discuss in a later section. One important area totally ignored in this analysis is the way women themselves responded to the challenges of colonial rule. Surely the problem of an identity-crisis is not the monopoly only of men?

We turn now to the interpretation by some Western feminist scholars of Indian women's public activities during this period. Gail Minault suggests that the concept of the extended family in Indian culture which could expand virtually indefinitely, was used to justify women's concerns beyond the kin group. The metaphor of the extended family certainly assisted middle class women's performance of some public roles through their associations.[69] Gail Minault and Geraldine Forbes argue that women adapted the institution of purdah or seclusion a custom which defined the separate worlds of men and women to form their own associations. The need to be effective required the avoidance of confrontation by not appearing to be a threat to the established order. By projecting the idea that women's needs and nature were special or different, women were able to mobilise themselves in a public sphere of their own, not open to men. Thus *purdah* otherwise a hindrance to women's mobility, was utilised for women's advancement through women's forums in which women could voice their concerns. Despite the restrictions of *purdah* and without challenging patriarchal structures, it was possible for this rudimentary women's movement to acquire a unique strength.[70]

Mediating structures between the separate female world and the world of public affairs extended the female space. From women's uplift to national uplift, from women's emancipation to national regeneration was an inevitable step, as social reform and the growth of nationalist consciousness became increasingly close in a complex-sometimes complementary, sometimes contradictory relationship. The politicisation of women in the newly extended female space was facilitated by the mediating role played by members of the female intelligentsia who had more time to absorb nationalist literature as most of them were not involved in working for a living. Many became leaders in both the women's and the national movements.

Pandita Ramabai was a delegate to the Indian National Congress in 1889 along with nine other eminent women. Sarojini Naidu believed that the fate of women was linked with the fate of the nation. She wielded tremendous influence on contemporary women and saw no conflict between tradition and women's participation in public affairs, in the world outside the home, as the world was an extension of the home. She appealed to women not to ignore their larger responsibility.[71] Sarala Devi Chaudhurani became an accepted mobiliser of youth in the nationalist cause, and was noted by official intelligence reports as 'far more dangerous' to the Raj than her husband, a well-known revolutionary.[72]

The partition of Bengal in 1905 galvanised and transformed women's participation in the national movement. The mobilisation of women was attempted through the publication of pamphlets, public meetings held exclusively for women and new nationalist associations (in contrast to the elite associations) which emerged during the swedeshi period.[73] Mass struggles militancy, armed struggle and political agitations mark this period. Women of different classes were involved in growing numbers in such activities in different parts of India, in both rural and urban areas. The Chief Secretary to the Government of Eastern Bengal and Assam reported confidentially to the Governor General and the Secretary of State in 1907, that the youth of East Bengal absorbed hatred of the alien rulers who had "drained Golden Bengal of her wealth, virtually with their mother's milk".[74] Some British women who made Indian nationalism their own cause, played important roles as 'helpers' as well as 'catalysts'. Among them were Annie Besant and Dorothy Jinarajadasa, both Theosophists, Margaret Cousins, an Irish feminist, and Sister Nivedita, the disciple of Swami Vivekananda.[75]

In 1901, Sarala Devi Chaudhurani formed the Bharat Stri Mahamandal after serious differences with the male leadership of the National Social Conference. After 1910, women experienced in organising and working in local women's associations, and convinced that women should take the leadership into their own hands, started provincial and national women's associations. This was possible through effective intra-elite, intra-regional networks and able organisms cadres. These associations, despite efforts to be national in orientation and representative of as many groups as possible, failed to be actually national in scope, lacking all-India structures, among other shortcomings. But their history is more or less identical with the history of the Indian women's movement. The associations were inevitably elite, bourgeois and urban, consisting of women from the upper crust, women with the advantages of social status, education and privilege but redeemed by their desire to serve all women. Obviously, the women's movement in this phase neither represented the masses nor counted among its members lower caste, illiterate, rural, peasant and poor working women.

The Young Women's Christian Association (YWCA) of India, established in 1875 in Calcutta, was the earliest of these bodies. It became a national body in 1896. Though its membership was confined to Christians, its objectives were broad in scope. The Women's India Association (WIA) was formed in 1917 in Madras. In the same year Sarojini Naidu led a delegation of women formed by Margaret Cousins to the Constitutional Reforms (Montagu-Chelmsford) Committee, demanding universal adult franchise. The Indian women's movement believed that the enfranchisement of women would lead to legislation for social reform. The delegation's memorandum asked for women's franchise on the same basis as men and improved facilities for women's education and health care.[76]

The National Council of Women in India (NCWI) was formed in 1925, and the All India Women's Conference (AIWC) in 1927. By the mid-1930s the WIA and the AIWC claimed a membership of over 10,000 women.[77] The NCWI developed eight provincial Councils by 1934 and had 180 affiliated societies with a membership of over 8000.[78] The WIA was a vigorous Organisation that undertook to widen its scope of activities beyond fund-raising, social service and women's education and sought to influence government policy on equal rights for women in some areas, and was involved with the issues of suffrage, education and social reform. The WINs founders included women like Margaret Cousins and Annie Besant, who were not merely suffragists, but political radicals and critics of imperialism in their own country.

Women's Role in Freedom Struggle

This international dimension of the Indian women's movement is totally ignored by analysts like Chatteijee who underestimate the impact of Indian nationalism on politically disaffected groups in the West. Apart from the Western women who chose to adopt India as their home, and identified themselves with the nationalist, anti-imperialist struggles, there were many other women who played a supportive role from their own countries. Vivekananda, Rabindranath Tagore, Mahatma Gandhi.[79] Jawaharlal Nehru, Subhash Chandra Bose, Bhikaji Cama etc. had many supporters among Western feminists who were politically radical. Unfortunately, the nationalist reaction to Catherine Mayo's Mother India has drawn a curtain of invisibility over these connections, and prevented historians of nationalism from examining the transformation of the women's question through the first three decades of the twentieth century, in India and elsewhere. This transformation influenced both the women's movement and a section of the nationalist leadership. Why else would a nationalist journal like Malayala Manorama carry regular reports of women's movements in different countries?[80]

The All India Women's conference, originally convened only to discuss women's education, became a permanent body which succeeded in developing branches all over India. It called itself an apolitical body; its constitution included a clause that declared that it would not engage in party politics. Its emphasis was on unity and women's uplift through education, and social and legal reform. It also emphasised women's contribution to national development. By 1932, however, the AIWC had become involved with women's political rights and all questions which affected women and children as well as with social problems such as untouchability. Although its major focus and priority remained the women's question and the elimination of women's backwardness, and stress was laid on the well-being of women and the family the future of India gradually became an important concern.[81]

Many members of the WIA were also members of the AIWC and many such members were members of the Indian National Congress, and leaders in the national movement as well. This factor led to close relations between the women's and the national movements.

Consequently, the two main actors in the women's movement, the WIA and the AIWC, were swept by a variety of influences. The women's question had gradually evolved from the perspective of uplift within the traditional framework to that of women's equality. But involvement in the struggle for freedom led the women's movement into dilemmas and contradictions, it was caught between the middle class character of its membership and the increasing radicalism within the national movement with its transformation into a mass movement from the 1920s onwards.

Even the most cursory examination of women's organised activism from the beginning of the twentieth century explodes the myth still being pursued by many that women's role in the national movements against imperialism was male-dictated or male-manipulated. Once mobilised, women moved on their own, acquiring new confidence and articulating new priorities.

Women's Inspirational Support

The number of women directly involved in the revolutionary movements that developed in Bengal,

Maharashtra, Punjab, Uttar Pradesh and the erstwhile Madras Presidency from the turn of the century may have been small but the inspirational support base of the revolutionaries included far more women whose names will never feature in the dictionaries of freedom fighters.

The women who provided shelter, food and cover, carried messages or arms, or instilled a passion to 'serve the country' among their children, telling them about the 'heroes' and 'martyrs' who had sacrificed their lives for the country's freedom did not all belong to the elites. Many were not educated, and still more were used to poverty. They played such roles without waiting for any 'social sanction'. They provided a communication channel for the message of nationalism, when nationalist literature, and even news of revolutionary activities were sedulously proscribed, censored and withdrawn from circulation. Even the writings of persons of the stature of Rabindranath Tagore, Sarat Chandra Chatterjee, Nazrul Islam and many others, did not escape such bans. But the stories continued to spread and the songs and poems were observed eagerly by young people, often from women in their homes.

The few who played such roles more overtly, like Sarala Devi Chaudhurani, were marked by the Raj's intelligence arm, but women's invisible participation which provided greater force has received little formal acknowledgment. The one source which tried to record this invisible role of women was creative literature—through fictionalised characters who could not be prosecuted.

Similarly, women's active, even militant roles, as participants and leaders in quasitionalist peasant and workers' struggles remained strangely invisible till farly recently.[82] Recent attempts to reconstruct life stories of women activists and to obtain oral history from the few surviving women freedom fighters provide little substance to the theory of male direction, guidelines or manipulation. The women continue to say that they felt "compelled to join the struggle". And repeatedly they acknowledge the support received-overt or covert-from other women in the family, the kin group, friends and neighbourts.[83]

Developments since independence have demonstrated time and again that women react to national crises more spontaneously than to routine politics, the present opposition from the women's movement to the communalisation of political life was anticipated in 1984. Prannoy Roy's pre-election study had sought answers. In order of priority, to a question on which were the most burning issues facing the nation. The respondents were given a choice-inflation, public corruption, or problems of national integration. Roy's own expectation was that the majority of women would identify inflation as the first problem. He was taken aback when 68 per cent of the women respondents, as compared to only 13 per cent of the men, placed national integration at the top of their priorities.[84]

We find it difficult to believe that the leaders of the national movement were not aware of the growing base of women's support and feelings for the national cause, and were 'surprised' at the intensity and degree of their response to the Civil Disobedience movements. What is more understandable is the initial expectation, even desire among many of the leaders, that women will remain content with supportive, constructive roles, but not seek involvement in direct action. In fact, women defied even Gandhi in confronting the forces of repression. The majority of the women who participated actively in different corners of the country did not seek anyone's permission to do so. Why then do we still have this persistent myth? Is it because women's participation left so many issues of women's subordination unarticulated or unresolved, or because the women's movement was believed to have lost its autonomous character by becoming involved with the national political struggle?

The nationalist movement was a multi-layered, multidimensional process, which involved different sections of people, with different aims and visions for the future. In the light of this fact, Partha Chatterjee's claim regarding the "resolution" of the women's question by nationalism presents a strange logical discontinuity. Firstly, which group of nationalists formulated that solution? Certainly not the women. Secondly, using his own definition of the nationalist project—which, we presume, included building a nation as one of its objectives—we may ask: was there only one model or vision of the nation? Even the cultural nationalists or revivalists, whom he appears to regard as the only other group distinct from the half—hearted liberals suffering from an identity crisis, did not have a uniform goal. Were there not other radicals who cannot be neatly classified into either of these camps? Finally, what was the women's question that the cultural nationalists are supposed to have "resolved"? There is no definition of this question in his paper.[85]

In an earlier book[86] he examines the evolution of nationalist consciousness through three thinkers: Bankim Chattopadhyay—representing the "moment of departure" from the apron-strings of colonial ideas, Gandhi—representing the "moment of manoeuvre", combining a "war of movement" with a "war of position", and Nehru-representing the "moment of arrival", engaging in a 'discourse of order' or 'rational Organisation of power'. Since he does not mention women in his discourse on any of the three thinkers, we are safe in presuming that he does not see the women's question as having any political significance—In the vision of the nation nurtured by any of these thinkers. Nor does he appear to attach any political significance to the incorporation of gender equality in the Fundamental Rights Resolution of 1931, or the shifts in Gandhi's statements about women through the 1920s.

Unlike the social reformers, Gandhi had realised some of the negative consequences of colonial rule on women's economic status[87]. This realisation strengthened his decision to launch the khadi movement which would offer to the masses of women an immediate, open channel for their participation in the national struggle. Even more, Gandhi used women's role in the khadi movement to convince men that women's participation as equals was essential if the Sivadeshi or boycott movement was to succeed, an argument that he extended later to the winning of full freedom for India, and nation-building.

> ... (women) are starving not because there is no food in their village but because they have got no work for which they could get money and for such money they could get food. These poor sisters of yours and mine are without work for nearly six months in a year because of your sins and my sins... these millions of sisters of ours at one time spun yarn... and it was woven into cloth that we used to wear.[88] 200 years ago, the women of India spun not merely for home demands but also for foreign lands. They spun not merely coarse counts but the finest that the world has ever spun. No machine has yet reached the fineness of the yarn spun by our ancestors.[89]

I do not know how much men in India will have to pay for keeping you, the women of India, in darkness about so many things of the highest importance in life both to men and women. But thanks to God that since the advent of the movement for reviving the spinning wheel thousands of women have learnt to come out of their homes....[90]

The full freedom of India will be an impossibility unless your daughters stand side by side with the sons in the battle for freedom and such an association on absolutely equal terms on the part of India's millions of daughters is not possible, unless they have a definite consciousness of their own power.[91]

> ...whether we wish to boycott foreign cloth through the means of khadi or through mill-made cloth it is women who are the spinners.[92]

> The entire khadi movement depends on the women. This movement would collapse today if the women were to refuse to extend their cooperation to it.[93]

Calling khadi essentially a women's movement served many purposes. It brought the women an income basic for their survival forced men to acknowledge women's higher skills in this activity, and unleashed women's aspirations to break through purdah and other barriers of inequality. It also enabled Gandhi to challenge the dominant upper caste and middle class value that equated the family status with women's non-involvement in productive work. He exhorted well-to-do women to support the movement in their dual capacity as consumers and producers, by criticising their lifestyles. It was their duty to help their poorer sisters who had lost their livelihood on account of the import of foreign cloth.[94] Why had they given up spinning, which "even queens used to do", and become idle dependents? Why had they abandoned a skill which brought them so much pride and happiness? Why should they not spin to earn something for themselves, contribute to the family's income, or at least gift it to the poor weavers? Such involvement in productive work would also contribute to the nation's wealth.

> You have two or three hours in which you do nothing. You spend them in temples. Telling the beads in temples is dharma, but at the present time real bhakti consists in this work for cloth.[95]

For women to provide leadership in the movement, feeling virtuous by wearing khadi was not enough. They had to understand the dignity that came from being productive and independent. Such an understanding would help them to identify with poor women, emancipate themselves and achieve the new identity necessary for nation-building. Gandhi believed that only women could influence the growth of that new identity, and better values in the next generations.[96]

In 1917 he stated that "woman... (is)... mother to the Nation..."[97]

The economic and the moral salvation of India thus rests mainly with you. The future of India lies on your knees, for you will nurture the future generation... The destiny of India to far safer in your hands than in the hands of a Government that has so exploited India's resources that she has lost faith in herself.[98]

The 1920s and 1930s represent a transition in Gandhi's views on women from the concept of women's rights to the far more dynamic one of role. Women's energy would be unleashed for the nation-building process through an assertion of their productive and creative roles as equal partners, participants, leaders, conscience keepers, and beneficiaries.[99] Between 1921 and 1925, Gandhi had added India's political salvation as a goal for women in nation-building.

> ... unless women of India work side-by-side with men, there is no salvation for India, salvation in more senses than one. I mean political salvation in the greater sense, and I mean the economic salvation and spiritual salvation also.[100]

This speech was made before a group of young Christian women, at a time when the fragile unity of the nationalist struggle was threatened by many divisive forces of interest groups based on religion, caste or class. Many years later, angry with some negative reactions to Indira Nehru's engagement to Feroze Gandhi, a Parsi, he commented, "As time advances, such unions are bound to multiply with benefit to society" and rebuked the critics for their ignorance, intolerance and prejudices species of untouchability, dangerous because not easily to be so classified.[101]

In comparison to Gandhi's evolving, even changing views on women and the nation-building process, Nehru's understanding of women's subordination was both limited and static. Though fully aware of the problems of building a democratic and egalitarian society on the foundations of a social and cultural structure divided by multiple allegiances (or identities) religious, linguistic, caste and tribal and hierarchical beliefs that prevented a "sense of equality",[102] he did not understand the critical connections between the controls over women and the maintenance of that differentiated and hierarchical social structure.[103]

While he certainly accepted, the emancipation of women as a value in itself, and claimed improvement in Indian women's status as his greatest achievement,[104] it has been argued in some recent studies that his approach to the women's question reflected the elitist vision of social reformers, relieved to some extent by his fascination for socialism, with little or no understanding of the deeper causes of women's subordination in India.[105] Though he piloted the 1931 Resolution on Fundamental Rights through the Congress, his actions or statements in the years that followed-before or after independence-reveal little understanding or observation about the complexities of the situation or aspirations of women in different sections of society. However, being more sensitive to international opinion, he reiterated his support for the removal of all disqualifications and hindrances imposed on women by law or custom on several occasions. While he introduced the emphasis on women's rights in the Constitution, he did little to reduce the controls of the collectives that determined the boundaries of women's lives and behaviour—the family, community, caste, class and religion.

The inequalities inherent in our traditional social structure based on caste, community, and class have a very significant influence on the status of women in different spheres. Socially accepted rights and expected roles of women, norms governing their behaviour and of others towards them vary among different groups and regions. They are closely affected by the group in the social hierarchy. All this makes broad generalisations regarding women's status unrealistic.[106]

One unfortunate legacy of colonial modes of thought is the continued—influence of the Raj's classification of Indian nationalists into the two neat categories of 'extremists' and 'moderates'. These terms only sought to define them by the methods they adopted for dealing with the colonial state, and not by their vision of the nation they sought to construct. Some post—independence analysts, while using the terms liberals and cultural nationalists, or radicals are still imprisoned by the old classification.

As a result, Gokhale remains a neglected, discarded liberal, because the Raj viewed him as a moderate while Tilak, Vivekananda, Gandhi and the revolutionaries all get clubbed together as extremists/revivalists. One wonders where such analysts would place M.N. Roy, Ram Manohar Lohia, lqbal Nazrul Islam. Faiz Ahmad Faiz. Subhash Chandra Bose and a host of others? Was Bhikaji Cama, a liberal or a revivalist? Some writers seem to have classified Sarojini Naidu as a revivalist and a supporter of women's traditional role, as she utillsed traditional language to urge women to enter the national movement.[107] One of her political associates, however interprets such behaviour as a necessary strategy to draw women into the national movement.[108] Had these writers ever seen Sarojini telling her Mickey Mouse (her name for Gandhi) where his authority ended, or known that she ignored or defied virtually all the rules in the code of cultural norms such a classification might not have been made.

Since the theoreticians have not cared to define the women's question-we have to adopt a common sense one, contextualised in the Indian historical process of change. To the nineteenth century reformers it represented an amalgam of social practices and issues (e.g. child marriage, child widows, sati polygamy etc.) that was a source of much humiliation for the Indian middle class from their colonial masters and models. For the nationalists, however, the question related to women's role and status In the nation-building project. Was their participation necessary? If so, in what capacity—as equal partners, leaders or subordinates?

Nation-building called for a resolution of the problems of a multi-ethnic, multi-lingual, multi-cultural and multi-religious population within a hicrarchical, social order. Gokhale, the 'moderate' liberal. identified the problem of the 'depressed classes' as standing in the way. Why would these people identify themselves with the new nation he asked, if they did not have a stake in that new identity? Equality all citizens was thus more than half-digested liberal ideology-it was a pragmatic political necessity. And eventually, it was Gokhale whom Gandhi acknowledged as his political guru not Tilak.

Cutting across class, caste, ethnic groups, language, culture and religion was the common attribute and problem of all women-gender inequality. The subordination of women, manifested in restrictions on their lives, occupational, marital and other relational choices, as Jyotiba Phule pointed out in the nineteenth century, was an "essential instrument" for maintaining caste hierarchy and Brahminical dominance in Hindu society.[109] But the status of higher class/caste women was more problematical than that of women of the lower classes/castes. The problems of widows' oppression, purdah and the growing gender gap in education which had preoccupied the nineteenth century reformers did not affect the majority of Indian women.

Nearly 90 per cent of the total female population was deeply involved in the agrarian, manufacturing, or the trading economies of the subcontinent-as partners in household or family based enterprises, or as independent workers producers or traders.[110] The rights and roles of women of these classes mainly depended on local or community customs,[111] which often gave them far more freedom than what was available to their higher caste/class sisters whose lives were defined much more by the Code of Manu.

As for the educational gap—the sex ratio among the illiterate population remained virtually at par till 1931, when illiterates made up 80.5 per cent of the total population. According to the three reports on the state of indigenous education in the 1820s-the gender gap in the traditional institutions for elementary education was not as high as it was become under the English system. Of the 36 schools started by Vidyasagar in the 1830s, twenty were for girls. And they taught the same curriculum as in the other 16![112] Demographic indicators like average life expectancy, mortality and work participation did not show such wide gaps as in the twentieth century, especially after 1921. In fact, while life expectancy was appallingly poor for the total population women were still slightly better off than men—a pattern which changed only after 1921.[113]

Neither Islam nor any of the other religions had really managed to radically alter the life styles, or the gender role prescriptions of this vast majority in the same way as the political economy of colonial rule did. Deindustrialisation, land alienation, deforestation and capitalist transformation of the economy, with monetisation of wages and revenue not only increased the impoverishment of the people, but forged new instruments for the devaluation and subordination of women through, for example, wage discrimination, exclusion from some sectors which had been open to them before, loss of usufructuary rights to community property and resources etc. without a compensatory gain in rights elsewhere. All these changes strengthened the age-old system of hierarchical patriarchal norms and values which enforced control over women to keep various groups separated from each other.[114]

Some of these facts many have remained unknown to the nineteenth century reformers, but they were not entirely unknown to the twentieth century nationalists. Gandhi did not win the response of poor working women—rural or urban —by his ideology alone. They recognised his awareness of much of their plight—a direct consequence of the economic depredations of colonialism. But while pleading for reviving khadi—an instrument of war against imported textile, and as a method of employment generation for the masses of the people—he preached gender equality in economic rewards and in political decision-making as well.

The cultural or religious revivalists, Hindus and Muslims alike, on the other hand, were totally apposed to gender equality. Their visions of the future nation demonstrate virtual unanimity on many issues, including women's roles.[115] Liberalism as practiced in the West too and no models to offer, since demands for gender equality had been defeated repeatedly during and since the French and the American revolutions. Suffrage, conceded in a few countries just before or after the Ist World War, did not promise equality in legal or economic rights.[116]

Some models of gender equality or women's emancipation, however, became available with the Russian Revolution (1917), its extensive to the Asian Republics in the 1920s[117] and Kemal's measures for the emancipation of women in Turkey in the same period.[118] In the last two cases, political strategy—to undermine established power structures based on clan organisations in alliance with a religious clergy—played as important, if not a greater role than ideology, Indian nationalist leaders were not altogether ignorant of these developments. The extent of such influence needs to be researched.

The 1920s represented a period of major changes affecting women in the subcontinent—internal socio-economic transformations which reinforced and heightened their opposition to alien rule, and external political changes that affected women's lives in other parts of the world, providing new ideas and challenges to the expanding women's movement. Nationalism, too, experienced numerious internal tensions of class, community, sectional interests, ideologies and organisations that threatened the carefully constructed, fragile unity of anti-imperialist forces. Set within this complex historical perspective, the women's question acquires totally new dimensions and political depth that most analysis have missed so far, because they continue to view it through the myopic, pale and static vision of nineteenth century reformers.

For example, there has been no research to trace the connections between the Fundamental Rights Resolution of the Congress in 1931—which accepted gender equality as a basic principle—the Lahore Congress of Asian Women for Equality, the Geneva International Conference on Women's Equality, and the Congress of the Chinese Communist Party which also adopted a resolution on gender equality. Since all these meetings took place in the same year, the absence of any enquiry into possible connections appears exceedingly strange.

The political significance of the women's question *vis-à-vis* the nation-building project, however, needed far more complex understanding. Articulation remained incomplete and unclear. An attempt to express and define a women's perspective on restructuring Indian society was made by members of the Sub-Committee on 'Women In a Planned Economy' constituted by Nehru as a part of his National Planning Committee (NPC) set up in 1939[119] but the Report was never considered in the entire history of planning in Independent India. The reasons for this strange omission also need to be researched.

In the history of Indian nationalism, the Fundamental Rights Resolution of 1931 was an attempt to defeat the forces of disintegration which threatened the nationalist movement. Most of its provisions, especially those rejecting inequalities based on gender, caste and religion, represented a total 'departure from the inherited social tradition' in the interests of constructing a new national identity.

REFERENCES

1. Dasgupta, Kalpana, 1976, *Women on the Indian Scene,* New Delhi, Abhinav Publications, p. 16.
2. Examples are: Tarachand, 1961-72. *History of the Freedom Movement in India.* 4 Vols., Delhi, Government of India. Publications Division: and E.M.S. Namboodiripad, 1986, History of Indian Freedom Struggle, Trivandrum. Social Scientist Press.
3. Pearson, Gail, 1981, 'Nationalism. Universalisation and the Extended Female Space in Bombay City". in Gail Minault (ed.), *The Extended Family: Women and Political Participation in India and Pakistan,* Delhi, Chanakya Publications. pp. 175. 188.
4. Manmohan Kaur, 1985, *Women in India's Freedom Struggle,* Delhi, Sterling Publishers, S.R. Bakshi, 1988, Mutiny to Independence, New Delhi, Deep and Deep Publications.
5. Majumdar, R.C., 1962, 1963, History of the Freedom Movement in India, 3 Vols.. Calcutta. K.L. Mukhopadhyaya, and 1969, *The Struggle for Freedom,* Bombay, pp. 998-99: J.P. Suda, 1969. *Indian National Movement,* Meerut; Bipan Chandra, 1971, *Modern India,* New Delhi, pp. 184-86 and 1988, *India's Struggle for Freedom 1858-1947,* Delhi, Viking, p. 528, Sitarani Singh, 1968, *Nationalism and Social Reform in India. 1885-1920,* New Delhi, Rampart: Sumit Sarkar. 1983, *Modern India,* Delhi, Macmillan India Ltd., p. 290.
6. Majumdar, R.C., 1963, *op.cit.,*Vol. 111, pp. 280-81, 414, and Suda, *op.cit.,* pp. 243-44.
7. Brown, Judith. 1972, *Gandhi and the Civil Disobedience Movement,* Cambridge, Cambridge University Press, pp. 146, 168.
8. Desai, Mahadev. n.d., The Story of Bardoli, among others and Jawaharlal Nehru, 1945, Discovery of India, Calcutta, p. 32.
9. Dasgupta, *op. cit,* p. 5.

10. Le Mesurier, Unrecorded Confidential Proceedings, Morley and Minto Papers, Home Department, Government of India, India Office Library, London, and National Library of Scotland, Edinburgh.
11. Bipan Chandra, 1971, *op. cit.*
12. Alexander, Rajani, 1984, "Participation and Perceptions: Women and the Indian Independence Movement", Samya Shakti, Vol.1, No. 22, pp. 1-5.
13. Politically radical and mass-based organisations and terrorists kept scant records for security reasons and even if they did keep them, these were destroyed in one way or another. Refer, for example, to Geraldine Forbes, 1981, "The Indian Women's Movement: A Struggle for Women's Rights or National Liberation?" in Gail Minault (ed.), 1981, *op.cit.*,p.77. However, a member of the Communist Party has used reports of samitis material from files of publications preserved in party archives and other papers including the memoirs of comrades. See preface in Renu Chakravartty, 1980, Communists in the Indian Women's Movement, New Delhi, People's Publishing House.
14. *Forbes*, 1981, *op.cit.*, p. 50.
15. Aparna Basu, 1976/1990, 'The Role of Women in the Indian Struggle for Freedom", in B.P. Nanda (ed.). Indian Women: From Purdah to Modernity, Delhi, Nehru Memorial Museum and Library (NMML) and Vikas/Radiant Publishers, pp. 16-40. This paper has utilised a variety of sources including transcripts of interviews which are available at NMML, New Delhi.
16. *Forbes'* 1981, *op.cit.*, p.50. See also Patricia Caplan, 1985, Class and Gender in India, Women and their Organisations in a South Indian City, London and New York, Tavistock Publications-, J.M. Everett, 1979, Women and Social Change in India, New Delhi, Heritage: Aparna Basu and Bharati Ray, 1990. Women's Struggle: A History of the All India Women's Conference. 1927-1990, Delhi, Manohar.

17. Desai, Neera, 1989, "Family Strategies in South Gujarat' (mimeo).
18. Some of these facts emerged during discussions which were recorded in 1983 in Calcutta by the Centre for Women's Development Studies (CWDS), New Delhi, Transcripts are available with CWDS.
19. The Report of the Committee on the Status of Women in India (CSM), Towards Equality, 1974, New Delhi, Government of India, Department of Social Welfare, Ministry of Education and Social Welfare, Chapter VIII.
20. *Ibid.,* Chapter V: Asok Mitra, Lalit Pathak and Shekhar Mukherji. 1980, 'Introduction', in The Status of Women Shifts in Occupational Participation, 1961-1971, New Delhi, ICSSR and JNU, Abhinav Publications.
21. Srinivas, M.N., 1978, *Changing Position of Indian Women,* Thomas Huxley Memorial Lecture, Delhi, Oxford University Press.
22. Mitra, *et.al., op.cit.*
23. M. Karlekar, 1991, *Voices from Within Early Personal Narratives of Bengali Women,* Delhi, Oxford University Press.
24. See CW, *op.cit.,* Chapter VI.
25. See CSWI, *op.cit.,* Chapter 1.
26. Mazumdar, V., 1985, 'Emergence of Women's Question in India and the Role of Women's Studies', Occasional Paper, 7. New Delhi, CWDS.
27. Mazumdar, V., 1976/1990, 'The Social Reform Movement in India—From Ranade to Nehru'. in B.P. Nanda (ed.), *op.cit.*
28. Majumdar, R.C., (ed.), 1974, British Paramountcy and Indian Renaissance, Bombay; Charles Hetmsath, 1964, Indian Nationalism and Hindu Social Reform, Princeton, Princeton University Press: S. Natarajan, 1959. A Century of Social Reform in India, Bombay, Allied Publishers; Partha Chatterjee. 1986, Nationalist Thought and the Colonial World, Delhi, Oxford University Press; T. Ray Chaudhuri. 1988, Europe

Reconsidered, Perceptions of the West in Nineteenth Century Bengal, Delhi, Oxford University Press.

29. Chatterjee, *op.cit.*, and Ray Chaudhuri. *op.cit.*, for example.

30. Bhattacharya, N.N., 1987, *History of the Tantric Religion*, Delhi, Manohar, and 1977. *The Indian Mother Goddess*, South Asia Books: D.D. Kosambi, 1982, *The Culture and Civilisation of Ancient India in Historical Outline*, Delhi, Vikas; O.R. Eherenfels, 1941, *Mother Right in India*, London, Oxford University Press.

31. Bhattacharya, *op.cit.*

32. CSWI, *op.cit.*, p. 77.

33. Mazumdar, V., 1972, Education and Social Change: Three Studies in Nineteenth Century Bengal, Shimla, Indian Institute of Advanced Studies and 1976/ 1990, *op.cit.* See also Ashok Sen, 1977, Ishwar Chandra Vidyasagar and his Elusive Milestones, Calcutta, Riddhi.

34. See Karlekar, *op.cit.*

35. Maulana Thanawi, n.d., Behesti Zewar. See Barbara Metcalf, 1984, "Islamic Reform and Islamic Women: Maulana Thanawi's Jewelry of Paradise", in Barbara Metcalf(ed.), Moral Conduct and Authority, Berkerley, University of California Press, pp. 184-95. Also Metcalf, 1983, "The making of a Muslim Lady: Maulana Thanawi's "Bihisthi Zewar", in Milton Israel and N.K. Wagle (eds.) Islamic Society and Culture, Essays in Honour of Professor Aziz Ahmad, Delhi, Manohar, pp.17-38.

36. Makarand Mehta's Study of the Swaminarayana cult in the nineteenth century, presented to the Indian history Congress in the early 1980s. see Arthat, (Gujarati), 1988, Journal of the Centre for Social Studies, Surat.

37. Karlekar, *op.cit.*

38. Mazumdar, V. and Kumud Sharma, 1990. "Sexual Division of Labour and the Subordination of Women: A Reappraisal from India", in Irene Tinker (ed.), Persistent Inequalities,

Women and World Development, New York, Oxford University Press,

39. Mazumdar, V., 1972, *op.cit.*, Swamny Madhavananda and R.C. Majumdar (eds.) 1982, Great Women of India, Almora, Advaita Ashrama; and A.S. Alterkar, 1959, The Position of Women in Hindu Civilisation, Delhi Motilal Banarsidass and 1982, "Ideal and Position of Indian Women in Social Life", in Swami Madhavananda and R.C. Mazumdar (eds.) *op.cit.*
40. Sita's second exile from the Ramayana and Shakuntala's rejection by her royal husband from the play by Kalidasa, Abhignana Shakuntalam.
41. Mazumdar, V., 1972, *op.cit.*, and Sen, *op.cit.*
42. Vohra, 1974, Liberal Thought in Maharashtra, Ph.D. thesis, University of Pune (unpublished).
43. Adhav, S.M., 1979, Pandita, Ramabat, Madras, The Christian Literature Society (Confessing the Faith in India Series, No.13).
44. Pushpa Joshi (compiled by), 1988, Gandhi on Women, Ahmedabad, Navajivan Trust, and New Delhi, CWDS. See also Mazumdar, 1976/ 1990 in B.R. Nanda (ed.), *op.cit.*, p. 56-60.
45. Kosambi, Meera, 1988, "Women's Emancipation and Equality —Pandita Ramabai's Contribution to women's cause", *Economic and Political Weekly*, 23(44), October 29, See also Basu, A., "A Century's Journey: Women's Education in Western India: 1820-1920", in K. Chanana, (ed.), 1988, Socialisation Education and Women, New Delhi, NMML, and Orient Longman.
46. Everett, 1979, *op.cit.*, pp.41-42. Everett cities John Broomfield, 1971, "The Regional Elites: A Theory of Modern Indian History", in T.R. Metcalf (ed.), Modern Indian: An Interpretive Anthropology, London, MacMillan, pp.60-72.
47. Refer to the collection of essays in Chanana, *op.cit.*
48. *Ibid.* See also Mazumdar, 1976/1990, *op.cit.*, pp.53,63.

49. Chanana, K., "Social Change or Social Reform: The Education of Women in Pre-Independence India", in Chanana (ed.), *op.cit.*, pp.96-128.

50. *Ibid.*, pp.110-114 and G. Minault, 1981. 'Sisterhood or Separatism? The All-India Muslim Ladies' Conference and the Nationalist Movement", in Minault, *op.cit.*, pp.85-89 and 1982, "Parda's Progress: The beginnings of School Education for Indian Muslim Women", in J.P. Sharma (ed.), Individuals and Ideas in Modern India, Calcutta, K.L., Mukhopadhyaya.

51. Chanana, *op.cit.*, p.113.

52. CSWI, *op.cit.*, Chapter VI.

53. Report of the First National Conference on Women's Studies, 1981, Bombay, SNDT Women's University: Women's Studies and Social Sciences in Asia: Report of a Meeting of Experts, 1983, Bangkkok, UNESCO, Office of the Regional Adviser for Social Sciences in Asia and the Pacific: Report of the Second National Conference on Women's Studies, 1984, Indian Association of Women's Studies Units in Indian Universities, 1985, Department of Political Science, Delhi University; V. Mazumdar and Balaji Pandey, 1988, National Council of Educational Research and Training, National Council of Educational Research and Training, National Specialised Agencies and Women's Equality, New Delhi, CWDS; Report of the National Seminar on Education for Women's Equality, November 1985, New Delhi, Government of India, Ministry of Education.

54. CSWI, *op.cit.*, pp.50-54, 69-77.

55. *Ibid.*, pp.234-235, 261-263; Mazumdar and Pandey, *op.cit.*, Chapter II.

56. CSWI, *op.cit.*, Chapters V and VI.

57. *Ibid.*, p.359.

58. Chanana, *op.cit.*, p. 98.

59 Everett, *op.cit.*, pp.45, 48-49, 51.

60. Everett, *op.cit.*, Basu and Ray, *op. cit*; Minault, *op.cit.*, Mazumdar 1976-1990, *op.cit.*; G.Forbes, 1979, "Traditional

Symbols and New Roles, The Women's Movement in India", in M.S.A. Rao (ed.), Social Movements in India, Vol.II, Delhi, Manohar, and 1982, "From Purdah to Politics; the Social Feminism of the All India Women's Organisations", in Hanna Papanek and Gail Minault, 1982, Separate Worlds, Delhi, Chanakya Publications.

61. Christine Dobbin, 1972, Urban Leadership in Western India, London, Oxford University Press, pp.53-77, 249-253, cited by Everett, *op.cit.*, p.59. Also Everett, pp.39, 51, 54-56, 59-61. See also Karlekar, *op.cit.*,

62. Everett, *op.cit.*, for a concise account, pp.57-60; Basu and Ray, *op.cit.*, pp.2-3; Basu, 1988, *op.cit.*, *Chanana, op.cit.*, and *Forbes*, 1979, *op.cit.*,

63. Natarajan, *op.cit.*

64. Murshid, Ghulam, 1983, Reluctant Debutante; Response of Bengali Women to Modernisation, 1849-1905, Rajshahi University Press.

65. Sarkar, Sumit, 1973, "The Complexities of Young Bengal", Nineteenth Century Studies, 4,pp.504-534, and 1975, "Rammohun Roy and the Break with the Past", in V.C. Johsi (ed.), Rammohan Roy and the Process of Modernisation in India, Delhi, Vikas.

66. Chatterjee, Partha, 1989, "The Nationalist Resolution of the Women's Question", in Kumkum Sangari and Sudesh Vaid (eds.), Recasting Women, New Delhi, Kali for Women, *op.cit.*, p.237

67. *Ibid.* pp.238-239.

68. *Ibid.* pp.247-249.

69. Minault, G. 1981. 'Introduction: The Extended Family as Metaphor and the Expansion of Women's Realm'. in Minault, *op.cit.*, pp.3-15.

70. Minault, G., 1982, 'Purdah Politics: The Role of Muslim Women in Indian Nationalism, 1911-1924" in Hanna Papanek and Gail Minault (eds.). *op.cit.* See *Forbes*, 1982, in the same volume, pp. 220-21, 236-38.

71. Sarojini Naidu said: 'It is well for us to remember that the success of the whole (nationalist) movement lies centred in what is known as the woman question. It is not you but we who are the true nation-builders", at a lecture delivered at the Indian Social Conference, Calcutta, December 1906. See Sarojini Naidu, 1925, Speeches and Writings, Madras, Natesan (quoted by Gail Pearson, *op.cit.*, p. 18 1, footnote 28). See also Manrnohan Kaur, *op.cit.*, pp. 175-176, Everett, *op.cit.*, pp.83-88, Forbes, 1979, *op.cit.*, pp. 155-160.

72. From Unrecorded Confidential Proceedings, Morley and Minto Papers *op.cit.*, cited in V. Mazumdar's unpublished Ph.D. thesis, 1962. Britain's India Policy 1905-1910, University of Oxford.

73. Everett, *op.cit.*, pp.54-55, 57.

74. Mazumdar, 1962. *op.cit.*

75. Barbara Ramusack, 1981. "Catalysts or Helpers?' in Minault (ed.), *op.cit.*, and Everett, *op.cit.*

76. Everett, *op.cit.*, p. 103, A.Basu, 1976/1990, *op.cit.*, p.34.

77. Forbes, 1981. *op.cit.*, p. 54.

78. Everett, *op.cit.*, p. 73.

79. Gandhi's writings in 1906 prove how powerfully he was impressed by the courage, heroism and sacrifice of British suffragists. See Joshi, *op.cit.*, pp. 3.5-8.

80. Saradamoni K., 1979, personal communication. See also Mazumdar, 1982. 'Another Development with Women: A View from Asia", Development Dialogue, Journal of the Dag Hanirnarskjold Foundation, Vol. 1-2.

81. Basu and Ray, *op.cit,*, pp.4-12, Forbes, 1981, *op.cit.*, pp.60-62 and 1982, *op.cit.*, pp.234- 236. Everett, *op.cit.*, pp.118-19.

82. Mira Savara, 1981, Changing Trends in Women's Employment: A Case Study of the Textile Industry in Bombay, Ph.D. dissertation, University of Bombay, Sunil Sen, 1985, The Working Women and Popular Movements in Bengal, Calcutta, K.P.. Bagehi and Co.: P. Custers, 1987, Women in

the Tebhaga Uprising-Rural Poor Women and Revolutionary Leadership 1946-47, Calcutta, Noya Prakash, Kapil Kumar, 1989, "Rural Women in Oudh." 1917-1947, Baba Ramachandra and the Women's Question', in Kumkum Sangart and Sudesh Vaid (eds.), *op. cit*: Stree Shakti Sanghatana, 1989, We were Making History, New Delhi. Kali for Women, Dipesh Chakravarty, 1983, Development of Class Consciousness among Jute Workers, Ph.D. thesis, A.N.U., Canberra..

83. For instance, Dr. Phulrenu Guha, personal communication. Also Dr. Guha, Oral History Transcript, NMML, New Delhi, and many others.
84. Prannoy Roy, 1984. personal communication.
85. Chatterjee, 1989, *op. cit.*
86. Chatterjee, 1986, *op.cit.*
87. Mazumdar, V., 1988, Khadi and Village Industries Commission, National Specialised, Agencies and Women's Equality, CWDS. pp. 2-15.
88. Gandhi's speech at a women's meeting in Karaikudi. 24 September 1927. *Me Hindu*, 26 September 1927 and in Collected Works of Mahatma Gandhi (CWMG)-Vol.35, pp. 26-28.
89. Gandhi, 'To the Women of India', *Young India*, II August 1921 (CWMG, Vol.20, pp. 495-97).
90. Gandhi's speech at a public meeting in Karatkudi, 25 September 1927. The Hindu, 27 September 1927 (CWMG, Vol.35, pp. 38-39).
91. Gandhi's speech at a public meeting in Pagancri, 27 September 1927. The Hindu. 29 September 1927 (CWMG, Vol.35, pp. 44-46).
92. Gandhi's speech in Olpad taluk, on or before 30 March 1930. Navajivan, 6 April 1930. (CWMG. Vol. 43, pp. 154-55).
93. Gandhi, "To the Women', Navajivan, 6 April 1930 (CWMG, Vol.43, pp. 189-191).

94. Gandhi's speech at Gujarati Women's Conference. Dandt, 13 April 1930. Praja Bandhu, 20 April 1930 (CWMG, Vol.43, pp. 251-252); Gandhi, "How to Remove the Blot', Young India, I October 1919 (CWMG, Vol.16, pp. 131-132). Gandhi's Message to All India Women's Conference-sent before 22 December 1938, The Hindustan Times. 28 December 1938 (CWMG, Vol.68, p. 230)

95. Gandhi's speech on Swadeshi at a Women's Meeting at Nadiad, 6 July 1919. Gujarat, 20 July 1919 (CWMG, Vol.15, pp. 439-445).

96. Gandhi, 'Women's Role", *Navqlivaii*, 3 October 1920 (CWMC, Vol.18, pp. 319-21).

97. Gandhi, Speech at Second Gujarat Educational Caderence, Broach, 20 October 1917 (CWMG, Vol.14, pp. 31-36).

98. Gandhi, 'To the Women of India". Young India, 11 August 1921 (CWMG, Vol.20, pp. 495-497).

99. Gandhi, Interview to Free Press of India, Dandi, 6 April 1930. The Amrita Bazar Partrika, 7 April 1930 (CWMG, Vol.43, p. 199).

100. Gandhi's Speech at Women's Christian College, Madras, 24 March 1925. *The Hindu*, 25 March 1925 (CWMG,Vol. 26, pp. 395-98).

101. Gandhi. 'Indira Nehru's Engagement'. *Harijan*, 8 March 1942 (CWMG.Vol.75, pp. 375-76).

102. Gopal, Sarvepalli, 1984, Jawaharlal Nehru: A Biography, Vol.111, London, Jonathan Cape, p. 280.

103. Mazumdar, V., 1989, 'An Unfulfilled or a Blurred Vision? Jawaharlal Nehru and Indian Women", paper presented at the International Seminar on Nehru and Non-Alignment, University of Sydney, Australia, 13-15 December.

104. Gopal, Barvepalli, 1979, Jawaharlal Nehru: A Biography, Vol.11, p. 313. See also Gopal, 1989, "The Problem', Seminar, No.363, (November) Special Issue on 'The Nehru Era'.

105. Mazumdar, V., 1989, *op. cit*, Lotika Sarkar, 1988, 'Nehru and Gender Justice", paper presented at a National Seminar on Nehru and the Constitution, Ministry of Law and Justice and Indian Law Institute, 30-31 December, and L. Sarkar, 1989, 'Empowering Women", Seminar, *op. cit*.
106. CSWI, *op. cit*. p. 3.
107. See note 71.
108. Phulrenu Guha, Personal Communication.
109. Vohra, *op. cit*. See also Mazumdar and Sharma, *op. cit*.
110. Buchanan, Francis. 1811-1833, Accounts of the Districts of Bihar and Bengal: A.I. Chicherov, 1971. India, Economic Development in the Sixteenth to Eighteenth Centuries: Outline History of Crafts and Trade, Moscow, Nauka Publishing House, Asok Mitra 1979, The Status of Women, Literacy and Employment, Bombay, Allied Publishers.
111. CSWI, *op. cit.*, Chapter 111. See also Smita Tewari Jassal, 'Women's Right to Land and Other Productive Resources in Rural Areas, An Historical Exploration", Part 1, New Delhi, CWDS (mimeo).
112. Mazumdar, 1972. *op. cit*.
113. Mitra, 1979, *Op. cit.*, CSWI, op-cit., Chapter II.
114. Mazumdar and Sharma, *op. cit*.
115. Mishra, Ish, n.d.. "The Women's Question' in Communal Ideologies, A Study In the Ideologies of Rashtriya Swayam Sevak Sangh and Jamaat-B-Islami. New Delhi, CWDS (mimeo). See also Everett, *op. cit.*, Chapter VII and Minault, 1981, *op. cit.*, pp. 83 108.
116. Mies, Maria and Kumart Jayawardena, 1981, Feminism in Europe: Liberal and Socialist Strategies 1789-1919, The Hague, ISS: Alice Rossi (ed.), 1973/1981. Me Feminist Papers, New York, Bantam Books.
117. Marshall, Gregory, 1976, The Surrogate Proletariat, Soviet Policy Towards Women in Central Asia 1919-1929, Princeton, Princeton University Press.

118. Abadan Unat, Nerirn. 1967, 'Turkey'. in Raphael Patat (ed.). Women in the Modern World. Glencoe. Ill. Also Deniz Kandiyoti and Mubeeceel B. Kiray (eds.). 1981, Women in Turkish Society, Leiden. See also Mazumdar, 1982, *op. cit*.

119. 'Document'. *Samya Shakti*, Vol.Vl, 1991-1992, pp. 110-12, and Everett, *op. cit.*, pp. 150-51.

3

WOMEN'S MOVEMENT AND EMPOWERMENT

Introduction

Among all the developing countries, India has one of the most complex forms of patriarchal system. The contemporary women's movement in India is one of the most burgeoning movements in developing countries, challenging caste, class, and gender inequalities. The resurgence of the women's movement in the 1970s in the context of the crisis of the state and the upsurge in social movements against growing inequality marked a significant shift in the analysis and understanding of women's issues and in redefining feminist politics (Agnihotri and Mazumdar 1995). The proliferation of women's action groups and grassroots organisations since the 1970s reflects the diversity and complexity of the women's movement.

The canvas of the contemporary women's movement is very large. It has moved beyond the traditional concerns with legislation, education and social welfare to a wide range of issues, such as access to land and natural resources, environmental degradation, media, reproductive health and population, gender violence (rape, dowry deaths, *sati* widow immolation, alcoholism, wife battering, etc.), communal and caste conflicts, representation of women in the *panchayati raj* institutions (village-level political councils), etc. Movement politics reflect organisational and ideological differences in articulation of what women's issues are and how the movement should proceed to focus on them (Calmen 1992). Though there are divisive, sectarian and vanguardist tendencies within the contemporary women's movement in India, different articulations around the category "women" and their issues could be seen as an expression of the plural Indian society with fragmentation of interests in terms of region, religion, language, ethnicity, caste, class, and gender.

The contemporary women's movement in India has played an important role in confronting the "politics of development" that marginalises poor women, and in creating grassroots organisations as "participatory and mobilising" mechanisms for women's empowerment (Sharma 1991-1992). At one level, the women's movement has contributed to bringing gender issues to the forefront of development planning and pressuring the state to enforce progressive legislation and devise gender-sensitive development policies and programmes. At another level, the "agitational politics" of the women's movement that draws from women's activism has redefined the conventional idea of "politics" that ignores women's political participation in larger social and political movements and women's struggles for women's rights and issues dealing with the "private" sphere.

Within the broader political agenda of the contemporary women's movement in India, how is the issue of women's education addressed? The role of the women's movement in promoting women's education is examined here in terms of the following questions: What role did the social reform movement and the nationalist movement play in promoting women's education? To what extent has the women's movement succeeded in changing school curricula and redefining knowledge? How has the women's movement perceived the role of education in women's empowerment?

Historical Antecedents

The contemporary women's movement in India is set against the historical context of the social reform movement and nationalist movement for independence (Mazumdar 1976). What was the contribution of these movements in promoting women's education? What role was played by the early women's movement in shaping the agenda of women's education?

The Social Reform Movement

The history of the women's movement in India can be traced back to the social reform movement in the early 19th century that attempted to ameliorate the conditions and status of women, particularly those from higher castes. Social reformers were the first to challenge the traditional subordination of Hindu women (Desai 1977). They fought to give women some degree of dignity and status, but within the framework of Hindu revivalism. They continued to emphasise the patriarchal ideals of Hindu women as self-sacrificing, selfless, and submissive wives and mothers.

The basic premise of the social reform movement was that women were oppressed because of social customs and traditions, such as child marriage, *sati*, purdah (physical seclusion) and lack of education. Only a few progressive thinkers, such as Jyotiba Phule and Ishvar Chandra Vidyasagar, perceived oppression of women as a traditional instrument for maintaining social inequality and the dominance of high castes in Indian society (Mazumdar and Sharma 1979). The first *mahila mandals* (women's groups), organised by the Hindu revivalist and reformist organisations—Arya Samaj and the Brahmo Samaj—created space for women for socialising and for education.

Social reformers, revivalists as well as liberals, perceived education of women as an instrument for changing their subordinated status in society. There was considerable debate among the social reformers with different ideological orientations regarding women's education.[1] Cultural revivalists perceived women as the custodians of the tradition and the family. Women's education was seen essentially as a means of strengthening traditional Indian culture and values to resist westernisation. The liberal social reformers advocated limited education for girls to make them enlighted companions for the emergent class of westernised men from upper castes and efficient mothers for the next generation. Thus, education for women was promoted to improve their traditional roles within the patriarchal family. Social reformers neither envisaged women's education as a means to equip them for playing a wider role in society nor emphasised the liberating potential of education to question the patriarchal oppression. Hence, the social reform movement opened up access to schooling for girls and women from the upper castes but the differences in access to the kinds and levels of knowledge remained throughout the colonial period.

The contribution of the social reform movement in improving women's education, however, cannot be underestimated. The efforts of social reformers along with the missionaries paved the way for the development of public female education in the early nineteenth century and provided impetus to the emergence of a group of educated women—such as social workers, teachers, academics and doctors—who later on became the vanguard of the early women's movement (Gandhi and Shah 1991).

The social reform movement also became instrumental in the growth of women's organisations, mostly in urban areas, during 1880-1930. The focus of the women's movement during this period was, however, on improving the status of women within the ideological framework of Hindu revivalists and the emerging class of Western-educated intelligentsia.

The Nationalist Movement

The merging of the social reform movement with the nationalist movement for Independence brought a marked shift in the perspective on women's issues. The democratic ideology of the nationalist movement and the need to broaden the political base of the nationalist struggle contributed to the acceptance of the principles of equality of rights, status, and opportunities for participation in the process of national development (Mazumdar and Sharma 1979). It was the increased political participation of women in the freedom struggle from the 1920s onwards that called for fundamental redefinition of gender roles.

Mahatma K. Gandhi, the leader of India's non-violent freedom struggle, played an important role in channelling the energies of the emerging women's movement into the nationalist movement. Gandhi's view on women synthesised the Hindu ideology on women with liberal Western ideology on "equality" in the public sphere.[2] Like social reformers, Gandhi perceived women as the oppressed group and opposed social customs (early marriage, dowry, purdah, etc.) that subordinated them. He envisaged a significant role for women in Indian society and advocated gender equality in legal, educational, social, and political spheres. To expand the mass-base of the nationalist movement, Gandhi made possible the involvement of women in politics. However, Gandhi's reconstruction of Indian women and feminity was not based on the deeper structural analysis of the origin and nature of gender subordination (Patel 1988).

Hence, Gandhi reaffirmed their traditional role in the family as wife and mother and did not assign any significance to women's productive role within the family or the economy. Thus, Gandhi projected women as the potential vanguard of the non-violent process of social and political transformation without questioning fundamental structures of patriarchy. Although Gandhi favoured female education for all sections of society, he too advocated women's education to improve their traditional roles as wives and mothers in the patriarchal family.

The Early Women's Movement

It was within the historical context of the social reform movement and the nationalist movement that the Indian Women's Association (1917), and the All-India Women's Conference (1927) known as the *Akhil Hind Mahila Parishad* were established to mobilise women for advancing their status through education, social reform and politics.

The All-India Women's Conference, an umbrella women's organisation, played an important role in pressuring the colonial government to give women political and legal rights and amendments in Hindu laws pertaining to marriage, divorce and property. But as it was dominated by Hindu women from upper and middle classes and castes, it lacked the mass-base and refrained from mobilising the rural women or women from the lower rungs of society in its campaign against the orthodox Hindu laws and practices. In practice, the dominant section of the women's movement during the colonial period shared the views of the social reformers and Gandhi on the status of women and did not question patriarchal social relations within the family and society. Although the communist movement was engaged in organising women workers on a small scale since the colonial period, its influence on the early women's movement was very limited because gender issues were subordinated within its broader political agenda of class struggle.

The concept of education as a prerequisite for women's equality was, in fact, the first demand of the early women's movement that developed during the 1920s and 1930s (Mazumdar 1987). The first All-India Women's Conference in 1927 emphasised the need for legal rights to deal with obstacles in promoting education for women and condemned the practice of early marriage as it interfered with women's education. However, education for women was perceived essentially as strengthening their roles within the dominant ideological framework of social reformers and nationalists. Given the elitist nature of the early women's movement, it hardly paid any attention to the question of female education among lower castes and Muslims.[3]

In summary, India's integration into the world economy via colonialism changed some of the forms of traditional patriarchy and introduced contradictions into it without substantially weakening it (Liddle and Joshi 1985). At the same time, the nationalist movement laid the foundation of the principles of women's equality and provided some legal rights in social, economic and political spheres for women. Acceptance of the equality principle by the constitution of India following Independence broadened the roles that women needed to play in society as citizens and opened up new avenues for women through education. Nevertheless, the ambivalence between the traditional view based on the sharp demarcation of the public and private roles of men and women continued in educational policy even after Independence.

Changing the School Curricula

The women's movement in India has played an important role in drawing attention to gender bias in school curricula. However, sporadic and weak efforts by the women's movement have not succeeded in bringing significant changes in school curricula or institutionalising gender-sensitive curriculum reform.

Challenging Curricular Differentiation

Following Independence in 1947, the liberal state, committed to the constitutional principle of equality of women, rejected the colonial educational policy of differentiated curricula between men and women.[4] The National Committee on Women's Education (1958-1959), appointed by the Government of India, recommended common curricula for girls and boys. The Committee on Differentiation of Curricula for Boys and Girls (1964) also rejected the curricular differentiation on the basis of gender and even suggested the inclusion of "home science" in the core curriculum for boys and girls in elementary schools to counteract traditional stereotypes regarding "feminine" and masculine" tasks (Government of India 1964). These recommendations were also endorsed by the Educational Commission (1966). Nevertheless, the basic assumption regarding the primary roles of women as housewives and mothers remained in the educational policy until the late 1970s. In spite of the rejection of the policy of differentiated curricula on the basis of gender, the practice of different curricula for girls and boys continued at the institutional level in many states.

The women's movement before 1975, influenced by the liberal state ideology, was politically too weak to challenge the state. The comprehensive report of the Committee on the Status of Women in India,[5] *Towards Equality,* highlighted that instead of changing social values and attitudes regarding women's roles, the educational system had contributed to strengthening and perpetuating traditional ideas of women's subordination through the "curricula, the classification of subjects on the basis of sex and the unwritten code of conduct enforced on their pupils" (Government of India 1974). In the 1970s, however, the women's movement did not challenge the practice of differentiated curricula because it was preoccupied with the issues of growing violence and atrocities against women and marginalisation of women in the economy (Mazumdar 1987).

Protest against Sexist Bias in School Textbooks

The issue of school curricula was picked up by the urban women's movement in the early 1980s in the context of widespread protest against different forms of violence, including degrading portrayals of women in the media.[6] Voices against gender stereotypes in school textbooks were raised by a few women's organisations as part of the protest against the mainstream media.

A few urban-based women's groups and organisations took up the task of critically analysing the depiction of women in textbooks for school children and their socialisation into gender-defined roles and activities (Gandhi and Shah 1991). They voiced their concerns about how most textbooks propagated gender division of labour and reinforced women's subordination and men's knowledge and authority. The report of the National Commission on Self-Employed Women and Women in the Informal Sector, also highlighted the invisibility of poor women workers and their stereotyped images in school curricula and adult literacy primers and suggested the revision of the textbooks and primers[7] (Government of India 1988a). Only a few organisations, however, pressured the state to change gender bias in textbooks for school children.[8] The task of developing alternative non-sexist material for school children was very limited.

The urban women's movement, dominated by middle class women, did not pursue or sustain efforts to change curriculum content in order to bring about systemic changes in school practices or alter gender differentiation in the selection of field of study at higher levels. Protest against stereotyped images in school textbooks subsided as the attention of the women's movement shifted to other burning issues of violence against Indian women, such as rape, dowry related deaths, foetal sex-determination tests, abortion of female foetuses, *sati,* and atrocities against women during communal unrest and riots.

The State's Response

The response of the Indian state towards the demand of the contemporary women's movement for changing school curricula has been ambivalent. The National Policy on Education (1986) reflects the liberal view of promoting women's education for equality (Government of India, 1986). It advocates the positive interventionist role of the national education system for the empowerment of women and development of new values through redesigned curricula and textbooks.

However, the policy goals are not fully translated into practice. Except for school textbooks, prepared by the National Council of Educational Research and Training (NCERT), the state has not succeeded in removing gender bias from school curricula. Despite an emphasis on women's equality as one of the core values of the literacy curriculum of Total Literacy Campaigns, literacy primers used in the states of Bihar, Gujarat, Madhya Pradesh, Maharashtra, Tamil Nadu and Uttar Pradesh promoted the ideology of domestication. Instead of challenging the gender division of labour in family and society, the content of these primers reinforced women's domestic role as mother and housewife. Thus, educational policy emphasises giving women opportunities to reach the same types and levels of education and training as men. However, there has been no concerted effort to pursue changes in curricular content or in institutional practices.

Redefining Knowledge

In India, research on women is not new. In fact, the debate on the status and conditions of women in the social reform movement and the nationalist movement have provided considerable impetus to research on women. What is new is the shift in emphasis and approaches to understand the changing roles and status of women in the broader context of Indian society.

Women, in general, have been historically excluded from mainstream knowledge production. Whatever knowledge women possessed was either not acknowledged or not given legitimacy. During the past two decades, however, there has been tremendous expansion in research, scholarship, and action related to women's issues in India.[9]

The revival of interest in research on women in the early 1970s can be attributed to a large-scale research project on the status of Indian women in the context of the International Women's Decade. Subsequently, the alarming findings of the Report of the Committee on the Status of Women in India, *Towards Equality* (Government of India 1974), contributed to the emergence of several streams of new scholarship and influenced research on women sponsored by the Indian Council of Social Sciences Research (ICSSR) and a few other agencies[10].

The formation of the Indian Association of Women's Studies in 1981 as a result of the increased interest in women's issues among the academic community and the activists, and the organisation of national/regional conferences of women's studies significantly contributed to forging strong linkages between the women's movement and women's studies[11]. It was through the establishment of women's studies research centres and women's studies cells in the university system that women's studies has become an integral part of the institutionalised system of higher learning.

Women's studies in India strives to promote equality, justice, and liberation through knowledge. While engaging in the "politics of knowledge", women's studies in India has not only made women visible to development planning and academic scholarship but has also broadened the horizons of knowledge to help understand the forces that marginalise women in Indian society. As in other parts of the world, women's studies in India has contributed new understandings in the fields of economics, history, sociology, and, particularly, development planning.

Making Women's Issues Visible

The major contribution of women's studies in the earlier phase was making women's issues academically visible and shifting the research agenda from the concerns of women from upper castes and middle classes to the needs and problems of poor women. The overriding concern of research in the earlier phase of women's studies was on population policy and planning and the issues of poverty, unemployment, inequality, and strategies for survival.

Women's studies has also contributed significantly to the ongoing critique of dominant approaches to development from the feminist perspective. Such critique has succeeded, to some extent, in generating interest in women's studies among development planners and in integrating some of the needs and concerns of women for full employment and distributive justice into development planning. In addition, women's studies has also reinterpreted women's contributions to history and highlighted their substantial role in the creation of culture. While mobilising poor women, women's studies has brought to the forefront their perspectives and knowledge and used this knowledge for intervention. It has reclaimed the history of women's protests and struggles in larger movements and made women's activism a legitimate area of enquiry in social sciences. An equally important aspect of women's studies has been blending academic research with action in various forums to influence public policy and public opinion in order to improve the status and conditions of women.

Women's studies has made an important contribution to understanding how gender socialisation and discriminatory practices adversely affect educational participation by women. The *Towards Equality* report was the first one to draw the attention of educational planners to how education has both reduced and widened the gender gap among different levels of the population. Mazumdar has identified three debates on women's education which have emerged since the publication of this landmark report.[12] The first debate shows how education has contributed to widening gender inequality instead of eliminating women's unequal roles and position in Indian society and has created a new division between educated and uneducated women. The second debate revolves around the issue of continuation of curricular differentiation in educational institutions despite the policy of non-discriminatory curricula.

Finally, the third debate challenges the role of education in promoting social development among women. The problems of dowry, domestic violence, and eve-teasing (verbal sexual harassment of women and girls) have not disappeared but in fact have prevailed among the educated middle class. Since the mid-1980s, the debate on women's education has shifted from gender discrimination in education to using the education system to promote new values and a new kind of social order. The challenge before women's studies is to change the institutionalised processes and organisational structures of the existing system of education.

On the other hand, the influence of women's studies on mainstream educational research has remained very limited. A descriptive study of educational research during 1950-1983 shows that though gender was used as one of the independent variables in several studies, research on women's education from the feminist perspective was very limited. The International Decade for Women provided some impetus to research on women's education. However, research on women's education was dominated by conventional normative and descriptive surveys and seldom reflected feminist perspectives. Women's studies has neither taken up women's education as a priority area nor succeeded in influencing mainstream educational research. Though feminist scholarship on women's education has grown over the years, it has remained on the fringe of women's studies and mainstream educational research.

With the changing political discourse of the women's movement since the mid-1980s, the issues of gender violence, reproductive health, fundamentalism and communalism, and political participation have come to the forefront of movement politics. The challenge before women's studies in the 1990s is, however, to search for an alternative paradigm that gives expression to the plurality and diversity of women's experiences and empowers women to gain autonomy and collective strength in order to change their social reality.

Integrating Theory and Praxis

Women's studies in India aims at promoting gender equality and justice by producing relevant knowledge that leads to action. It is based on the premise that knowledge is not "value-neutral". It is an instrument for domination as well as transformation. Hence, women's studies is aptly described "as the intellectual arm of the women's movement" not only for changing state policies, but also for transforming women's perceptions about themselves. Transformation of the existing intellectual tradition, which has also contributed to maintaining patriarchal social relations, is emphasised equally by women activists and academics.

In India, there is a close linkage between women's studies and the women's movement. Women activists and academics have worked together to redefine knowledge. Women's groups have played a vital role in the expansion of knowledge and generation and dissemination of information. Activists from women's groups and organisations are also active participants in all public forums pertaining to women's studies. They have made a significant contribution by giving expression to the silent voices of ordinary women and integrating their concerns into the research agenda of women's studies. They also have played an important role in articulating the need for developing feminist methodology on the basis of experiences of the women's movement in order to understand the social reality of women at the grassroots.

Women's studies has also striven to break the isolation of academia and learn from the experiences of others. This is evident from the close involvement of many academics with the activities of the women's movement. Research inputs of women's studies have also enriched the women's movement by providing conceptual and analytical tools to interpret forms and mechanisms of women's oppression. Women's groups and organisations working at various levels also look to alternative knowledge produced by women's studies to develop strategies for empowering women. Thus, women's studies in India contains the potential of bringing substantial change to the position of women by linking academic visibility of women's issues with political action.

With the growth of women's studies, however, opinions have become divided regarding its role and focus. Women activists fear that the excessive academicisation of women's studies will alienate it from the women's movement. On the other hand, women's studies scholars are apprehensive that excessive preoccupation with action can lead to the dilution of scientific endeavour. Instead of acting as a catalyst to change all disciplines and shake the foundations of existing knowledge, it could be marginalised as a discipline in the university system. Against the twin danger of excessive academicisation and activism, the key challenge facing women's studies is how to blend research and action, theory and practice without losing its broader political goals.

In the 1990s, women's studies faces the challenging task of pursuing its goals of gender equality and social justice in the context of globalisation and liberalisation. Until now, women's studies has survived in the university system with the financial support and patronage of the government and donor agencies. However, the further growth and sustainability of women's studies research centres and cells are constrained by the present fiscal crisis in higher education. Given the rigidities of the university system, the institutionalisation of women's studies is in danger of losing its transformative and critical role. Thus, in the changing context it remains to be seen to what extent the committed academic community can pursue knowledge that transforms policies and builds perspectives to empower women.

Women's Empowerment for Equality

The women's movement in India has come a long way from its earlier focus on improving the status of women through welfare-oriented activities to demanding social justice and equality in democratic society. It has been with the active involvement of non-governmental organisations (NGOs) and women activists with grassroots women since the mid-1970s, as well as through increased research and documentation of their situation, that the issue of empowerment of grassroots women has come to the forefront of the contemporary women's movement in India (Banerjee 1995). This section highlights salient issues emerging from this debate.

Defining Women's Empowerment

The term "empowerment" has been used widely by the government, donor agencies, NGOs, women activists, and academics since the early 1980s.[13] However, there are apparent differences between development planners and the women's movement in how the concept of empowerment is understood. While working closely with grassroots women, the contemporary women's movement in India has played an important role in giving dynamism to the static interpretation of the concept of empowerment.[14] It has used "empowerment" as a strategy for changing prevailing gender inequalities through transformation of structures of gender subordination.

The present debate on women's empowerment through grassroots groups has emerged from the debate on organising women in the informal sector (Sharma 1991-1992). The term empowerment in India was confined to organising for collective bargaining and improving their capacity to receive essential basic services (education, health care, training, etc.). Over the years, however, the concept of empowerment has broadened to include the growing concerns of the women's movement for gender equality and social justice.

While reviewing the debates on the dynamics and role of grassroots organisations in women's empowerment, Sharma summarises the concept of empowerment as follows:

> The term empowerment refers to a range of activities from individual self-assertion to collective resistance, protest and mobilisation that challenge basic power relations. For individuals and groups where class, caste, ethnicity and gender determine their access to resources and power, their empowerment begins when they not only recognise the systemic forces that oppress them but act to change existing power relations. Empowerment, therefore, is a process aimed at changing the nature and direction of systemic forces which marginalise women and other disadvan-taged sections in a given context.

Thus, women's empowerment is essentially about changing power relations that subordinate women in the family and society. It is an enabling process that seeks to redistribute power between genders and involves resistance, conflict, and accommodation.

Empowerment also involves disempowerment of some structures, systems, and institutions. Given the powerlessness of marginalised women, women's empowerment is more often an externally induced process. Grassroots organisations and intermediary NGOs play an important role in empowering the poor. However, empowerment is not a top-down or one-way process. It is through the continuous and gradual process of conscientisation that women understand the systemic structures of power that dominate and subjugate them, and develop the capability and strength to influence the direction of social change. Empowerment is not, however, simply a change of mindset. It also involves collective action for transforming structures of gender subordination. In the ultimate analysis, individual women's empowerment cannot lead to radical restructuring of power relations in society unless women's mobilisation and collective action through grassroots groups become a political force—an organised mass movement—that challenges and transforms existing power structures.

The interest of the women's movement in empowering women is derived from its recognition of their citizenship and their civil and political rights to transform their social and material conditions. There has been a great deal of debate within the women's movement in India on how women's empowerment can be undertaken (Banarjee 1995). The key questions addressed in this debate are: How can poor women be mobilised through grassroots organisations? Who will empower women? What should be the thrust and the indicators of empowerment? It is within the context of the wider debate on empowerment that the women's movement in India has oriented its actions and attention to education.

Education for Women's Empowerment

Women's groups and organisations in India, working with poor men and women at the grassroots level, recognise the powerful role of formal education in reinforcing social and gender inequalities. At the same time, they have worked towards creating empowering forms of education for poor women. Education is perceived as a critical component of the strategy for women's empowerment.

Unlike the conventional approach to education, empowering education is perceived as a process that does not start with a mechanical transfer of knowledge and skills. It neither rejects women's knowledge and experiences nor imposes new ideas and information on them. But it values women's traditional knowledge and skills. The focus of such education is on broader educational strategies of awareness-building, social analysis, critical reflection, and organisational skills for mobilisation. Educational strategies for women's empowerment are often linked with organisational strategies for mobilisation. Hence, women's groups *(mahila sanghathan)* form the nuclei for the process of empowerment. An attempt is made to create a non-threatening environment for learning for poor women, who are probably learning for the first time.

On the basis of a study of approaches to women's empowerment through NGOs in South Asia and an analysis of materials used in gender training, Batliwala (1993) describes the educational process as follows. In general, gender training begins with ice-breaking exercises to create a climate for open communication among women. This is followed by sharing of experiences of patriarchal domination and powerlessness as well as strength and courage. Such sharing brings out catharsis and helps in building trust and solidarity among the group members. Then, gender and societal analysis helps poor women to understand the structural forces of their oppression. The process of collective reflection is followed by individual or collective actions to change their situation. Finally, they are introduced to new knowledge and information to influence their environment through local organisations. Thus, the basic educational strategy for empowering women includes development of critical consciousness (of both society and one's self), reaching out to new bodies of knowledge and information, development of analytical skills for critical reflection and action, and learning organisational strategies for change.

The transformatory form of education goes hand in hand with the mobilisation strategies in order to bring sustainable changes to women's lives. Hence, the role and process of building women's collectives is emphasised all throughout the educational process. Furthermore, the core content of empowering training/education must be situated within a broader understanding of the ways in which the state and patriarchy construct, mediate, and reinforce gender relations.

Contributions of the women's movement in mainstreaming popular education for women's empowerment are visible in the space created within the state for innovative educational interventions for poor, rural women. For example, the state-sponsored programmes of the Women's Development Programme of Rajesthan and the *Mahila Samakhya* (Education for Women's Equality) in some of the districts of Andhra Pradesh, Gujarat, Karnataka, and Uttar Pradesh can be seen as early attempts at operationalising the strategy for women's empowerment through education.

The starting point in these programmes is not to impose literacy or traditional education on women, but to allow them to seek education at a point when its meaning and value become evident to them. Education is used as an intervention to facilitate the process of collective reflection and action through *mahila sanghas* and to improve women's access to development activities.

While criticising traditional educational and training programmes that focus merely on imparting literacy skills to women, women activists working closely with grassroots women have also attempted to redefine women's literacy for empowerment. Literacy is perceived as a strategic intervention for empowering women in the wider struggle against inequality and injustice in society. Thus, literacy for poor women is advocated as a means of acquiring knowledge and skills through which they begin to understand and analyse unequal gender relations in society and to change the nature and direction of systemic forces that marginalise them.

Experiences of empowering women through government-sponsored educational programmes, such as the Women's Development Programme in Rajasthan, the *Mahila Samakhya* Programme and Total Literacy Campaigns, show mixed results. At one level, these programmes have created some space to work in partnership with the government and have given women's groups greater outreach and access to resources for women's empowerment. However, the state coopts the political agenda of women's literacy when its interests are threatened. Empowered women have been able to address collectively the problems of drinking water, primary health services, child care, bus services, wages, and work conditions. Though they have not always been successful in obtaining these services and facilities, the process of collective action has strengthened their groups and built resilience. In some places, women have gone beyond practical gender issues and taken up strategic gender interests related to domestic and social violence against women, such as alcoholism, wife-battering, sexual exploitation, and marital disputes.

Over the last two decades, the contemporary women's movement has moved away from improving the status and conditions of women through welfare measures to enabling them to become economically self-reliant and empowering them to change unequal relations of power in society. On the basis of the grassroots women's struggle for equity and social justice, the women's movement in India has broadened our understanding of education for women's empowerment.

Empowering education is essentially political, seeking to change unequal power relations in society. The women's movement in India has attempted to interface between the feminist focus on individual empowerment and the emphasis of grassroots organisations on collective empowerment through women's collectives. Rigorous analysis of the educational process of empowerment will help us understand the meaning and parameters of empowerment in different socio-political contexts and how grassroots mobilisation gives poor women space to redefine their priorities within the women's movement in India.

Summing up

The main concerns of the contemporary women's movement in education appear to be improving women's access to all levels of education and using education as an instrument to transform values and attitudes for the creation of a new social order. The contemporary women's movement has played an important role in making the dismal educational situation of poor women visible in development planning. It has also made a significant contribution in giving a strong meaning and actual form to the concept of women's empowerment. In the 1990s, however, the contemporary women's movement faces new challenges to promote women's education in the context of worsening economic conditions, growing gender violence, rising religious fundamentalism, and identity politics.

Until now, the state as a mediator has responded to some of the demands of the women's movement and passed progressive legislation to promote the goal of gender equality. However, the process of economic stabilisation and structural adjustment (SAP), initiated by the government in the early 1990s, will have far-reaching impacts on the status and conditions of women. The government issues assurances that women and the poor will be protected through social safety net measures during the transitional period of economic restructuring. However, the new development approach with its emphasis on economic growth through globalisation, privatisation and liberalisation is likely to sharpen existing inequalities in society. In the changed scenario, it remains to be seen to what extent the women's movement can pressure the state for interventions to promote gender equality.

The issue of women and religious fundamentalism came to the forefront in the 1980s. Growing communalism and factional politics based on caste, language and ethnicity, have posed new challenges for the women's movement (see Sharma 1992; Agnihotri and Mazumdar 1995). The women's movement has extensively debated the relationship between religion and patriarchy. While religion is criticised as an obscurantist and oppressive force reinforcing women's subordination, the question of "cultural identity" is not seriously debated.

In the changing economic environment, the nature and direction of women's education is shaped by the dominant development paradigm that perceives women as an inexpensive source of labour and as consumers of the products of global markets. What is needed is a deeper understanding of the impact of macro-economic policies and their impacts on women's education in order to create more spaces within the mainstream education system to address deeper causes of gender inequality.

Except for women's studies in higher education, most of the efforts of women's education are concentrated in developing alternatives and innovations outside the formal system of education.[15] Though the contemporary women's movement has shifted attention away from the discriminatory role of education to the transformatory potential of education, it has not made concerted efforts to change the direction of the new educational reform nor to create spaces to change the mainstream system of education.

The National Policy on Education (NPE), formulated in 1986 and revised in 1992, has provided a separate and protected space for women's empowerment through the Mahila Samakhya Programme, an educational programme aimed at promoting women's education for equality. However, such space within the state has remained limited and not extended to the larger system of education. Under the social safety net approach, the focus of educational policy has shifted from higher education to basic education (elementary education). Such a policy is, however, likely to restrict women's access to higher education and constrain the space given to women's studies in higher education.

The women's studies centres within the university system have created some space to question knowledge that makes women and their concerns invisible and to generate new knowledge not only to understand the forces that marginalise women, but to transform their consciousness and values, and enlarge the horizons of feminist praxis.

Until now the women's movement has built its agendas around women's issues. Though women's education has remained a low priority for the movement, it has brought to our attention the feminist vision of education. However, the women's movement has succeeded neither in carrying this vision to the people's movements nor in influencing the concepts and strategies of the Total Literacy Campaigns in which women's participation has been high. Ideological differences regarding women's subordination have prevented the women's movement from forging strong and longer alliances with the people's movements and from using the space created through large-scale mobilisation of women in literacy campaigns. It is essential for the women's movement to build linkages with other people's movements and struggles in order to raise feminist concerns for women's education within other movements and develop a broad-based support for changing the dominant system of education.

In conclusion, the challenges before the women's movement are enormous. What is needed is to address multi-faceted and long-term perspectives and approaches. It is crucial to develop alternatives outside the formal system of education to promote women's empowerment. However, it is equally important to develop strategies and mechanisms to change the institutionalised practices and organisational structures of the existing system of education that reproduce gender inequalities. If women's education for equality is not only a women's issue, but a political issue, then the women's movement can develop multi-pronged and long-term strategies and approaches with the help of broad-based support from grassroots organisations and other movements.

REFERENCES

1. Refer to Kishwar (1986) and Karlekar (1986) for the debate over women's education among social reformers and internal contradictions in their views.
2. For a detailed discussion of Gandhi's view on women refer to Kishwar (1985a, b) and Patel (1988).
3. Refer to Hassan (1992) for a brief discussion on Muslim women's education during the colonial period. She argued that the vast majority of Muslim women remained on the fringe of the colonial educational system due to socio-religious oppression. The Muslim social reformers in the early 19th century also questioned oppressive social customs (polygamy, early marriage, ban on widow remarriage, and dowry) and advocated female education to make them more conscientious and religious and to improve their roles as wives and mothers. Muslim women from the upper class also actively participated in the nationalist movement and advocated female education. However, educational participation of poor Muslim women remained very limited.
4. There was considerable debate on the issue of curricula for both the sexes in the early post-Independence period (see the Government of India 1974: 274-75).
5. This comprehensive report on the status of Indian women was commissioned by the Government of India for the International Year for Women in 1975. Feminist social scientists in India participated actively in the Committee's investigation.
6. In the early 1980s, several women's groups, activists and media professionals expressed their concerns about the negative trends in the portrayal of women in the mainstream media (print, films and television) that reinforced ideological and cultural reproduction of women's subordination in society. They organised some protests and campaigns against sexism and obscenity in the mainstream media (Bhasin and Agarwal 1984).

7. With the active participation of feminist researchers and activists, this commission played an important role in highlighting the situation of poor working women in the informal sector.
8. Ahmedabad Women's Action Group undertook in the mid-1980s a gender analysis of the school textbooks and worked with the Gujarat State School Textbook Board to improve the textbooks. Refer to Shah et al. (1987) for the details.
9. Vyas and Singh (1993) for detailed information on published and unpublished sources relating to women's studies in India. Women's studies owes its growth to a group of committed academics, official patronage, and the support of international donor agencies (Krishna Raj 1988).
10. Mazumdar (1989) for a detailed discussion on the ICSSR's Programme of Women's Studies.
11. The Indian Association of Women's Studies was established with the primary objective of integrating women's issues into teaching and research and providing a common platform for increasing interactions between the academic community, activists, and others engaged in action programmes for women's development (Vyas and Singh 1993).
12. These debates have emerged in the specific historical context of the state and the women's movement in India.
13. Although the term "women's empowerment" was not used in India until the 1980s, the notion of empowerment was implicit in discussions on women's devel opment and women's equality in the 1970s (Banerjee 1995).
14. Sharma (1991-1992) and Banerjee (1995) for discussion on the con temporary debate on women's empowerment and grassroots organisations.
15. The draft report on "National Consultation on Education", organised by the Coordination Unit, World Conference on Women, Beijing. Nirantar: National Institute of Adult Education and Ankur, New Delhi 20-22 July, 1995.

4

GENDER DISCRIMINATION

Introduction

Gender is a common term where as gender discrimination is meant only for women, because females are the only victims of gender discrimination. Gender discrimination is not biologically determined but it is determined by socially and the discrimination can be changed by the proper and perpetuate efforts. Denial of equality, rights and opportunity and suppresment in any form on the basis of gender is gender discrimination.

Half of the world's population is females. They are doing two-third of work of the total work in the world but received only one-tenth of the world's total income. Nearly two-third of the women is illiterates and they have possessed only one per cent of the total world's assets. In the world, only one-fourth of the families are headed by female. India is a male dominant society and gender discrimination is customised habitually.

The beginning of any systematic women's studies in India is usually dated to the publication of the report *"Towards Equality' in 1974* (Government of India, 1974). This document, by scanning available data, was able to establish the size and the significance of gender gaps in post-Independence India, and stimulated a wide spectrum of both analytical and empirical work. It is customary to start any discussion on gender by distinguishing between the terms 'sex' and 'gender'. 'Sex' being a biologically determined attribute is not easy to change while 'gender' refers to socially constructed roles, which are likely to vary from one society to another, and which change significantly as societies develop and evolve over time. The construction of gender roles in any society is influenced by several factors, most of which are largely independent of the sources of poverty or growth.

An important contribution of the report Towards Equality was its clear articulation of the two sets of factors that play a role in the construction of gender in a society. These two sets of factors are those that determine 'achieved status' and those that determine 'ascriptive status. Achieved status is 'a status acquired by an individual through her efforts, often through competition and the use of special abilities, knowledge and skill.' Ascriptive status refers to 'any status not based on individual ability, skill, efforts or accomplishment but on inherited positions in society' (Govt. of India 1974. "Achieved status' is determined by such attributes as education, health, work participation and so on, essentially characterised by the fact that these are individual attributes, and are amenable to change through individual decision. In contrast, 'ascriptive' status include factors that are not in the control of the individual and represent a collective consciousness or community norms, such as family and kinship norms, the nature of the conjugal contract, levels of seclusion, religion etc.

Over the years, with changes in patterns of living, and the economic and demographic characteristics of society, the influence of ascriptive factors has undoubtedly come down. The fact remains however, that the roots of gender inequality are to be found in the 'black box' of whatever constitutes ascriptive status.

The influence of disciplinary rigour on research in the area has meant that, by and large, economists have confined themselves to the analysis of quantifiable factors, and the study of ascriptive status has remained within the domain of sociology. A second major influence on the work of economists has been the search for policy interventions that would have maximum impact. It would not be correct to suggest that research attention has been directed to 'achieved status' variables alone. But if we confine ourselves to the work of economists, then this statement is not too far from the truth.

The basic motivation behind research in this area is to identify the best points of intervention that would help to bring about change in gender relations, in the direction of greater equality, in a context of economic growth and human development. Development, in the simple sense of increasing material welfare, has dominated discussion and planning for growth since the 1950s, although the strategies recommended have changed considerably over the years. But it is only since the 1970s that gender equality has been an objective in the formulation of national macro policy, and this owes much to the advocacy and intervention of international bodies, specially the UN system.

Clearly, one can think of gender equality ('equal access and opportunities for men and women') as being realised only within an enabling framework of equal rights and equal access. The legal and constitutional framework of rights therefore forms an essential component in any discussion. It can be argued that economic equality is needed to make other equalities real. Indicators frequently used to measure gender equality include life expectancy, education, and earnings. These give an indication of the degree of access to food, health, education, and the means of livelihood. Other indicators are sometimes suggested to give a more direct measure of the extent to which women have control over their lives: one is the degree of seclusion expected from women. Interpretation of change is equally complex.

However, unless the ascribed roles of men and women change, gender equality will remain a distant goal. It is this understanding that forms the point of departure for this paper.

This introductory section is followed by a review of gender indicators such as education, health, employment and asset ownership which broadly demarcate the 'achieved status' of women. Section III reviews a set of less 'conventional' indicators such as violence against women reflecting their 'ascriptive' status. Section IV provides some quick comments on interventions. Section V provides an analytical assessment of the complementarity of 'conventional' and 'non-conventional' indicators in the study of gender discrimination. Section VI looks at the issue of gender equality under changing economic policy regimes. The concluding section provides some pointers to a possible research agenda.

Commonly used Indicators of Gender Discrimination: A Selective Review of the Literature

Indicators of gender discrimination seek to go beyond description, and to identify policy measures for improving women's status or autonomy. These terms are not synonymous. Status has the connotation of relative social standing, and improving status may not increase autonomy, a term that suggests the ability of self-determination, independence and control over one's life. However, knowledge of status is important in defining norms of behaviour, and permissible deviations from such norms. Demographic studies have tried to explore the extent to which women have control over their fertility behaviour by using various measures of 'autonomy'. Proxies used for female autonomy include female age at marriage, age difference between spouses, female secondary school education (Abadian 1996).

An interesting dimension of autonomy, draws attention to the difference between autonomy that is culturally 'granted' and that which is sought. Most of the measures above reflect a social consciousness rather than individuality. Women do not 'choose' where to have their children, how long to stay in school, or when and whom to marry. In fact, real autonomy in a majority of Indian households may be closely related to age, so that in a very real sense older women have the power to 'give' greater autonomy to young women. As Basu puts it, "The real pity often is not that men wield so much domestic power, it is that during the prime reproductive years female power is at its lowest" (Basu 1996: 54). "The 'socialisees' rather than the already 'socialised' represent the potential agents of change" (Epstein 1982)

There seems to be an increasing recognition in the literature of the interdependence of different variables. At the same time, it is important to identify a single or a small set of interventions from which one could try and improve women's status/autonomy. The same variable(s) may not be equally effective in all situations.

Education and Employment

Education and employment are undoubtedly the most popular choices of ways to improve women's well-being. The cause of women's education, in particular, has received much support from the findings of demographers.

'A number of empirical studies indicate that the extent of anti-female bias in survival is substantially reduced by various influences that give women more voice and agency within the family. One of these influences is female education. Another is the ability to earn an independent income through paid employment.'

The schooling-fertility link has been found to be strong in all empirical studies, although the lines of causation are not always clear. A recent study of Palestinian women re-affirms the power of education to secure better employment and economic independence and lead to more equitable gender roles. South East Asian experience also yields similar conclusions. The drawback of an excessive reliance on schooling as education is that usually it re-affirms gender roles and stereotypes; while formal schooling as a route to formal sector occupation is not substitutable, it is not always the case that educated and employed women are necessarily 'empowered' in the sense of having greater autonomy. Much depends on the content of the schooling.

In the context of Eastern Europe and transition to a liberal market economy, educational systems that favour learning by rote have been compared unfavourably to those which emphasise problem solving. If independent critical thought is the essence of 'success' of schooling, this is by no means ensured in South Asian schools, with very few exceptions. Equally important is the number of years spent in school. There is scattered evidence to suggest that little difference is made to employment or other decisions unless 8-10 years are spent in school. However in India only 8.6 per cent of adult females, and 15.3 per cent of adult males have completed middle school, as against 40 per cent and 66 per cent who are literate (Shariff 1999). Moreover, even higher levels of formal education may be needed for the kind of exposure to new ideas and strategies that questioning of gender roles will need.

Employment as a route to empowerment is equally complex. Work participation levels of women are high, if an extended labour force definition is used, although the majority are in informal sector jobs, crowded into the low skill end of the spectrum, and usually in part time work. The uncertain impact of paid work on women's welfare is closely related to their continued home responsibilities. Does earning an independent income increase a woman's bargaining power? The answer is yes if she has real control over it. In many situations however women work in response to household needs, and have been variously described as 'target earners' or as a 'flexible resource of the household'. It is unlikely that earning an income will alter the balance of power substantially; more likely, it will reflect the pre-existing balance of power in a household. If this is reasonably good (a complex of individual and cultural attributes) work may be empowering; if bad, it can lead to higher levels of stress and continued exploitation.

A recent analysis finds that regions with higher initial levels of female labour force participation have experienced larger growth of per capita expenditure and also faster poverty decline. In identifying the possible reasons behind this finding, the authors suggest that 'First, female labour force participation can be seen as having an important insurance role, in so far as a household with more earning members is less exposed (other things being equal) to downward income fluctuations resulting from illness and related events. Second, higher levels of female labour force participation leads to greater flexibility in occupational choices at the household level. Third, female labour force participation can be interpreted as an indicator of the general involvement of women in economic, social and political matters, with faster poverty decline being more likely in a society which gives greater scope for women's agency in general.' The same study finds little connection between literacy and poverty reduction.

The first two of the possible links suggested are relatively uncontroversial. The third, however, requires substantiation.

As Ramu puts it, "The choice of employment by urban wives is neither indicative of deviation from past practices nor a signal to future change in domestic and personal life. When women realise that they cannot satisfactorily resolve the conflict between new economic and old domestic roles, they not only compartmentalise these two roles but also scale down their occupational aspirations in favour of maternal and conjugal obligations."

Much of the feminist analysis that has tried to address this question has revolved around analysis of time use. In both rural and urban India, women spend a large proportion of time on unpaid, home sustaining work. With economic development many of these activities (fetching water for instance) should in theory be provided through public utilities or the market. At present, these are still the responsibility of the individual. One estimate shows that 88 per cent of rural women and 66 per cent of urban women are engaged in one or another self-provisioning activity. Investment in infrastructure, specially the provision of facilities of drinking water, sanitation, and fuel and fodder, will result in a reduction of time on unpaid work. Other things remaining the same, this will contribute to an increase in women's welfare. But without any reduction in unpaid work, paid work is unlikely to be liberating.

A second issue is that of labour mobility. Increased demand for women's labour, particularly in export oriented and labour intensive units, is a frequent outcome of structural adjustment programmes. But women may not be able to respond to new opportunities and to shift to new occupations, because their mobility tends to be low, even where migration is not involved. This is partly attributable to intra-household allocation of responsibilities. Rights and obligations within a household are not distributed evenly. Male ownership of assets and a conventional division of labour reduce incentives for women to undertake new activities. In addition, child bearing has clear implications for labour force participation by women. Time spent in bearing and bringing up children often results in de-skilling, termination of long term labour contracts, and in poor households can also result in deterioration of health. The behaviour of women in seeking work, and how entrepreneurial they are in the face of new opportunities, is also affected by the presence or absence of role models; so new jobs that get taken up by men easily get to be seen as the rightful preserve of men (Collier 1994). Despite this, the East Asian economies witnessed a dramatic increase in women's labour force participation in the 1960s and 1970s. However, it is only where the labour surplus situation no longer exists, as in Singapore, that women workers in the export sector can be said to have distinctly better employment prospects subsequent to industrialisation.

Household needs change over the life cycle, and women's labour force participation in different age groups shows varying patterns in different countries: single peaked, double peaked or plateau (as in India). The 'peaking' is caused by women dropping out of the labour force during the period that they have young children. Whether or not they return to work depends on labour market institutions as well as social supports and conventions. Studies suggest that women in the urban informal sector need to supplement family income once they have children, since it is not possible for the man to increase his earnings any further. Peak reproductive demands lead to an increased participation in paid activity, further increasing the vulnerability of women already at a vulnerable point in their lifecycle.

A clear distinction needs to be made between women whose work participation goes up in response to new opportunities (usually those who are educated, urban, and very often young enough not to find family responsibilities a constraint) and those whose work intensity goes up as a result of excessive demands on time. The latter is specially likely to happen to older women, who are not as mobile, usually illiterate and unskilled, who are unable to find alternative employment in a situation of re-structuring. Such women may find themselves moving to less and less productive work, and longer hours, and probably increasing the quantum of unpaid work in an effort to save household resources. Greater mobility will benefit the one group but not the other.

Demographic Transition and Access to Resources

While demographic transition has accompanied, or facilitated, economic growth in most countries, certain demographic characteristics that indicate the low status of women seem very resistant to rising incomes. Son preference that characterises India, and Asia in general, does not disappear with rising incomes. The discrimination evident in a declining sex ratio and in the large numbers of 'missing women' suggests that there is no reduction of gender bias in a context of economic growth (Dasgupta and Bhat 1998). Indicators reflecting the health status of women show the same patterns. First, the perception of poor health itself varies across gender. Second, there is some evidence that medical intervention is sought more often for boys than girls. Third, there is very inadequate allocation for health needs special to women.

The Cairo Conference on Population and Development (1994) recognised the need to address health and demographic concerns in a broader framework. The programme of action recognises the need for sustained economic growth in the context of sustainable development; education, especially for girls; gender equity and equality; infant, child and maternal mortality reduction; and the provision of universal access to reproductive health services, including family planning and sexual health.

Adequate investment in infrastructure and in social development characterised the growth of East Asia, and has been held up as a lesson to India. Growth with poverty reduction has been shown to be possible. The poverty estimate in China in 1978 stood at 33 per cent and at 10 per cent in 1985. In Malaysia and Indonesia, the poverty ratios continued to decline in the three or four years post-reform. One common aspect of growth in these countries is investments in infrastructure and in health. But such investments are in themselves unlikely to be enough either to improve the relative status of women or to confront the patriarchal structures developed over centuries. Agarwal argues that it is ownership and control of land that holds the key to empowering women and to more equitable gender relations in South Asia (Agarwal 1994). Agarwal extends and modifies the bargaining approach, and Sen's cooperative conflict model, to develop a framework within which questions relating to women's empowerment can be analysed. Women in uncomfortable situations tend to use the 'weapons of the weak': covert resistance rather than confrontation. What might be needed, then, especially in the South Asian context, is more emphasis on their ability to pursue their self-interest, rather than better perception of self-interest which is possibly high. As she points out, quite apart from the process of bargaining, the issues that are open to bargaining will vary from one society to another. The crux of the empowerment-through-land argument lies in the ability to exert real control, and not just in having legal title.

Less conventional indicators

How far do the above 'conventional' indicators succeed in capturing unequal gender relations? As one observer noted, 'Most of the world views Hindu women as degraded, downtrodden slaves. Yet, the percentages of Indian women in the professions compare favourably with those of the West: Indian women comprise 7.1 per cent of the doctors, 1.2 per cent of the lawyers and 10.9 per cent of the scientists, in spite of incredibly low literacy rates for the overall female population...Clearly, Indian women present a paradoxical situation for the interpreter of South Asian society. The view of the Hindu woman as downtrodden represents one behavioural reality; her participation in the highest political and social arenas is another undeniable reality'.

Speaking on the subject of the changing position of Indian women in 1978, M.N. Srinivas was optimistic about the mingling of traditional support structures and new roles, concluding that "migration to urban areas, female political participation, education, the activities of social reformers, and the inequities of dowry, all resulted in enabling women to make a relatively easy transition to new roles and responsibilities". Among the enabling factors in this transition, Srinivas suggests that the availability of servants and of kin-networks are probably crucial in reducing conflicts between job pressures and home management. In addition, Indian men have not opposed feminine emancipation".

One way of measuring the extent to which such a transition has taken place, from women being purely domestic entities, essentially playing a supportive role to men, to equal participants in economic and politi cal activity, would be to look at measures of education, and employment. However the success of the transition will depend on its acceptability. If educated working women face high levels of stress, this may be the result of inadequate support structures and of low responsibility and emotional support from families. Measuring stress will require monitoring of less quantifiable indicators, including the degree of seclusion enforced upon women, domestic violence, and the prevalence of depression/ anxiety.

Domestic Violence, Stress and Depression

Domestic violence and depression are reported from very diverse societies. The form of the violence may vary—from dowry demands and bride burning to credible threats. Domestic violence needs a clear definition: it includes actual and threatened violence, psychological abuse and sexual assault, and its defining characteristic is that it tends to be repetitive in nature, but difficult to anticipate or avoid.

The reluctance of women to acknowledge or address violence is hardly surprising, since it is usually associated with low self-esteem, a sense of personal inadequacy, and an erosion of coping strategies over time. Even more, family/kin are unwilling to acknowledge its existence unless it crosses some threshold level. In a study of wife beating practices in Karnataka, Vijayendra Rao reports that "Mild forms of wife-beating seemed commonplace. Many men and women admitted to it in informal conversations, often claiming that it was justified if the wife did not 'behave herself'. However, in the context of the survey interview, only 22 per cent of women admitted to have been physically assaulted by their husbands... Only the women for whom beating was a serious and chronic problem admitted to it." And further, that "Wife abuse, while widely tolerated and often even considered necessary by the community, has to happen under circumstances that are considered legitimate. Disputes over dowries, a wife's sexual infidelity, her neglect of household duties, and her disobedience of her husband's dictates are all considered legitimate causes for wife beating. A husband who beats his wife when he is drunk, but is otherwise a 'good' husband, is also tolerated by the community, which believes that any sanctions they might impose would not have much effect on his drinking. However, husbands can suffer significant social disapproval when they batter their wives beyond levels considered tolerable by the village, or beat them for reasons not considered legitimate by the community".

Violence is not unique to Indian or South Asian society, but the form it takes and the acceptable threshold, probably vary from one society to another. For instance, it is often remarked upon that Indian women may more often choose, even where economic independence is not the issue, to stay with or return to violent husbands, and in extreme situations choose 'suicide over separation.' The psycho-sexual basis of domestic violence itself is probably culture specific. Without venturing too far into this field, some recurrent images which help to explain the persistence and acceptance of domestic violence in India, are reported here. On the one hand, the Indian version of the Freudian mother-whore dichotomy ('mother-whore-partner-in-ritual') apparently continues to have a strong hold on men. This 'describes the separation of sexuality from tenderness, the object of desire from the object of adoration'

The result is that, as Sudhir Kakar puts it, "Given the perception of the man as someone who is infantile in his attachments, volatile in his affections, and cruel in his anger, the woman's choice in love is limited to appeasement and masochistic surrender." At the same time women continue to derive their identity from the *jodi*', (literally, 'pair') with the result that 'burning rage' is less often seen than 'aching disappointment' 'In the ideals of the traditional culture, the 'good' woman is a *pativrata,* subordinating her life to the husband's welfare and needs in a way demanded of no other woman in any other part of the world with which I am familiar.' The relevance of these culture-specific images to psychiatric intervention is clear. Most often, it is depression and anxiety for which women seek help. What needs to be emphasised is that there is no conclusive evidence of the role of biological/hormonal factors, with the single exception of post-partum depression, and social factors have generally been underestimated (Abel et al 1996). The implications for forms of intervention are explored further in the next section.

Interventions: Some Quick Comments

Policies directed at eliminating or at least reducing gender disparities are an integral part of Indian policy documents today. The interactions between the various instruments are assumed to be mutually complementary. However, experience suggests that without adequate social supports, both psychological and physical, the outcomes are difficult to predict.

Education

Policymakers have generally been receptive to such goals as higher levels of education and employment. An emphasis on girls' schooling, hostels for working women, and other such measures increase opportunities for women within existing economic structures. It is also accepted generally that enhancing capabilities in this manner is not always possible through market mechanisms. A World Bank publication concludes that the persistent gender gap in education is an example of market failure and government action is needed here (World Bank 1995 a, b; Summers 1994). In India, state interventions to promote access to schooling, work and health facilities take some note of constraints specific to women. But such interventions do not address the broader structural constraints on women.

Work

From observation and small samples, it does not seem that work outside the home increases women's agency, at least not on its own. In fact, clinical observation suggests that it can result in an increased risk of depression in women. The nature of the work, the extent to which women are in supportive relations, the presence of young children, whether husbands are employed or not: these are some of the many factors that determine whether or not work is beneficial or detrimental. It has been suggested that it is probably not the presence or absence of particular roles in women's lives that predispose some of them to more distress, but a particular combination of roles. There is evidence that multiple roles can be good for women's mental health. Women who have multiple roles, but who also have social support and financial security, are less likely to get depressed than either women with few roles or sources of self-esteem/power, or those with multiple roles with many demands and little support.

The central point is that developing economies are also changing societies. 'Western' notions of a mind at peace with itself include concepts of self-sufficiency, personal autonomy, efficiency and self-esteem; 'eastern' notions emphasise integration and harmony, social integration, balanced functioning and protection and caring. These make an impact on how one would treat the incidence of stress-related disorders. The western approach would emphasise control, understanding by analysis, problem solving and separation of body and mind. An eastern approach would seek understanding by awareness, acceptance, harmony, contemplation, and a body-mind-spirit unity (Fernando 1995). Therapy that takes the form of meditation or prayer may begin to have limited relevance where changing gender roles are involved. Or, to put it in another way, a form of intervention is needed that can address both personal anguish and social/cultural oppression. This is a big task to undertake, requiring the development of 'a series of options, each one more socially connected than the last, in a progression from private symptom to public action' (Holland 1995).

Law

In India, considerable emphasis has been placed on the law as a tool for social change. But how judges will interpret the law, and how far the intentions of social reform movements are translated into practice, is difficult to predict. Two decades ago, women activists did not hesitate to condemn dowry, or offer divorce as a way out of oppressive situations. Today, there seems to be a general feeling that no 'quick' solutions are possible, and that much more sustained action is needed. Dowry must be abolished, but women's rights to property must also be ensured. Divorce must be made possible, but the stigma attached to it must also go; women's ability to earn and live alone or to seek a new partner requires social consent and approval.

Counselling

It is here that institutions to provide support and practical alternatives acquire their importance. Today, there are a large number of counselling centres in Delhi, for example, responding essentially to problems that arise in the wake of changing gender roles and aspirations, family structures and economic opportunities. An analysis of cases handled at the ISST Counselling Centre suggests that earlier patterns of arranged marriages are simply unable to cope with situations where personal initiative is needed and nuclear families are the norm. (Jaishankar 1997). At the same time, marriages of choice between individuals from different castes/regions/ cultures, which are becoming increasingly common, face even greater problems, with clashing cultural norms and role expectations that take a while to surface. One of the recommendations of the ISST report was the need for extensive pre-marriage counselling, for both men and women, to help in an informed assessment of likely compatibility in attitudes, expectations, awareness, self-esteem and values. In addition, there is need for easier access to referral services and legal help for clients. These suggestions are more radical than they might appear: they require open discussion of sex, individuality and questioning of norms, none of which forms part of the normal socialisation of Indian children.

Social Networks

Autonomy for women should not imply irresponsibility on the part of others. Hence, the continued importance of support networks and group solidarity (Abadian 1996). Of relevance, here is the distinction that has been made between the role of human capital, Chuman resource endowments with physical health determining capacity to work, and skills and education determining the returns to labour') and social capital ('inter-household and intra-community level reciprocity drawing on social resources'.

Empowerment of women, in the Indian context, unquestionably requires some change in the norms of behaviour. This in turn, calls for new structures providing emotional and psychological guidance, something that kin networks would normally do when norms are stable. The multi-layered institutions that make up the social capital of a community do provide a fabric of support and a safety net for the vulnerable. However, while all societies permit some deviance, in transitional situations 'permissible' and 'actual' deviance come into conflict with each other.

In devising development strategies that are sensitive to the need for greater gender equality, both the more individual route to empowerment (education, health, employment) and the 'institutional' route (e.g. via construction of social capital) are potential tools.

An analytical assessment of the complementarity of 'conventional' and 'non-conventional' indicators in the study of gender discrimination

One of the criticisms leveled against the Gender Development Index (GDI) popularised by UNDP's Human Development Report (1995) has been that it is not contextualised, so that comparisons across countries or regions, may not be very meaningful. Much of the literature that has been spawned subsequently in the field on the contrary, has been in the direction of adding on to the list of possible indicators from a wide range of areas of concern, spanning economic, social, political and demographic dimensions of gender inequality, both within and outside the family.

With increases in income, one would expect some conventional disparities (e.g. in education, health) to go down. The HDI 1995 attempts to record the achievements of countries using two alternative indices, the GDI and the GEM. Subsequent work on constructing indices has shown that using different estimates can generate very different rankings (Seeta Prabhu 1996). The popularity of conventional measures (education, employment) is based on the assumption that (1) they are amenable to policy intervention and (2) they have an influence on the underlying structural determinants of gender discrimination.

Our categorisation of indicators into 'conventional' and 'non-conventional' ones does not follow this pattern. Although, the review touches on only a few commonly used indicators of gender discrimination, the category of 'conventional' indicators will include almost all the measured and directly measurable indices of gender discrimination that are found in the literature. The difference between the 'conventional' indicators and the 'non-conventional' ones is not simply that one is more amenable to measurement while the other is not; we feel that the latter are in some sense one step closer to that unobserved and unobservable category, i.e., gender discrimination that one is seeking to measure.

The study by Seeta Prabhu et. al. raises an objection against the choice of variables in the construction of GDI since they feel that gender discrimination in Indian society would have been captured better through differences in indicators other than 'per capita income', 'educational achievements' and 'life expectancy'.

What are these other indicators? More pertinently, is it useful to use the same set of indicators under all conditions? It has been argued that gender relations in Indian society get "influenced" by "traditional hierarchies" based on patriarchy, caste and ethnicity, and compounded by inequalities of wealth and power — that poverty "accentuates the problems faced by women." This suggests that caste, ethnicity and poverty can shape the observed manifestation of gender discrimination. This is inclusive of the possibility that the interaction of these factors can influence the nature of gender discrimination. Also, since caste and ethnicity are in some sense indelible categories, or signals, and poverty is not so, the dynamic implications of moving in and out of poverty groups could be quite different from cross sectional differences between caste or ethnic groups. Prabhu et al believe that indicators such as access to fuel and water, property rights and incidence of violence against women would have served as better indicators. This may well be the case, but the question remains how such a conclusion is justified.

There is a case for arguing that in some sense discrimination against women is a social problem which manifests itself in different forms under different situations. It is fine to try to find proper indicators for gender discrimination; the problem occurs when one forgets that these indicators or deficiencies indicated by them in themselves are not the disease but only the symptoms. Many attempts at fighting gender discrimination in the past have had limited impact because of this misplaced identity.

The single-minded emphasis on income-generation activities in the 1980s to boost women's status, to the exclusion of other dimensions of control and access, is a case in point. Increased labour force participation again is one such indicator. It is not necessarily the case that the labour force participation by itself is emancipatory. It may simply be a reflection of a changed manifestation of gender discrimination. Many educated married women who are employed do so to enhance household income packets on which they have little control and end up doubling their daily workload at the same time. Middle-class educated families in urban India might not discriminate in basic education or health care, but may still demand and provide dowry as a basic right and inflict bodily harm, even death, on young brides for not bringing in enough of it. The husband in such families may continue to demand hot meals and all comforts from their wife despite the fact that they may be loaded with the responsibility of earning supplementary household incomes as well as do all household chores. Questioning of such perceived rights or any deviant behaviour from the norm may invite violence.

Anthropometric data from various Asian countries suggest that with rise in household incomes, health and nutritional status of girl children does go up but so do gender differentials, at least up to a level of incomes, and then after a point the differentials start declining. Is this information to be interpreted as a genuine decline in gender discrimination, or looked upon as a result of poverty reduction, and greater availability of food for everybody in the household? If one identifies gender discrimination with its simple observable index, it will have to be interpreted as the former. However, it may well be that under the changed conditions, the overt manifestation of gender discrimination will come up in some other form, like for instance in reduced mobility, lower workforce participation, in more stringent compulsions of dowry giving, in stricter surveillance on female sexuality, and womanly duties.

On the other hand, the reduction in gender differentials in the area of basic needs, such as nutrition, health care and literacy, might set about forces that may lead to an ultimate reduction in the strength of patriarchal values and bring about more equitable gender relations. If the idea is to capture the strength of patriarchal values as a determinant of gender discrimination, then using the same formula (read indices) for every situation will be unacceptable, since as has been argued above, the overt manifestation of gender discrimination might be different for different social groups and at different levels of economic well-being. The problem, therefore, is to devise a formula which will capture the strength of gender discrimination under different situations.

It is important, therefore, to demarcate clearly gender discrimination as a concept from the overt manifestation of its presence in a particular context as measured by one or the other indicator. The question then boils down to whether it is possible to identify one or a set of indicators which can measure gender discrimination independent of the context, or whether it is useful to identify different sets of indicators which may serve as better indicators of gender discrimination under different contexts.

Many studies have shown that violence against women within the household cuts across income classes and often, social groups. Dowry deaths are as much an urban middle class phenomenon as it is in rural areas, perhaps more. The outcome in one situation may appear to be more outrageous because perhaps the stakes are higher. Should one say that gender discrimination is lower in the former situation because all three accepted indicator components of GDI happen to have better values?

The essence of gender discrimination is unequal power relations. The social instruments for perpetuating such unequal power relations is restricting access to property, and skill/education and ensuring control over female sexuality through restrictions on mobility and such other institutions like early marriage. The norms of social acceptability change. It is important to monitor the objective state of social acceptability on women's situation. But it is equally important to monitor the reaction to deviant behaviour from socially acceptable norms of womanly behaviour. This is the reason why violence against women and the extent of its acceptability in society, both as a means of ensuring the continuity of such acceptability as well as a method of punishment for deviation is a very important indicator of presence of gender discrimination.

If one agrees that the phenomenon of gender discrimination can manifest itself in different forms under different situations, then there is no guarantee that if and when one set of measured disparities are removed by external policy interventions, gender discrimination will go away automatically. Kerala and Sri Lanka show little disparity in educational qualifications for boys and girls. But this does not necessarily mean that gender discrimination does not exist in these places. It is instructive to note that in spite of being repeatedly sighted as a model of social development and gender equality, the higher levels of formal education and labour force participation of Keralite women have not been able to stem the rapidly rising incidence of violence against women in Kerala, both inside and outside the family.

According to one report, crime against women in the state has doubled in the five years between 1991 and 1995. At 275 per 100,000, the crime rate at Kerala stands way above the national average of 181.7 (Menon 1997). Higher household incomes might trigger off a higher desire to educate the girls in the families, but female mobility may be much more restricted in households with higher economic status as compared to poorer ones. Female autonomy in terms of decision-making in personal matters might also be higher in such households. There may be no overt gender disparities in provision of basic needs in urban middle class families, but persistence of dowry demands might be much higher in these households than elsewhere. All depends on what use the increased access to basic needs like health and education are put to. If these lead to greater self-esteem and autonomy for women and concurrently, if it is also associated with a higher degree of concurrence of the self-image of the women with the image of her that the family and community has, it is only then that one could perhaps say that gender discrimination is decidedly lower in one situation as compared to another.

Thus, although conventional indicators of gender discrimination are useful to chart for two reasons, i.e., (a) they are easier to measure, and (b) they are more amenable to policy interventions, the task of measuring overall gender discrimination is a much more complex one than is suggested by studies that map out the same set of conventional indicators, however large and detailed the set is, independent of the context.

Violence is not a very easy phenomenon to measure, or even to identify. Gender violence could take any of the following forms:

(a) Overt physical abuse (battering, sexual assault at home and workplace),
(b) Psychological abuse (confinement, forced marriage, credible threats)
(c) Genderised deprivation of sources for physical and psychological well-being (health, nutrition, education, means of livelihood, psychological support),
(d) Commodification of women (trafficking, forced prostitution etc.)

While violence might take a wide variety of forms, in each case it can be traced to an understanding of unequal power relations in society. Patriarchal values predispose certain positions to women in different life cycles within particular social contexts. Such positions are also associated with certain presupposition about expected norms of behaviour.

Gender violence, or its credible threat, could come about in either of two circumstances. In one set of circumstances, it could be an expression of shared perception of woman's lowly status. In another, violence against women can be triggered by an intolerance towards deviations from presumed norms of womanly behaviour. Thus, it is very important to trace out the feedback effect of higher access of resources of whatever kind on the psychic and the material conditions of not only the woman herself but also of the family and the community. It is therefore necessary to analyse what we have called the less conventional indicators of gender discrimination over and above mapping out the conventional indicators. This is important for two reasons.

One, because these are one set of indicators which cut across socio-economic and cultural contexts, making them in some sense more useful for cross-contextual comparisons and two, because these could be used to signify the non-concurrence of perceptions on women's situation between different members of the household and between the woman and the community she lives in. The degree of dissonance or divergence between the woman's perception and the perception of others can be traced through the discordance within the family which is reflected in violence. Nothing brings out the existence of unequal power relations more than violence or its credible threat. Thus, one can conceive of four broad categories of cases:

(i) Low levels of observed gender disparities by conventional indicators as well as low levels of perceptional differences in gender roles by self and others. Only when both characteristics are low that one could say that gender discrimination is low.

(ii) The most common example of this would be traditional patriarchal societies where men and women share the same perceptions about women's low status.

(iii) Asymmetric perceptions of gender roles coupled with low levels of observed gender disparities in terms of conventional measures. A transitional society; could be violent.

(iv) Highly discriminatory by conventional standards and also violent.

It is only when gender disparities in 'conventional' indicators is low and when violence or its threat is low, that one can say that gender discrimination is also low. If either one or the other condition is not satisfied, it signifies that power relations are tilted against women.

A study of gender discrimination under changing conditions (economic reforms) should involve not merely a mapping out of a whole set of conventional indicators under specified contexts, but also a concurrent assessment of the degree of violence or its credible threat, along with a measure of tolerance or its absence to deviation from accepted norms of gendered behaviour.

Gender Equality and Structural Reforms

Much concern has been voiced about the likely ill-effects of macro economic reforms on the situation of women. Liberalisation has been seen to lead to increased feminisation of poverty. Privatisation has generated fears of reduction in state responsibility in the provision of social goods and services, resulting in an increase in the burden on women in the private domain to that extent. While increased feminisation of the workforce appears to be a global phenomenon, it has been pointed out that the increase in female work participation has been taking place in low-paying and unprotected jobs, leading to a rise in the casualisation of the female workforce.

The main components of a structural adjustment programme are aimed at altering the long-run growth dynamics of an economy by operating on the supply side, while stabilisation measures are generally geared to reduce excess demand by curtailing deficits in external accounts and containing inflation in the domestic sector. The usual package of structural adjustment measures consists of measures to allow greater 'free market' operations, free trade and enhanced convertibility of the domestic currency, privatisation and de-licensing of industry, reduction in tax and tariff rates, introduction of uniform rates of taxes and tariffs, abolition of price controls and subsidies and measures to improve labour market 'flexibility'. Stabilisation measures usually consist of domestic credit squeeze, curtailment of budgetary deficits, reduction in money supply and devaluation.

The impact of such macro policy measures on the gender distribution of costs and benefits both within and outside the market sphere is clearly not something that can be directly discerned or estimated. To a large extent, it will depend on the existing scenario in gender equity to start with, and also the dynamics of changes in gender equations that may be propelled by the forces of economic reforms. Although, a number of authors have argued that the likely impact of these measures on women is predominantly negative (Commonwealth Secretariat 1991; Elson 1992; Ghosh 1996; UNDP 1995), rarely have the lines of transmission of macro policy impact on gender balances in various spheres of activity been clearly demarcated or the complex of feedback impulses systematically contextualised within a proper format. If stabilisation measures usher in a recession, both men and women will suffer. Gender differentials of such suffering can be traced out only when it is contextualised within a particular socio-cultural milieu and it will be different under different contextual conditions. Changes in the structure of employment, level and composition of social sector outlays etc. affect both economic and social arrangements. Gender relations are therefore likely to show some change, although as stated earlier, these changes are mediated by pre-existing conditions, so that outcomes can vary from one part of the country to another, and from country to country.

Thus the propositions regarding the effect of reforms on gender discrimination detailed earlier are, in the present state of knowledge, simply a set of propositions, with mixed empirical evidence. Reforms would be judged as successful if they could eliminate poverty, and strengthen the processes of economic and social change that lead to increased welfare. An intrinsic component of greater welfare is higher status of women.

Although, it is possible to justify interest in how gender relations might change with economic growth on purely economic grounds, this would be a narrow perspective. It is important to understand whether the pattern of growth being followed holds the potential for developing capabilities and enhancing the quality of life for all citizens. The intensification of work, discontinuation of education (especially of girls), increases in time spent on home maintenance, higher levels of stress and violence, are all ways in which economic restructuring can affect women adversely.

Using conventional indicators of equality, India's developmental experience has involved a gender gap. According to the 1991 census, the male literacy rate was 63.9 per cent, as against 39.4 per cent for females; school enrollment as a percentage of the corresponding age group, was estimated at 108.8 per cent for boys in the age group 6-11, in 1985-86, and 77.1 per cent for girls in the corresponding age group; the difference in enrollment is greater in the age group 11-14, being 65 per cent for boys and 38.1 per cent for girls. This understates the actual gender difference, since attendance is far lower for girls, as observed in micro studies. Despite the fact that women are biologically the stronger sex, an estimate of age and sex specific survival rates shows higher rates for males over females up to the age of 40, possibly reflecting inadequacies in nutrition inputs and care to young children/nursing mothers.

However, there has also been an improvement over time. How much the improvement actually has been largely depends on the particular combination of indicators used. One attempt to measure the behaviour of the gender gap (defined as educational achievements + life expectancy) with economic development suggests that it is only in South Asia and in Sub-Saharan Africa that this gap increased in the two decades upto 1984. The same study finds an inverted U pattern of rising gender inequality in the initial stages of human resource development and then a declining phase; the implication possibly being that labour scarcity forces higher investments and positive action to reduce gender bias (Jalan and Subbarao 1994). It has, at the same time, also been observed in India that even communities that traditionally paid a bride price upon marriage now demand a dowry; the incidence of 'dowry deaths' is widespread; and reports from family counselling centres suggest that role conflicts are high as is the incidence of depression, anxiety and domestic violence.

Changing gender relations is tantamount to a questioning of established norms. As a consequence, this may be associated with increased violence, or threat of violence, and attempts to force a return to established norms, or at any rate to ensure that new norms do not radically alter the balance of power. Measuring gender discrimination in a situation of change requires tools appropriate to a dynamic context.

Summing up

What transpires from the analysis above is that measuring gender discrimination is no easy task. The problem arises not simply because the phenomenon can manifest itself in myriad form, thus necessitating the tracking of different "indicators", but also because there is no guarantee that these indicators will move in roughly the same direction under all conditions. Thus determining the context—specificity of different indicators becomes important, as is the need for establishing systematic patterns of linkages between them for informed analysis.

As argued above, equally important is the need to do such analysis in conjunction with the "not-so-conventional" indicators of mental health, such as stress and anxiety that is caused by gender related factors. Most available studies of violence against women are concerned with acts of actual perpetrated violence. Apart from the problem of reporting bias, the actual acts of violence may be only the tip of the iceberg. Credible threat of violence is an equally potent measure of women's subjugation. Only a properly conceived psychological assessment of gender-related stress can hope to bring out this incidence. Such assessment needs to be done in the context of other, more conventional measures of women's status in society.

Mapping these complex sets of issues against the background of changing economic policy regims poses another set of challenges. Changes in macro policy would generally get manifested in changes in external economic opportunities and constraint for households at various levels. These may trigger gender-differentiated changes in labour use patterns, both within and outside the households, generate some new pressure points and relieve some other. Tracing them systematically to track the changing nature of gender relations in a particular context is a challenge in itself. It is not clear at this point whether it is even a doable research agenda. What propels the inquiry is the belief that it is important to start by asking the right questions.

REFERENCES

Abadian, Susan. 1996. 'Women's Autonomy and its Impact on Fertility'. *World Development* vol. 24, No. 12 pp. 1793-1809.

Abel, Kathryn, Marta Buszewicz, Sophie Davison, Sonia Johnson and Emma Staples. (ed). 1996. *Planning Community Mental Health services for women.* London: Routledge.

Agarwal, Bina. 1994. *A Field of One's Own: Gender and Land Rights in South Asia.* Cambridge: Cambridge University Press.

Banerjee, N. 1996. 'Technological Change and the Feminisation of Work'. Paper presented at workshop on Gender and Employment in India, Indian Society of Labour Economics and Institute of Economic Growth, New Delhi Dec. 18-20.

Banerjee, Nirmala. 1998. "Household dynamics and women in a changing economy", in Maitreyi Krishnaraj, Ratna M. Sudarshan, Abusaleh Shariff (eds.). *Gender, Population and Development*. Delhi: Oxford University Press, pp. 245-63.

Barr, Nicholas. 1996. 'People in Transition: Reforming Education and Health Care'. *Finance and Development,* September.

Basu, Alaka M. 1996. 'Girls' Schooling, Autonomy and Fertility Change: What do these words mean in South Asia?' in Jeffery, Roger and Alaka Basu. (ed.) Girls Schooling, Women's Autonomy and Fertility Change. Delhi: Sage Publications. pp. 48-71.

Behrman, Jere R. and Zheng Zhang. 1995. 'Gender Issues and Employment in Asia'. *Asian Development Review* Vol. 13 No. 2 pp. 1-49.

Beneria, Lourdes. 1995. 'Toward a greater integration of gender in economics'. World Development Vol. 23, No. 11, p. 1839-50.

Collier, Paul. 1994. 'A Theoretical Framework and the Africa Experience' in Horton, S., Kanbur, R. and Mazumdar, D. (ed). *Labor Markets in an Era of Adjustment.* Vol I. Washington: The World Bank. pp. 279 - 307.

Commonwealth Secretariat. 1989. 'Engendering adjustment for the 1990s': Report of a Commonwealth Expert Group on Women and Structural Adjustment, London: Commonwealth Secretariat.

Dasgupta, Monica and P.N. Mari Bhat. 1998. 'Intensified gender bias in India: a consequence of fertility decline' in Krishnaraj *et al (op cit)* pp. 73-93.

Dreze, Jean and Amartya Sen. 1995. *India: Economic development and social opportunity.* Delhi: Oxford University Press.

Dreze, Jean and P.V. Srinivasan. 1996. 'Poverty in India: Regional Contrasts and Female Labour Force Participation'. Paper presented at workshop on Gender and Employment in India, Indian Society of Labour Economics and Institute of Economic Growth, New Delhi Dec. 18-20.

Elson, Diane. 1994. 'Micro, Meso, Macro: Gender and Economic Analysis in the Context of Policy Reform' in Bakker, I. (ed.) *The Strategic Silence: Gender and Economic Policy.* London: Sed Books p. 33-45.

Elson, Diane. 1987. 'The Impact of Structural Adjustment on Women: Concepts and Issues'. Discussion Papers in

Development Studies, DP8801. Manchester: University of Manchester.

Epstein, T. Scarlett. 1982. 'A Social Anthropological Approach to Women's Roles and status in Developing Countries: The Domestic Cycle' in Anker, Richard, Mayra Buviniv and Nadia H. Youssef (ed) *Women's Roles and Population Trends in the Third World.* London: Croom Helm pp. 151-70.

Fernando, Suman. ed. 1995. *Mental Health in a Multi-ethnic Society: A Multi-disciplinary Handbook.* London: Routledge.

Floro, Maria Sagrario. 1995. 'Economic Restructuring, Gender and the Allocation of Time'. *World Development* Vol. 23, No. 11, pp. 1913-29.

Ghosh, Jayati. 1996. 'Trends in Female Employment in Developing Countries: Emerging Issues' in UNDP Background Papers - Human Development Report 1995. New York: United Nations Development Programme. pp. 71-88.

Govt. of India. 1974. 'Towards Equality'. Report of the Committee on the Status of Women. Delhi: Government of India.

Govt. of India. 1990. 'Results of the Fourth Quinquennial Survey on Employment and Unemployment (All India), National Sample Survey 43rd Round (July 1987-June 1988)', Sarvekshana, special number, September.

Jacobson, Doranne and Susan S. Wadley. 1997. *Women in India: Two perspectives.* New Delhi: Manohar Publications.

Jaishankar, Shobha. 1997. *Coping with Crisis: A Review of Experience in Family Counselling.* Delhi: Institute of Social Studies Trust.

Jalan, Jyotsna and K. Subbarao. 1994. 'Gender Disparity in Human Resource Development: Cross Country Patterns'. ESP Discussion Paper Series. Washington: The World Bank.

Jeffery, Roger and Alaka Basu. (ed.) 1996. Girls Schooling, Women's Autonomy and Fertility Change. Delhi: Sage Publications.

Kakar, Sudhir. 1989. *Intimate Relations: Exploring Indian Sexuality.* Delhi: Viking Press.

Menon, Leela. 1997. 'Second Sex'. Indian Express, March 31, 1997.

Mukhopadhyaya, Swapna. 1995. 'Women in the informal sector'. Paper presented at National Seminar on Employment Promotion in the Urban Informal Sector, Institute of Applied Manpower Research, New Delhi December 14-15.

Olmsted, Jennifer. 1996. 'Women 'Manufacture' Economic Spaces in Bethlehem' *World Development,* Vol. 24 No. 12 pp. 1829-40.

Phongpaichit, Pasuk, 1988. 'Two roads to the factory: industrialisation strategies and women's employment in South East Asia' in Agarwal, Bina (ed) *Structures of Patriarchy: State, Community and Household in Modernising Asia.* Delhi: *Kali for Women,* pp. 151-163.

Ramu, G.N. 1989. *Women, Work and Marriage in Urban India: A Study of Dual and Single Earner Couples.* Delhi: Sage Publications.

Rao, Vijayendra. 1998. 'Wife Abuse, its Causes and its Impact on Intra-Household Resource Allocation in Rural Karnataka: a 'Participatory' Econometric Analysis' in Krishnaraj *et al. op cit.* pp. 94 - 121

Saith, Ruhi and Barbara Harris-White. 1998. 'Gender Sensitivity of well-being indicators'. UNRISD Discussion paper No. 95. Geneva: United Nations Research Institute for Social Development.

Seeta Prabhu K. 1996. 'Gender-Related Development Index for Indian States: Methodological Issues': EPW Volume 31, No. 43.

Shariff, A. NCAER. 1999. *India Human Development Report.* Delhi: Oxford University Press.

Srinivas, M.N. 1966. *Social Change in Modern India.* Delhi: Orient Longman.

Srinivas, M.N. 1978. *The Changing Position of Indian Women* Delhi: Oxford University Press.

Summers, L.H. 1994. 'Investing in all the People: Educating Women in Developing Countries'. EDI Seminar Paper No 45. Washington: The World Bank.

UNDP. 1995. *Human Development Report*. New York: Oxford University Press.

Wadley, Susan S. 1992. 'Women and the Hindu Tradition' in Jacobson and Wadley, *op cit* pp. 111-35.

World Bank. 1995a. *Toward Gender Equality: the Role of Public Policy.* Washington: The World Bank

World Bank. 1995b. *Advancing Gender Equality: From Concept to Action.* Washington: The World Bank.

5

EMPOWERING RURAL WOMEN

Economic growth and technological advancement in India in the last decade is very impressive. Technology, market and development are considered gender-neutral. But there is pronounced urban bias and rural neglect in the development process of India. Modernisation of the economy or advancement of the society is a semi-myth for village women. The gender division of labour within the rural household has remained culturally stubborn. Women as a class are oppressed and subdued by the hegemony of social patriarchy. Economic growth has failed to improve the situation either. Rather technology and labour market imperfections have accentuated the concentration of women in domestic works with non-market roles and activities, generating a new process of 'housewifisation', not 'feminisation of jobs' in the rural sector. Although gender empowerment has been a buzzword in development circles, the concept remains ambiguous. Gender concerns and discourses survive within the development bureaucracies dominated by men. It is easier for them to ring-fence gender issues as a problem of poverty and to argue against 'feminisation of poverty' than to admit the gender disadvantage which crosses the boundaries of class and ethnicity.

Since the beginning of planned development, women have been viewed as a deprived section requiring welfare measures. Most studies and reports on women have only remained as a source of data, which rather endorses the passivity of the state. This chapter is based on a primary survey of 900 households of two villages of Orissa. It studies the impact of technology on various social parameters of village economy. It examines the link between technology and occupational pattern of women, the level of female education, and identifies the factors that influence women employment.

It assesses employment potentials and opportunities for women in both farm and non-farm activities in the villages. It attempts to reveal the real scenario of the rural sector, and argues that rescuing gender from poverty trap means we need poverty-independent gender analyses and policies. Education and technology should ensure liberation and freedom of thought for all human beings. It should break gradually the shackles of tradition that binds women in the man-made gaol. The gender issue should be delinked both from myopic economics and insensitive politics.

Developmentalism and Rural Sector

There is a global economic movement of economic integration through technology. The impact of this globalisation process has become all pervasive and inexorable. All sectors of developing countries seem to be vibrating with economic buoyancy. It has generated an impervious atmosphere of over optimism of instant economic growth. There is expansion of trade, investment, market, and increase in GNP, productivity, per capita income, profit, efficiency, salary etc. Lifestyles of metro people in India have become more attractive, comfortable and fashionable than ever before. There is worldwide process of overproduction but unemployment and dramatic contraction of purchasing power of people. The global economic system is thus characterised by two contradictory forces: the consolidation of cheap labour economy on the one hand and the search for new consumer markets on the other. Unfortunately, the former undermines the latter in the long run. It generates social apartheid and undermines the rights of women. It is an insidious and inscrutable process, which is conducive to globalisation of markets, which ultimately undermines human livelihood and destroys civil society in the south.

After India's Independence and a long period of planning and development exercise, spanning over more than 62 years of in India, it is saddening to observe that the incidence of poverty and livelihood insecurity have remained as grave as ever. There is pronounced urban bias and rural neglect in the development process. The economic development has created an urbanisation process, which is dysfunctional, and an industrialisation pattern, which is regionally concentrated. The development planners have remained broadly myopic and complacent with trickledown effect for the rural sector. The result of the development exercises have been the persistence of a huge low productive primary sector, slender industrial sector and a bloated tertiary sector. All the benefits of the welfare measures have gravitated willy nilly towards the elite class and such other groups with political visibility. The rural sector of India has remained closed to the subsistence level and sensitive to the vagaries of nature—flood, cyclone and drought etc.

With the euphoria of 'high-tech civilisation', the concern for rural development, rural poverty, hunger and inequality virtually are dismissed as an obsession of egalitarian romantics. This insolent attitude and insouciance have generated dangerous consequences. It has spreaded an excitement of over optimism of instant change and pragmatism of high-tech-efficiency. It appears to be very logical and attractive. But its socioeconomic impact and implications are not uniform across social groups, genders, regions, sector and generations. Its statistical mirage underestimates the ground reality and depicts a misleading picture. When one aims at gender equity, neither the earlier panacea of central planning nor the virtues of free marketism appears to carry much conviction for the common man of backward regions of India. The problem of economic vulnerability, livelihood insecurity and malnutrition among village people is becoming more pronounced.

Women and Economic Development

The millennium development Goals (MDG) aims at eradicating poverty and promote gender equality and empower women by 2015. There is need to improve the policies and implement them with greater impetus. But poor women in India remain in traditional fields of employment. When traditional jobs become unavailable due to number of factors, women are forced to seek employment in other areas, which may have no relationship with their original experience and expertise. Women have a marginal role in family decision making, they are primarily responsible for keeping the hearth going. They are occasionally consulted on marriage negotiations but not on any financial matters in the villages. Women's economic contribution has been invisibilised in the industrial process of economic development.

This trend is not linear or unidirectional. Women are also displaced and lost their share in the industrial workforce due to upgradation of technology, and reduction of labour intensity of production through automation and adoption of high-tech. Employers in the private sector, in the process of modernisation, eschew the responsibility for workers well being in the name of eliminating market distortions. Moreover, in the current globalised economy, women's social subordination coincides with the absence of economic alternatives. Employment of women in industries has been accompanied with deregulation of labour protection. Women fail to defend or promote their interest both as women and as workers. Even male-led labour unions either ignore or consider women's demand as divisive and irrelevant to the interest of the 'real working class'. The women-heads in the families face serious challenges in village economy due to low literacy levels, low asset holdings, lower productivity of land, lesser access to avenues of income-earning and governmental help and the declining kinship supports.

The differential social evaluation of the sex roles, the male-orientation in running households coupled with rural poverty and household poverty enmesh in narrowing choices open to women heads of households. The capital intensive technology has rather trivialised the gender issue. The whole host of economic and social structures and processes that reinforce patriarchy, devalue and commodify the women. The confluence of modernisation does not improve the fate of women.

Technology and Women of India

Modern technology is supported and directed by powerful institutions and interests. Men gravitate to science and technology. We must question, whether technology is male dominated because it demands some essentially masculine traits, or 'simply' because technology is where the power is?. Technology is socially constructed, or co-produced, alongside gender. Technology itself gets gendered in the eyes of would be technologists. The continued male dominance in science and engineering is due in large measure to the enduring symbolic association of masculinity and technology by which cultural images and representations of technology converge with prevailing images of masculinity and power. The use of technology is always discriminatory.

Technical prowess is what defines them as engineers *and* what gives them a sense of power. The symbolic gendering of technology extends beyond the artifactual, but it has material consequences. Within the masculinity-technology association, one can discern a series of highly gendered dichotomies. Most obvious of these is the distinction between being people-focussed and machine-focussed. It corresponds to the division between feminine expressiveness and masculine instrumentalism. Most women routinely interact with people and technologies. For example computer is implicitly rather than explicitly gendered. 'Hard' technology is inert and powerful, while 'Soft' technology is smaller scale. So the world of technology is made to feel remote and overwhelmingly powerful because of the hard-soft dualism. The hard-soft dichotomy also extend to styles of thought in technology. On the masculine side of those dualisms we have an objectivist rationality associated with emotional detachment. On the feminine side we have a more subjective rationality associated with emotional connectedness. Males have dominated the 'internet culture' since its inception. The Internet culture can be discomforting and alien to females.

India has achieved higher technological advancement during last decade. The Green Revolution, which focuses on increasing yields of rice and wheat, entails a shift in inputs from human to technical. Women's participation, knowledge and inputs are marginalised, and their role has shifted from being "primary producers to subsidiary workers." Women work longer hours and their work is more arduous than men's, albeit their work is unrecognised. Men report that "women, like children, eat and do nothing." Technological progress in agriculture has had a negative impact on women. There is tremendous effects of information technology on women's employment and the nature of women's work in all third world countries including India.

But in areas of technology, till today women represent about 10 per cent of researchers and about 5 per cent of manager. The impact of information technology on society has not been uniformly beneficial, and the technological divide is being increasingly felt, especially in the developing countries. Serious obstacles still continue in achieving gender equality. The gender implications of digital divide is very serious in India. Access to and use of the Internet has important economic, educational, and social benefits, and those who are excluded from Internet participation will also be excluded from several benefits. Lack of training does not allow them to escape from their sex-typed slots.

The women from poorer families face challenges as they adjust to new technologies. Their jobs do not reintegrate them, leveling the hierarchies and adding responsibilities. It is still believed by the elite class of Orissa that science improves their role and make them better mother, better wives, enriching their domestic lives. They do not think beyond that. Women still face subtle resistance to their participation in science and technology, no matter how talented she is, from all corners, particularly from the husband, howsoever educated he may be. Women are expressly excluded from many activities. Because marriage has remained indispensable goal for the women, particularly in Orissa. All her achievements culminate in a good marriage and proving her motherhood. Not being married is a great social stigma both for the family and the girls.

Not becoming mother is considered greater ominous. Therefore getting higher education for girls is an accident. Ninety per cent of marriages are caste-based, arranged by the parents. Therefore, parents feel it as a burden or duty. Girls continue their studies till the parent get a good boy for them. Education reduces the set of choice for the parents. So, it is perceived as a problem for many girls. It is increasingly difficult to marry and get a partner. A good girl student experiences very encouraging motivation from the teachers, but cold attitude from the parents and relatives. Besides this, the amount of dowry offer proportionally increases with the girls schooling for the parents. Even today, many educated people (including the potential husbands) think that educated women would engage in deviant social and political behaviour. It is perceived that she would refuse to do household work and disobey their husband, if their education is too higher than the husband. They would become musculinised and expect to be included in men's activities. Advocates of women's education argue that education will help women to fulfill their God-given duties toward their husband and family. Therefore women suffer greater subordination and deprivation both at home and in society. Oppression of women in Orissa can be described as hypocritical at its worst and schizophrenic at its best.

Women should be given various (both farm and non-farm) training to escape from their sex-typed slots. The aim with jobs should be to reintegrate them wherever possible, leveling the hierarchies, adding responsibilities to lower grade jobs and building in more interaction with the technologies in the case of routine operations and jobs. It should provide pathways for lower skilled women workers to learn and progress. The aim of training should be to encourage women of any age or occupation to consider on-the-job or off-the-job training for more technical work. Otherwise they are more susceptible to displacement and deskilling by emerging push-botton technology. Technology should liberate women potential instead of hooking them up, or tying them in side the virtual prisons. Community-based women's organisations should be instrumental in the process of enabling women to cross the so-called digital divide. Technology should be powerful tools for women to overcome discrimination, achieve full equality and higher well-being.

STATUS OF WOMEN IN VILLAGES

Although, gender empowerment has been a buzzword in development circles, the concept has been used in so many different ways by different agents that it remains ambiguous.

Conceptualising power and gender adequately entails understanding its multi-dimensional nature, the complex ways in which women experience subordination and the ways in which they negotiate or manage this state of affairs. The gender-gap in indices such as life expectancy, literacy and earning has in fact increased from sixties to eighties in entire south Asia. The UNDP developed Gender Development Index (GDI) as a tool to capture gender inequality. It notes the inequalities between men and women on the same variables that make up the Human Development Index related to the over all achievements in that society. It considers only three variables: health, education and income. It fails to take into account important dimensions such as the quality of community life access to basic amenities and human rights. Important dimensions relevant for women such as safety and security, household allocation of resources, unpaid labour, mobility constraints and on sexual and reproductive freedom by patriarchal ideology do not find any place. Raising income of women may not indicate improved status for women. The GEM (Gender Empowerment Measure) is again based on three variables. It is built on a very narrow conception of empowerment. It does not include legal and human rights nor does it reflect the ways in which cultural constructions of gender identity are made.

Thus, it is clear from the above discussion that if one attempts to assess the impact of economic reforms differential on men and women, the conventional parameters used to measure gender disparity is not enough. It is therefore necessary to consider research methodologies that go beyond the quantitative in order to do justice to the complexity of these phenomena.

Self-help Groups (SHGs) are playing a major role in rural India today. The group-based model of self-help is widely practised for rural development, poverty alleviation and empowerment of women. Self-help as a strategy for social development places emphasis on self-reliance, human agency and action. It aims to mobilise people, to give them voice and build people's organisations that will overcome barriers to participation and empowerment. Central to the idea of self-help is the formation of groups, concept of a 'community' and the development of egalitarian relationships that will promote people's well-being.

The self-help model in India facilitates institution-building in the form of people's organisations in the form of groups, clusters and federations. The poor, however, seldom organise themselves. It is an assisted self-help (Uphoff & Esman, 1984) process where the State, the financial institutions and the non-governmental organisations (NGOs) play an important role in mobilising and assisting the poor and the needy. While the policies of the external agents of development place emphasis on building institutions to assist the poor and women, the practice-oriented reality has to deal with the structural barriers that people, women and the organisations face. At the level of practice, the outcomes of self-help depend on building mutually beneficial relationships, negotiating power and gaining control.

In this book, we will examines the main approaches to the building of women's self-help in India, its implications for practice and effect on women's ability to exercise agency. This will be examined through an analysis of the strategies adopted by the various development sectors to promote women's development, and the possibility to change gender and power relations. The book is based on fieldwork done in two districts of India during the period 2003-2004: Sonipat in Haryana and Kolar in Karnataka.

Self-Help and the Group Model for Women

Alternative development thinkers emphasise participation, self-reliance and self-help as basic human rights. Development involves changes in the awareness, motivation and behaviour of individuals, in the relations between individuals as well as between groups within a society. These changes can come from within individuals and groups through self-help, and not necessarily from outside. The experiences of self-reliance have led to attempts to build local level organisations like, cooperatives, credit societies, neighbourhood or community development associations, water sharing associations or women's groups. The Neo-liberal paradigm has also incorporated self-reliance as a strategy for building people's entrepreneurial spirits and absorption into the capital market.

People's participation in self-help organisations is not new. In Kenya, local self-help development efforts - *harambee*; in Vietnam, Tontines or Hui with 10 to 15 members that are involved in financial activities through cash or kind; and in Indonesia, self-help efforts through credit unions, fishermen groups, village-based banks, irrigation groups etc. have been in existence. In the areas of urban development and housing, self-help takes the form of neighbourhood groups, tenant groups, slum development committees and so on. In rural development, it is through credit groups, development committees, user groups and so on. Group-oriented efforts in the form of micro-credit groups in different countries of Latin America, Africa and Asia are examples of current self-help efforts. The grameen groups in Bangladesh and the self-help groups (SHGs) in countries like Thailand, Nepal, Sri Lanka and India are forms of micro-credit groups.

The SHGs in India are small, informal and homogenous groups of not more than twenty members each. The groups are kept informal to minimise their association with bureaucracy and corruption, unnecessary administrative expenditure and profit constraints. The size of twenty is devised as any group larger than that would need to be registered under the Indian legal system and that brings a whole range of regulatory constraints. After a group is formed, it starts collecting a fixed amount from each member for about six months. During this period, the groups are expected to open a savings account with a financial institution which would like to extend credit. After accumulating a reasonable amount of resources, the group starts lending to its members. As the group members develop the experience of handling resources, understand the value of credit and the importance of repayment and accountability to the group, it can approach the financial institution for term loans. The group becomes jointly liable to the bank for repayment and it is expected to assume responsibility in monitoring the members. This joint liability provides incentives or compels the group to undertake the burden of selection, monitoring and enforcement that would otherwise fall on the lender.

The roots of the SHG model lie partly in indigenous savings systems of India and partly in the group-based model of Grameen Bank in Bangladesh, though it differs from it in several aspects. The Indian experience is distinctive in that the groups are mostly formed by women, they are formed through grassroots mobilisation with the help of NGOs and they are engaged in both poverty alleviation and empowerment activities. Through the selective incentives of benefits in the form of savings and credit the SHG model seeks to build collective action and enhance people/women's power. The State and the voluntary sector play an important role in mobilisation through facilitation and linking the groups to credit. The promotional strategies of the external agents can impact on how the participants develop their expectations from the system and what they gain.

The spread of SHGs in India has been phenomenal. It has made dramatic progress from 500 groups in 1992 to some 1,618,456 groups that have taken loans from banks. About 24.25 million poor households have gained access to formal banking system through SHG-bank linkage programme and 90 per cent of these groups are women only groups. The NABARD homepage declares that more than 400 women join the SHG movement every hour and an NGO joins the micro-finance programme every day. There are also agencies which provide bulk funds to the system through NGOs. Thus organisations engaged in micro finance activities in India may be categorised as Wholesalers, NGOs supporting SHG Federations and NGOs directly retailing credit borrowers or groups of borrower. The spread of the SHGs again show that it is highly concentrated in the southern part of the country with very few in the north and the east. Over half a million SHGs have been linked to banks over the years but a handful of States, mostly in South India, account for almost 60 per cent of this figure. Andhra Pradesh has over 42 per cent, Tamil Nadu and Uttar Pradesh have 12 per cent and 11 per cent respectively, and Karnataka has about 9 per cent of the total SHGs. Thus, the rise of the movement has been very high in the Southern States, and very minor in Haryana and in the North-East.

The widespread formation of the SHGs means that it has also taken the form of a movement for women's social development in India. Self-help groups, as a strategy for women's development, have arisen out of the perceived problem of women's lack of access to resources at both the household and the village level. Women's development has to go beyond the economic and place emphasis on issues relating to equality, autonomy and self-reliance at the individual level and on solidarity of the community at the group level. As a group-oriented model, SHG is a mechanism for women's development to bring in individual and collective empowerment through improvement in both 'condition' and 'position' of women. Women are organised as collectives towards the overall goal of achieving gender equality as well as sustainable, comprehensive community development. As women experience powerlessness in and through the interaction of multiple social, political and economic institutions, the self-reliance model for women's development aims to empower them.

Thus, an important aspect of SHGs is the implicit assumption that through participation in the groups, women will gain, generate and acquire power, and improve their 'position' within the family and the society. Psychological empowerment or the inner processes are given importance for the development of self-esteem and self-confidence so that women are able to motivate themselves into action. The SHGs, however, work within an existi·.g socio-cultural structure and there is a need to look at SHGs as an emerging structure of women in a patriarchal society. The SHGs have to be able to address the structural inequalities in which women are located, yet affect the hold of patriarchy in a manner that does not work to the detriment of women unlike other structures that are dominated by patriarchal interest.

In a study of the role of self-help in Kenya, Thomas found that self-help is politicised, but powerless. It does not alter fundamental power relationships within the political and economic system, but self-help groups have some positive impact. The benefits shared within a group cut across socio-economic lines, thereby promoting both gender and intra-community equity. Unlike the self-help projects in Kenya, the SHGs in India are primarily micro-credit groups and the direct objective of micro-credit is to improve the 'condition' of women.

There is, however, conflicting evidence as to whether micro-credit groups improve the 'position' of women. Social 'position' or status of women is an aspect of positional power that refers to the power or authority assigned to specific positions and roles in a society. Studies have found positive indicators of the cost effectiveness and economic potential of micro-credit loans (Pitt, Khandker & Cartwright 2003; Montgomery, Bhattacharya and Hulme 1996), but their positive social impact remained doubtful. Literature review points to conflicting evidence of women's ability to achieve control over decision-making and loans, incidence of increases in violence and dowry and evidence of economic and social empowerment.

The link between access to credit for women and that of transformation in gender and power relations was not found to be automatic. Goetz and Sengupta's study of Bangladeshi women's actual control of the credit received by them from the banks had found that a significant proportion of the loans are actually controlled by male relatives. Mahmud found that the group fund provides an economic base that holds the groups together. The group fund fosters a sense of unity and solidarity since it represents a source of collective bargaining power for women in the market place. While it provides a base from which to assert control and autonomy, it is only within a particular configuration of male power relationships in the family or village.

Rahman found that financial sustainability was taking precedence over women's socioeconomic empowerment (and women were not acting as autonomous agents in any meaningful sense). The pressure to return loans can increase tension and frustration among household members, produce new forms of dominance over women and increase violence in society. Providing resources to women and encouraging them to maintain control over these resources may provoke violent behaviour in men. Rahman concluded that loans alone, without viable opportunities for women to transform the power relations and create their own spaces in the prevailing power structure, make equitable development and empowerment of women unattainable in the society. Similarly, as Mahmud found, micro-credit participation did not improve women's access to material resources nor did it expand women's choice a great deal. Women's participation in the public sphere that could become choice enhancing remained limited, as they were not able to overcome the structural barriers.

In aiming to improve women's rights and status and thereby, responding to not only their practical interests, but also strategic interests, the self-help efforts enter the realm of the Indian women's movement. The Indian women's movement is influenced by various efforts to characterise the specificity of women's oppression and the links with other forms of social oppression (Omvedt, 2004:181). Women are mobilised to protest against domestic violence, legal discrimination, rising prices, prohibition of liquor, rape, dowry, child marriage, female infanticide, sexual abuse and so on. In dealing with women's strategic interests, women participate in collective activities through SHGs to address these strategic needs.

In the process, it aims to empower women with several forms of power. SHGs are nascent organisations that are supposed to achieve 'power to' (increasing capacity) through NGO facilitation, 'power within' (internal change) through self-empowerment, 'power with' to gain 'power over' (challenge and change subordination). Development for women through SHGs, thus, aims at transformation of power relations so that the disempowered can achieve increased control and choice.

It becomes, therefore, important to analyse the meanings of self-help to the promoters of SHGs, the strategies adopted to assist the SHGs, and the manner in which women exercise agency through SHGs to address powerlessness. It is also pertinent to understand the paradigms through which the external agents look at women's development—from Women-in-Development (WID) to Gender-and-Development (GAD).

Assisting Women's Development through SHGs

There are three main sectors promoting the SHGs in India: the voluntary sector including the non-governmental organisations, the government sector and the financial sector.

The SHG system was initiated by NGOs, such as Myrada in the mid-1980s in India. In the Indian voluntary sector, there are two types of NGOs that that take the initiative to organise

SHGs for linkage with the banks: development NGOs and empowerment NGOs. For development NGOs, micro-finance is a core activity, while empowerment NGOs combine their financial role with issue-based struggles. In promoting SHGs, the primary task of the NGOs is to mobilise, form and nurture the groups so that they can reach maturity. They form and train the groups, and assist them through the qualifying process of saving and internal lending. The groups are introduced to a bank to open a savings account, and later to take a loan. The NGO may remain heavily involved, assisting the members to manage their affairs, and possibly promoting higher-level clusters and federations of SHGs, or it may withdraw and work with other groups. Thus, the NGOs play an important role in linking the SHGs to banks.

Prior to the developmental role of today's NGOs, some NGOs had taken up advocacy and begun to emphasise empowerment of local communities and the poor in the 1960s and 70s. A wide range of women's issues, such as rape and violence, were taken up as part of their efforts to influence public policies and practices. Empowerment NGOs today mobilise people for such social issues and advocacy. Credit or micro-finance did not start as a core activity even for organisations like Myrada. It was used to supplement other activities aimed at providing sustainable livelihood to the people. The adoption of group model, like, the SHGs, *mahila mandals* (women's groups) and others for women's development represents a form of women's collective action through which gender specific issues are taken up. These issues are, alcoholism, male violence and dowry deaths, rape and sexual harassment.

Direct policy advocacy and developmental works undertaken by NGOs are different from the wider phenomenon of social movements concerning women's issues. But they are inter-related, as policy advocacy can be considered to be one of the many strands of a movement.

The NGO approach theoretically combines both the developmental (WID) and empowerment (GAD) perspectives with the objective of building equitable social relations. NGOs emphasise the social dimensions of poverty and the self-help groups (SHG) are one such medium through which the NGOs work for economic and social empowerment of women. The poverty alleviation paradigm underlies many NGO integrated poverty-targeted community development programmes. Some NGOs act as banking intermediaries, channeling finance to different SHGs, others have formed collectives of several SHGs forming federations and linking them to banks. According to one estimate, NGOs have promoted about 80 per cent of SHGs linked to banks. Others adopt the GAD framework to challenge patriarchal structures. Thus, NGOs range from service-provider, developmental to empowerment-oriented. However, very few in practice follow the feminist empowerment model of organisations like, SEWA and WWF.

The launching of NABARD's Pilot phase of the SHG-Bank Linkage programme in February 1992 was a landmark development in rural banking with the poor. For financial institutions, such as, the Banks, SHGs form the basic constituent unit of the microfinance movement. The SHG model with bank lending to groups of (often) poor women without collateral has become an accepted part of rural finance. Self-help for the banks is understood through the performance of SHGs in savings and credit activities. As the women learn the nuances of financial discipline, bank credit becomes available to the groups to augment their resources for increased lending to members. The objective is to attain financial sustainability through fees charged and interests earned from borrowers of the group fund including interests paid by banks on the money deposited. The activities associated with SHGs are part of an overall arrangement for providing financial services to the poor in a sustainable manner.

It needs to be emphasised that NABARD sees the promotion and bank linking of SHGs not simply as a credit programme but also as an exercise in capacity building for the members of these SHGs. It is assumed that increasing women's knowledge and access to micro-finance services will lead to individual economic empowerment through enabling women's decisions about savings and credit use, enabling women to set up micro-enterprises, and increasing incomes under their control. This in turn is assumed to enable women to initiate broader social and political changes. Within the guise of poverty alleviation and empowerment, the financial sustainability paradigm assumes importance for the banking sector.

For Government, self-help is the act of contributing to growth by active involvement of the poor through a process of social mobilisation, encouraging participatory approaches and institutions and empowerment of the poor. It is the contrary of waiting for government to deliver services and has a collective connotation (Krause, 2004:38). Three main strategies guide this approach: involvement of NGOs, group-based approach for mobilisation and rights-based approach for women's development.

In the Government of India's discourse, the Sixth Five Year Plan recognised that development programmes aimed at the transformation of rural societies would be meaningless if they do not involve the rural women, but it was only during the Seventh Plan that women's ability to form groups and participate in economic activities was recognised. It was also realised that the role of voluntary organisations would be crucial in organising women and to supplement government efforts. The Eight Five Year Plan went further and recognised that 'women must be enabled to function as equal partners and participants in development and not merely as beneficiaries of various schemes.... Social, cultural and administrative constraints to the realisation of women's full potential need to be removed and there has to be greater societal awareness of their contribution to national well-being'. This approach specifically laid emphasis on building women's agency through the formation of women's groups and participation in income-generating activities. The main strategy adopted was to facilitate the access of poor women to employment, skill up gradation, training, credit and other support services so that women as a group could take up income generating activities for supplementing their incomes. Assistance was to be given either to individual woman or to those organised into homogenous groups to take up economically viable activities together with the provision of support services and child-care facilities for the women so organised. This approach of welfare and poverty-alleviation within the paradigms of WID culminated in the DWCRA programme.

The discourse at the Government of India level has moved from poverty alleviation to incorporate elements of gender justice from the GAD framework. The Ninth Five Year Plan (1997-2002) is the most vocal about women's empowerment and Government's direct efforts at formation of SHGs. The Plan (section 3.8.27) committed itself to empower women as agents of social change and development, to create an enabling environment for women as equal partners with men, where women can freely exercise their rights both within and outside home and organise women into SHGs marking the beginning of a major process of empowerment. Government, however, plays a passive and indirect role in SHG formation and functioning. The entry of government into the SHG movement was through the Rashtriya Mahila Kosh which funds NGOs for forming and nurturing SHGs. The Plan also placed emphasis on women's concerns from the perspective of gender equity in terms of cognizance to the existing gender inequalities in land inheritance laws and ceiling laws. The equity concerns expressed in the Plan are also reflected in the National Empowerment Policy, 2001 for social empowerment of women. Apart from education, health etc. it recognised the needs of women in difficult circumstances, violence against women, rights for the girl child and gender sensitisation at all levels of governance.

The Tenth Plan aims to continue with the process of empowering women through translating the national policy for empowerment into action with a three-fold strategy: economic empowerment, social empowerment and gender justice. Economic empowerment would ensure provision of training, employment and income-generation activities with the ultimate objective of making all potential women economically independent. Social empowerment aims at creating an enabling environment through various affirmative development policies and programmes for development of women besides providing them easy and equal access to all basic minimum services so as to enable them to realise their full potential. Gender justice aims at eliminating all forms of gender discrimination.

The formation, stabilisation, growth and expansion of SHGs take place under the overall philosophy of 'empowerment' of the poor women. Empowerment is understood as one aspect of a multi-dimensional definition of poverty. The assumption is that increasing women's access to micro-finance will enable women to make a greater contribution to household income, either through their own economic activity or equally becoming a channel for loans to household activity. This contribution and subsequent increase in status in the household will in turn give women the support they need to enable women to bring about wider changes in gender inequality in the community.

The policy approaches in practice, however, still have the dominant thrust of either the financial sustainability paradigm or the poverty-alleviation paradigm. Financial sustainability and poverty-alleviation paradigms very easily fit into the WID approach, and can leave the gender aspects to women's own agency. Though gender sensitisation is incorporated for government and bank officials through the GAD paradigm, the process is slow and the embeddedness of women's social reality make it difficult to negotiate existing structural barriers and achieve social transformation. There is a tendency to see gender issues as cultural and hence not subject to outside intervention. This is what prevents the promoters from raising gender awareness issues in the Muslim villages of Kolar or the issue of land rights in Sonipat. Any prioritisation of women's interests from a feminist paradigm is seen as inherently divisive. This also often brings resistance to the role of the fieldworkers as facilitators of gender equality, when they have to face abuses from the villagers.

The State's role in implementing empowerment enhancing programmes for women and weaker sections of society is often indistinguishable from other poverty alleviation programmes, like, income generation, assets creation and health and education. For government, SHGs also represent an important mechanism through which to deliver subsidy to the weaker sections. As a result, subsidy amount under programmes such as SGSY can be used as a mobilising force for forming SHGs of scheduled caste (SC) and scheduled tribe (ST) people. In both Kolar and Sonipat, SC groups with poor members got loans easily and it is used as an incentive for others to form groups with them. Some SC members even have the option of changing membership in groups, as they are much sought after by others.

The practices of development NGOs remain service-oriented, as they can gain access to the women only with male permission. As a result, the development NGOs pay more attention to credit, leaving the issues of gender and women's position to women's own efforts. At the same time, there is very little political space available to NGOs for a feminist engagement with the State at the local level (Cornwall, Harrison & Whitehead, 2004). NGOs act as an ideological partner of the State when giving training to women on legislations that are women-friendly. Empowerment NGOs do work against the State when they mobilise women to demand services from the State or to protest against any harmful State policy, such as, policy on the sale of alcohol. Yet, the State remains the main player. At the local level, networking and coordination among the NGOs with each other is weak in India. This gives the Deputy Commissioner, as the local level representative of the State, the power and authority to arbitrate for NGOs in the case of conflicts and disputes among NGOs or public complaints against NGOs.

Further, the banks' role is confined to sanctioning credit for financially viable schemes. Due to the limited economic opportunities available for rural women, very few non-traditional occupations are available. Thus, local may remain limited to getting some 'free fund' from the government (through subsidy and grants) or even fatigue with too much loans when members realise the futility of taking too many loans for unproductive purposes. This was observed in both Sonipat and Kolar. Gender sensitisation trainings for field officials emphasise the triple role of women (Kabeer 1994), but biases about women's appropriate role in society can come into play or an approach of non-interference in household matters can rule the decisions of the external agents. The distinction between the public and the private (Walby 1990) is not overcome in the dealings between the women and the bank officials.

Indian Women, SHG Practices and Power

What matters in women's social development is whether women could improve their 'position' and not 'condition' alone; how and at what level SHGs answer to women's strategic needs and not their practical needs alone. In women's development through self-help, social changes should result in a form of social power that gives identity, improves social status and equalises gender relations for women. This section discusses SHG members' experiences in the bank-linkage model to negotiate existing power relationships through the assertion of identity, improvement in status and changes in gender relations.

The emphasis on the SHG-bank linkage in both Sonipat and Kolar meant that most of the practices were based on the dominant material incentive, that is, bank loan. The primary emphasis placed on fulfilling practical needs—through both the mobilisation strategies and the formation of people's expectations—meant that credit was the primary motivation for seventy nine per cent of the women to join the SHGs. This was, no doubt, an important concern for the poor. Few of the older women gave importance to the social aspects of SHGs, and the educated ones acknowledged the utility of trainings.

The practices of participation in the bank-linkage model for an SHG involve different activities and they go through different stages. The required activities of the SHGs can be divided into three processes: regular, occasional and infrequent. Regular processes include meetings, savings, activities related to lending and borrowing. Recording minutes, keeping accounts, opening bank account, and going to bank for deposit of collected amount are some of the regular processes. Occasional processes include trainings and participation in joint activities geared toward fulfilment of practical interests. Trainings and participation in inter-departmental activities organised by the NGO, like, exposure visits, themes camps etc. are occasional processes in which women participate. Infrequent processes include acts relating to social movements or social change that are oriented to strategic interests. Such activities involve, running for elected offices, peace building efforts in times of conflict, help to distressed member or other villager, overseeing government programmes, fighting against the alcoholism of husbands and other male members in the village and so on. From the point of trategic needs, such socially empowering activities are important, but they are informal and take place infrequently.

These are also the stages through which a group has to travel before it is considered mature. Wilson (2002:223) identifies four stages through which a group has to travel in its path toward financial development—savings, interlending, linkage and sustainability. Corresponding to these, the development process of an SHG's life can be said to go through three stages: *forming, functioning and sustainable.* Groups that have started saving, inter-lending and deal with bank loans can be said to have moved from the forming stage to the functioning stage. Within the formal rules of SHG formation and bank linkage, groups have to accumulate sufficient experience in inter-loaning and account keeping before they are eligible for bank loans. The functioning groups are the ones that have started inter-lending at the minimum. These groups supposedly help in social development through knowledge of organisational functioning, women's physical and mental well-being and experience in economic as well as non-economic activities. Sustainable groups give wider exposure to women through their links with clusters and federation—the ultimate philosophy of group sustainability.

Though the women interviewed belonged to SHGs in different stages, yet groups in both the areas had some form of group or collective identity. The SHGs form a community that is distinctive by its gender and task. It is also an informal credit-based organisation for the women. Through emphasis on the independent and self-reliant nature of group functioning, the participants negotiate an identity that is separate from their identity as a member of any particular family. The focus on women's rights and awareness of their inner power is an attempt to produce a new subjectivity and identity for the women, which is a form of a politicised woman.

Rural Women

This was not easily achievable within the existing patriarchal social reality of Kolar and Sonipat. A woman's identity in rural India is through her position in either her natal or marital home as daughter, sister, wife, mother and/or mother-in-law. At the societal level, the identity of the individual women is also structured on the basis of her caste, class and family status. This was particularly significant for married women at the village level in Sonipat. During fieldwork, individual woman could be located only as somebody's wife or daughter-in-law. An independent identity of one's own by a young, married and illiterate woman is not easily achieved unless the woman can negotiate it through her new role in the SHG. As the SHGs formed were still in their evolving stage in Sonipat, this aspect was not achieved by the women. The few women who had an independent identity were the ones who were also *Anganwadi* (child care) workers. As one member in Sonipat explained, 'we only belong to somebody, we do not learn to be individuals... it takes for us to be mothers-in-law to open our mouths in front of others'. For women in Kolar belonging to sustainable groups, this had changed through their association with the SHGs. Laxmiamma in Bandakote village very confidently said: Now-a-days, people identify me as an SHG member.

In the area of participation, satisfaction and perceived feelings of self-worth can be used as indicators of women's feelings of self-empowerment. Seventy-one per cent women in Sonipat and ninety-one per cent in Kolar expressed some form of satisfaction from their participation in the SHG activities, but it reduced when it came to their perception of increase in social status through participation in the SHGs. In Sonipat, it was 40 per cent; whereas in Kolar, it was 86 per cent. The changes in perception were higher in Kolar due to the higher maturity stage of the SHGs as shown in the table 1.

TABLE 1
SHG Stage and Members' Perception

SHG Stage	*Feelings of satisfaction* **Sonipat**	*Feelings of satisfaction* **Kolar**	*Increase in status* **Sonipat**	*Increase in status* **Kolar**
Forming	17	8		
Functioning	43	5	26	5
Sustainable	68	64		
	60 (71%)	73 (91%)	34 (40%)	69 (86%)

As far as status was concerned, the responses clearly show that women in Kolar had a greater perception of increase in their status than in Sonipat. This was directly related to access to credit and other benefits through SHGs. In the absence of credit, women felt no difference in their status. One woman in Kolar remarked:

> "Our status has not changed as we have got no loan... without loan, who thinks we have done something? If I can open a shop, they will think I have done something and there will be a future. My husband is very old, he cannot work much and I have nothing."
>
> This perception was again coloured by the societal norms on women's appropriate role. In Sonipat, the women remarked, "They see us going from here to there, but get nothing... some think we are loafers....".

In Kolar, access to bank loans and other resources made a visible impact on the status of the group members of the sustainable groups. They were no longer confined to household activities alone. They moved around from village to village, attended meetings and participated in joint activities with other groups. It was an ability to take on more responsibility and more work that added to their visibility and status. Nagaratnamma in Kolar claimed, "our status has increased. When one works hard, then only one will gain. Now we get help from the men... we also get better treatment from the officials - we respect them and they respect us." This was corroborated by another woman who saw her status improved: "Wherever we go now-a-days, we get lots of respect. Earlier people criticised a lot, but when they saw the benefits coming, nobody says anything now".

In the relatively less rigid patriarchal system of Kolar and with access to loans, women were able to negotiate relationships to some extent. This had to do with the fact that men and other villagers' attitudes towards the position of women changed as they saw the women's ability to obtain credit from the banks. Chouramma of Kashettipalli village explained:

> "Earlier when we used to go out for training for 3-4 days and return, our men will be angry and ask, 'what have you brought? Sometimes other members will fight with us because they thought that the ones who went for training are hiding something. Now people have understood."

> Another member elaborated: Earlier we had to keep asking our men to let us go to meetings... now we ask him what to do with the money... if there is a dispute between the husband and wife, and as a result there is a problem in returning the loan, the wife will not be entitled to the second installment. So, husbands also learn to behave'.

Thus, the capacity to negotiate gender and power relations increased with access to loans and gradual changes in gender allocation of work at the household level occurred among the members of sustainable groups

Women's social recognition increased with the ability to bring in loan. Aspiration for increasing material condition was by itself not bad if women experienced any form of social power as well. There is a belief that as women in the SHGs receive loans, they become empowered. Their confidence, collective acts and mobility outside the house are cited as examples. Access to resources had, no doubt, given the option of independent decision-making to a majority of the women in Kolar. They were able to claim public space through holding meetings in the DWCRA or gram panchayat (village council) buildings. Access to public spaces had opened their participation at village level decision-making. Pappamma in Kolar informed that villagers give them respect as SHG members and they get invited to meetings. Men and other family members willing to provide women with time to attend meetings and trainings when they see their credit expectations fulfilled.

While important, these do not necessarily transform the hierarchical power structures that place women's position below that of the men and give women social power. Male permission remained a crucial factor for participation in SHG activities. Married women in Kolar unanimously said, 'we are here (participating in SHGs) only because our husbands have agreed'. Along with credit, collective activity against alcoholism and male violence was undertaken not only to assert identity, but also as a means to increase status. More than 80 per cent in Kolar participated in some form of collective activity, but less than 40 per cent did so in Sonipat. Power had been gained temporally when women interacted with the State informally through group activities. Women in Kolar could organise such activities through their interaction with other members at the cluster level meetings. Sometimes, women from several groups in the same village organised such activities as, when demanding a bus service to their village or removal of an alcohol shop. They were, however, aware of the limits of the power generated in women's collective acts against alcoholism, when they said,

> "All of us went to the DC's office and demanded the removal of the liquor shop. It was removed, but after six months, it opened again... it should be at least far away from the village, so that even if our husbands drink.... it wears off by the time they reach home."

The custom of observing *purdah* or *ghungat* (veil) is a cultural constraint for the women in Sonipat (Chowdhry 1994:283). Ironically, it is also construed as a symbol of respect for elders. On the question of removal of *ghungat,* it clashed with the older women's expectations of respect from the young. An elderly widow in village Rajlubhogipur, Sonipat explained:

> "What is purdah? It is just covering your face when some elders are around and then forget about it as soon as they are gone. Getting an opportunity to work is more important. There is nothing bad in being bound in a few social customs... purdah is not such a bad thing."

It was the educated young lady who could express that they do not face any problem with the practice of *ghungat.* What was of more importance is economic independence:

> "If we could have had a shop in the village, it would have benefited more. Men say that these ladies are just roaming around—they have not achieved anything."

In both the cases, the constraints of informal practices, lack of information and uncertainty about the future meant that women chose to save money for their daughters' dowry. Within the existing societal framework, that was the only option for a girl to have a 'good' marriage and the bride's family does not have much option in it. Even in the homogenous scheduled caste village of Seetharampura, it depended on the groom's side to take the final decision. The social entrepreneur informed that they could only take steps to reduce dowry, but it was not possible to stop it. Women felt that "all these talk about stopping dowry is for Nagarajan (the trainer) only... if a girl does not take dowry on her marriage, she should be prepared to die or to come back to her mother's house." From the perspective of both men and women, marriage is the only viable option for girls for her upward mobility, security and stability in life. In this regard, women showed a process of rational decision-making within the existing institutional structure of patriarchal norms and a weak judicial system.

Women's identity, perception of changes in status and gender relations was mostly higher with the higher stages of the SHGs to which they belonged. The ability to reach the higher stage was, however, a result of many interacting factors and not dependent on women's agency alone.

The SHG movement is a micro-finance movement and it is no doubt, the largest in the world, but can it be a (social) movement that can change gender and power relations? A movement is a collective effort to seek change. Social movements generally arise when individuals act collectively, agreeing on a goal and on an ideology (Katz, 1993:103). The self-help model incorporates many of the elements of the social movements that seek to create a (political) sphere that is "directly controlled by the community rather than the state, and share the belief that the way in which change is pursued will largely determine the result."

Viewed from the perspective of the contemporary women's movements, SHGs are informal organisations that fall under the 'empowerment' wing of the movement. Through the SHGs, women are coming together for credit and other benefits, and seek to promote self-reliance for themselves and enhance development. They are also a form of directed collective action where women are mobilised with an implied commitment to advance their interests, but within the broader development goals of the nation-state. The successful groups do articulate a belief system of personal power through savings, improving condition, social entrepreneurs who give leadership for improving position, there is a feeling of collective identification and loyalty to the groups; cluster and federation provide the organisational structure through which it is expected to grow to provide support to a wider range of women and work collectively. Self-help groups (SHGs), in rural areas, have provided an alternative to prevailing gender roles for women at the local level and federations of SHGs can create a movement of women's solidarity. Women's federation *(Grameena Okkutta)* in Mulbagal, Kolar has taken a step in this direction. Whether they will provide resistance to patriarchal norms and values is not yet clear.

Most of the SHGs and their activities remain oriented toward becoming good savers and good creditors. As social and socialised beings women's choices are inextricably linked with the family and SHGs as an emerging structure has to still function in a patriarchal society. Family norms and values are often designed by patriarchal preferences and approval or permission as per these preferences remain a crucial factor. The common identity of these SHGs is formed around the issue of working for material benefits. The changes in gender relations were very much benefit-based, susceptible to pressure and women had to justify their action in terms of benefits received. The identity achieved is temporary as many SHGs show a tendency to disintegrate when credit is not forthcoming or members change groups with the expectation of getting benefits.

SHGs are designed to stand on two pillars—credit (condition) and social reform (position). Self-help as practised from the economic perspective of credit management requires entrepreneurship and competitiveness at the individual level. On the one hand, "It is important to help the women think big." One of our star entrepreneurs is Vijaya Mayuri, a woman who went from making pappads to power cables. That is the kind of growth that is possible. Women should be aware of that. The individual entrepreneurial approach can come in conflict with the collective approach required for empowerment. Fulfilling strategic interests require women's solidarity, perception of common interest and sisterhood from a feminist perspective. The self-help movement incorporates liberal feminism which struggles for equality with men from within the existing the social structure. This again needs sustained enthusiasm from 'social entrepreneurs' and periodic motivation by NGOs to make sure that the feminist aspirations are not compromised. Unless handled carefully, empowerment through self-help groups becomes a double-edged sword as the initial enthusiasm is not sustained among both the members and the villagers, and the real interests of the women are forgotten.

Mayoux suggests that it is only through organisations mobilised for rights that can aspire to achieve genuine form of power for women. This is, however, not easily achievable due to the limited political space available to NGOs (mentioned above) and the differences among women both at the local and regional levels. Self-help signifies local aspirations and grassroots development, but these do not necessarily overcome existing differences. Women have multiple identities based on class, caste, education and other such categories and they are constantly required to negotiate the terrain of these overlapping identities. The diversity within the SHGs is not always acknowledged and divisions of caste and class remain. Even in homogenous groups, older women's interests can be different from the younger ones. Leadership remains with the educated and relatively better-off who can afford the time to devote in social activities. Difficulty of reconciling practical needs with what are strategic needs can give preference to the former, as when a woman has to decide between getting a daughter married or getting her educated.

What is often overlooked is that, the SHG efforts remain context-bound, localised and dependent on the facilitator. It needs to be recognised that women's needs and interests can be different in different areas of the country. The condition and position of women in different areas and even within the same group are not the same. Kinship and marriage patterns, caste and class differences, differences in the capacity of facilitating organisations would require different approaches to SHG formation and functioning in different areas of the country. Due to dependency, the SHGs are functioning more as micro-credit groups and not as social empowerment or social action groups for women. Most of the external agents play an instrumental role by being developmental and service-oriented. Burra, Deshmukh & Murthy's (2006:332) study found that where the NGOs or the facilitating organisations organised women around multiple issues by simultaneously expanding several spaces, the impact of empowerment has been higher. Such attempts are through simultaneous dealing of issues, such as, domestic violence (body space), savings and credit and livelihoods (Physical and economic spaces), contesting elections (political space), and fight against caste and tribal atrocities (socio-cultural space). This is, however, a slow and a difficult process.

The SHGs have the possibility of developing groups of organised, assertive and empowered women at the grassroots level. There is truth in understanding that the economic is political, but this can be limited in failing to take account of the existing differences, structural inequalities and the relationships of power at the local level. The SHGs can make women contribute to the economy; it has changed the lives of many in India. Group power has been found to be a potent force in giving collective empowerment and voice to the poor women in rural areas, but has not necessarily empowered them beyond the confines of patriarchy. There is a long way to go before reorientation of power relationships, both in the household and at the societal level, will take place.

Summing up

Although gender empowerment has been a buzzword in development circles, the concept is being used in so many different ways that it remains ambiguous. All studies and reports on women status have only remained as a source of data, which rather endorses the passivity of the state. We should reject the touristic observations of women in metro society, dispel misconceptions and portray the real scenario of Orissa. Effective policy design requires an accurate understanding of the gender issues within a broad social framework. We need poverty-independent gender analyses and policies in order to rescue gender from poverty trap. Women's income earning activity should not be temporary, exploitative and reversible. Education and technology should ensure liberation and freedom for all human beings. It should break gradually the shackles of tradition that binds women in the man-made gaol. Technological development can be both a threat and an ally to women in their various roles. Therefore, we should integrate gender into technology and development. More nuanced discussion of the complex interrelationships between gender and technology is needed. Training programme for successful technology transfer is necessary to derive the benefits of existing market-driven technological promotion. The new technology should be used as a vehicle for gender equality in the backward societies like Orissa.

The gender issue should be delinked both from myopic economics and insensitive politics. There is no substitute for a gender analysis, which transcend class divisions and material definitions of deprivation. Therefore, 'adding women' is not necessary, but an insight and rethinking development concepts and practices as a whole through a gender lens is necessary. We have to initiate debate on state non-action on gender issues. Despite several rules and acts in place, all rights of women are being violated and they have been suffering in silence. A vigorous multi-pronged and multi-professional effort is needed to establish the woman as a human being in her own right. With the hosanna of modernisation, it is imperative to dispel myths, superstitions and misconceptions about woman and her duties and adopt a rational attitude towards the woman as a human being.

Despite jamboree of techno culture we need a meaningful social transformation, which gives the equal independent human status to women. Economic citizenship is not sufficient for transforming existing asymmetric gender relations. In all backward states like Orissa, girls are educationally very successful but socially women are not. The wife may be happy but the women is not. The real progress should occur when the women become the producers of their own welfare and bounty, not the recipients of charity. The chance for a social transformation should begin and end with the womenkind in the ground, because, nothing grows from the top. Effective policy design requires accurate understanding of the gender issues within a broad social framework. Women development is a social process to be evolved from the society but not a technological product to be achieved by a triggered policy.

REFERENCES

Agarwal, Bina (1988) *Structures of Patriarchy: State, Community and Household in Modernising Asia.* Sed books, London.

Agrawal, Bina (1997). Bargaining and Gender Relations within and beyond the Household, *Feminist Economics,* 3 (1), pp. 454-87.

Berry, K. (2003) 'Developing Women: The Traffic in Ideas about Women and their Needs in Kangra, India' in Sivaramakrishnan, K. & Agarwal, Arun (ed.) *Regional Modernities: The Cultural Politics of Development in India.* Stanford University Press, Stanford, California, pp.75-98.

Boserup, Ester (1990). "Economic Change and the role of women" in *Persistent Inequalities: Women and World development,* (ed) Eren Tinker, Chapter-2, Oxford U. press, New York.

Burkey, S. (1993) *People First: A Guide to Self-Reliant Participatory Rural Development.* Sed Books, London.

Burra, N., Deshmukh-Ranadive, J. & Murthy, R. (2005) (ed.) *Micro-Credit, Poverty and Empowerment: Linking the Triad.* Sage Publications, New Delhi.

Byrne, Eileen M1993, Women and Science: The Snark Syndrome, Falmer Press, Bristol.

Calman, L. J. (1992) *Toward Empowerment: Women and Movement Politics in India.* Westview Press, Boulder, USA.

Carr, M., Chen, M. & Jhabvala, R. (1996) (ed.) *Speaking Out: Women's Economic Empowerment in South Asia.* Intermediate Technology Publications, London.

Chakrabarti, R. (2004) The Indian Microfinance Experience - Accomplishments and Challenges, in Debroy, B. & Khan, A. U. (ed.) *Integrating the Rural Poor into Markets.* Academic Foundation, New Delhi.

Chowdhry, P. (1994) *The Veiled Women: shifting gender equations in rural Haryana, 1880-1990.* Oxford University Press, Delhi.

Cornwall, A., Harrison, E. & Whitehead, A. (2004) 'Introduction: Repositioning Feminisms in Gender and Development'. *IDS Bulletin,* vol. 35, no. 4, pp. 1-9.

Curie, Bob (2000), *The Politics of Hunger in India,* Macmillan India, Chennai.

Das Kumar (1997) Asian Profile of Underdevelopment and Poverty, *Asian Profile,* Canada, 5(1).

Dewan, Ritu (1996), Gender: conceptual overview, *Economic and Political Weekly* April,19.

Dorward, Andrew et al (2003) Markets, Institutions and Technology: Missing Links to Livelihood Analysis, *Development Policy Review,Vol.21(3)* pp. 313-32.

Dube, S.C. (1988) *Modernisation and Development - The Search for Alternative Paradigms.* Sed Books Ltd., London.

Dyson, T. & Moore, M. (1983) Kinship structure, female autonomy and demographic behaviour in India. *Population and Development Review,* 9, 35-60.

Edwards, Paul N. (1996). The closed world: Computers and the politics of discourse in cold war America, Cambridge, Mass: MIT Press.: 167-72.

Faulkner, Wendy. (2000). The power *and* the pleasure? A research agenda for "making gender stick" to engineers. *Science, Technology, & Human Values, 25(1),* 88-120.

Fernandez, A. P. (1994) *The Myrada Experience: Alternate Management Systems for Savings and Credit of the Rural Poor.* MYRADA, Bangalore, India.

Fernando, J. L. (2006) *Microfinance: Perils and Prospects.* Routledge, London.

Fisher, T. & Sriram. M.S. (2002) (ed.) *Beyond Micro-Credit: Putting Development Back into Micro-Finance.* Vistaar Publications, New Delhi.

Friedmann, J. (1992) *Empowerment: The Politics of Alternative Development.* Blackwell, Cambridge, USA.

Gaonkar, R. (2004) 'Role of Self-help groups in Empowerment of Women'. Paper presented at the ISTR Sixth International Conference, Toronto, Canada.

Geisman, Donna (2000). *Women, Science and Technology,* Routledge, London.

Goetz, A. M. & Sengupta, R. (1996) 'Who Takes the Credit? Gender, Power, and Control over Loan Use in Rural Credit Programmes in Bangladesh'. *World Development,* vol. 24, no 1, pp. 45-63.

Government of India (1985) *Seventh Five Year Plan, 1985-1990.* The Planning Commission of India, New Delhi.

Government of India (1992) *Eight Five Year Plan, 1992-1997.* The Planning Commission of India, New Delhi.

Government of India (1997) *Ninth Five Year Plan, 1997-2002.* The Planning Commission of India, New Delhi.

Government of India (2001) *National Policy for the Empowerment of Women, 2001.* Department of Women and Child Development, Ministry of Human Resources, New Delhi, India.

Government of India (2002) *Tenth Five Year Plan, 2002-2007.* The Planning Commission of India, New Delhi.

Gran, G. (1983) *Development by People: Citizen Construction of a Just World.* Praeger Publishers, New York.

Hardiman, M. & Midgley, J. (1982) *The Social Dimensions of Development: Social Policy and Planning in the Third World.* J. Wiley, New York.

Harper, M. (2002a) 'Self-help Groups and Grameen Bank Groups: What are the Differences'? in Fisher, T. & Sriram. M.S. *Beyond Micro-Credit: Putting Development Back into Micro-Finance.* Vistaar Publications, New Delhi, pp. 169-198.

Harper, M. (2002b) 'Promotion of Self Help Groups under the SHG Bank Linkage Programme in India'. Paper presented at the Seminar on SHG-Bank Linkage Programme, New Delhi, India.

Hoff, K. and Stiglitz, J. E. (1990) 'Introduction: Imperfect Information and Rural Credit Markets - Puzzles and Policy Perspectives'. *The World Bank Economic Review,* Vol. 4.

Hunt, J. & Kasynathan, N. (2001) 'Pathways to empowerment? Reflections on microfinance and transformation in gender relations in south Asia', in *Gender and Development,* vol. 9, no. 1, March 2001, pp. 42-52.

Jannet (1998). *Women and Girls Last: Females and the Internet,* IRISS '98 International Conference: 25-27 March 1998, Bristol, UK.

Kabeer, N. (1994) *Reversed Realities: Gender Hierarchies in Development Thought.* Verso, London.

Kabra, K. (2000). Indian Economy 98-2000, *Alternative Economic Survey,* Rainbow Pub.Delhi.

Kanitkar, A. (2002) 'Exploring Empowerment and Leadership at the Grassroots: Social Entrepreneurship in the SHG Movement in India', in Fisher, T. & Sriram. M.S. *Beyond Micro-Credit: Putting Development Back into Micro-Finance.* Vistaar Publications, New Delhi, pp. 234-262.

Kannan, R. (2004) 'SHG Movement Aiming at Giving Women Larger Role', in *The Hindu,* March 8, 2004.

Karlekar, Malavika (1995), Search for Women Voices, *Economic and Political Weekly* 29 April

Katherine Jellison (1993) Entitled to Power: Farm Women and Technology, UNC Press.

Katz, A. H. (1993) *Self-Help in America: A Social Movement Perspective.* Twayne Publishers, New York.

Kiesler, S., etal (1985). Pool halls, chips, and war games: Women in the culture of computing. Psychology of Women Quarterly, 9, 451-62. Turkle, S. (1984). The second self: Computers and the human spirit. New York: Simon & Schuster.

Krause, P. (2004) 'Institutional Framework for Poverty Alleviation in Krishna and Nalgonda Districts of Andhra Pradesh' in Rajasekhar, D. & Biradar, R.R. (ed.) (2004) *Reluctant Partners Coming Together? Interface between People, Government and the NGOs.* Concept Publishing Company, New Delhi, pp. 35-56.

Mackenzie, L. (1992) *On our feet: Taking Steps to Challenge Women's Oppression: A Handbook on Gender and Popular Education Workshops.* Centre for Adult and Continuing Education, University of the Western Cape, Belville, South Africa.

Mahmud, S. (2002) 'Informal women's groups in rural Bangladesh: operation and outcomes', in Heyer, J., Stewart, F. & Thorp, R. (ed.) *Group Behaviour and Development: Is the market Destroying Cooperation?* Oxford University Press, Oxford, UK, pp.209-26.

Mahmud, S. (2003) 'Actually how Empowering is Microcredit?' *Development and Change,* vol. 34, no. 4, pp. 577-605.

Mayoux, L. (2001) 'Women's Empowerment Versus Sustainability? Towards a New Paradigm in Micro-finance Programmes', in Lemire, B., Pearson, R., & Campbell, G. (ed.) *Women and Credit; Researching the Past, Refiguring the Future.* Berg, Oxford, pp.247-69.

Mazumdar, V. (1986) 'Women's Studies in Indian Perspective: Summary' in Raj, M. K. (ed.) *Women 's Studies in India: Some Perspectives.* Popular Prakashan, Bombay, pp. 23-33.

Michel C. (1997). *Globalisation of Poverty,* Madhyam Books, New Delhi.

Molyneux, M. (1985) 'Mobilisation Without Emancipation? Women's Interests, the State and Revolution in Nicaragua'. *Feminist Studies,* vol. 11, pp. 227-54.

Molyneux, M. (1998) Analysing Women's Movements. *Development and Change,* vol. 29, pp.219-45.

Monkman, Karen (1998) 'Training women for change and empowerment' in Stromquist, N. P. & Monkman, K. (ed.), *Women in the Third World: An Encyclopedia of Contemporary Issues.* Garland Publishers, New York, pp.498-509.

Montgomery, R., Bhattacharya, D. & Hulme, D. (1986) 'Credit for the Poor in Bangladesh: The BRAC Rural Development Programme and the Government Thana Resource Development Employment Programme', in Hulme, D. & Mosley, P. (ed.) Finance Against Poverty. Routledge, London.

Moser, C. (1989) Gender Planning in the Third World: Meeting Practical and Strategic Gender Needs. *World Development,* vol. 17, no. 11, pp. 1799-1825.

Murthy, R. K. (2004) 'Organisational Strategy in India and Diverse Identities of Women: Bridging the Gap'. *Gender and Development,* vol. 12, no 1, May 2004, pp. 10-18.

MYRADA (2001) *The Myrada Experience: A Manual for Capacity Building of Self-help Affinity Groups.* Myrada, Bangalore, India.

NABARD (2005) *Annual Report, 2004-2005.* National Agricultural Bank for Rural Development, Mumbai, India.

Olson, M. (1965). *The Logic of Collective Action: Public Goods and the Theory of Groups.* Harvard University Press, Cambridge, Massachusetts.

Omvedt, G. (2004) 'Women's Movement: Some Ideological Debates' in Chaudhuri, M. (ed.) *Feminism in India. Kali for Women,* New Delhi, India.

Pieterse, J. P. N. (2001) *Development Theory: Deconstructions/ Reconstructions.* Sage Publications, London.

Pitt, M.M., Khandker, S.R. & Cartwright, J. (2003) 'Does Micro-Credit Empower Women? Evidence from Bangladesh'. World Bank Policy Research Working Paper 2998, Washington DC.

Purushothaman, S. (1998). *The Empowerment of Women in India.* Sage Publications, New Delhi.

Rahman, A. (1999) *Women and Microcredit in Rural Bangladesh: Anthropological Study of the Rhetoric and Realities of Grameen Bank Lending.* Westview Press, Boulder, Colorado, USA.

Rahman, Md. A. (1993) *People's Self-Development: Perspectives on Participatory Action Research.* Sed Books, London.

Rajasekhar, D. (2000) 'Non-governmental Organisations in India: Opportunities and Challenges'. Working paper no. 66, Institute for Social and Economic Change, Bangalore, India.

Rowlands, J. (1999) 'Empowerment Examined', in Eade, D. (ed.) *Development with Women: Selected Essays from Development in Practice.* Oxfam, Oxford, UK, pp.141-50.

Sa-Dhan (2001). *Microfinance Regulation in India.* Sa-Dhan, New Delhi.

Satish, P. (2001) Institutional Alternatives for the Promotion of microfinance: Self-Help Groups in India. Journal of Microfinance, vol. 3, no. 2, pp. 49-74.

Schuler, S. R., Hashemi, S. M. & Badal, S. H. (1998) 'Men's violence against Women in Rural Bangladesh: Undermined or Exacerbated by Microcredit Programmes?' *Development in Practice,* vol. 8, no. 2, May 1998, pp. 148-57.

Shankar, S. (2000) *India: Partners in Empowerment: NGOs and Government in the Maharashtra Rural Credit Project.* Report submitted to The International Fund for Agricultural Development, Asia and the Pacific Division, Project Management Department, January 2000.

Sriram, M. S. & Upadhyayula, R. S. (2004) The Transformation of the Microfinance Sector in India: Experiences, Options, and Future. *Journal of Microfinance,* vol. 6, no. 2, Winter 2004, pp. 89-112.

Stamm, L. & Ryff, C. D. (ed.) (1984) *Social Power and Influence of Women.* Westview Press, Colorado.

Swasti, Mitter (1997). *Women Encounter Technology(ed)* Routledge, UK.

Thomas, B. (1985) *Politics, Participation, and Poverty: Development through Self-Help in Kenya.* Westview Press, Boulder, USA.

Titus (2002) 'Costs in Micro-finance: What do Urban Self-help Groups Tell Us?' in Fisher, T. & Sriram. M.S. *Beyond Micro-*

Credit: Putting Development Back into Micro-Finance. Vistaar Publications, New Delhi, pp. 199.

Uphoff, N.T. & Esman, M. J. (1984) *Local Organisations: Intermediaries in Rural Development.* Cornell University Press, Ithaca, USA.

Walby, S. (1990) *Theorising Patriarchy.* Blackwell, Oxford.

Wilson, K. (2002) 'The New Microfinance: An Essay on the Self-Help Group Movement in India'. *Journal of Microfinance,* Vol. 4, No. 2, pp. 217-45.

6

WOMEN AND AGRICULTURAL DEVELOPMENT

Introduction

Regardless of the level of development achieved by the respective economies, women play a pivotal role in agriculture and in rural development in most countries of the Asia-Pacific region. Evidently, there are serious constraints which militate against the promotion of an effective role for women in development in those societies which were bound by age-old traditions and beliefs. Patriarchal modes and practices motivated by cultures and/or interpretations of religious sanctions and illiteracy hinder women's freedom to opt for various choices to assert greater mobility in social interactions. Resulting from these situations, women's contribution to agriculture and other sectors in the economy remain concealed and unaccounted for in monitoring economic performance measurement. Consequently, they are generally invisible in plans and programmes. They were, in fact, discriminated against by stereotypes which restrict them to a reproductive role, and denied access to resources which could eventually enhance their social and economic contribution to the society.

In terms of the ratio of membership of women in agricultural cooperatives, the percentage is rather low, but they have a strong influence on them—through the heads of the households. Certain obvious barriers restrict their direct and formal entry in agricultural cooperatives. Even in countries like Japan, the ratio of women membership in agricultural cooperative is extremely low. Only very few women serve on the Boards of Directors. Their simple and clear perception is that the administrative and decision-making domain rests with the men and women do not wish to overburden themselves with financial responsibilities in case something goes wrong with the cooperative. They, of course contribute significantly in farm operations. However, the women are very active in Women's Associations of Agricultural Cooperatives which organise their activities around the life and style of farm household members.

Regardless of the level of development achieved by the respective economies, women play a pivotal role in agriculture and in rural development in most countries of the Asia-Pacific Region. Evidently there are serious constraints which militate against the promotion of an effective role for women in development in those societies which were bound by age-old traditions and beliefs. Patriarchal modes and practices motivated by cultures and/or interpretations of religious sanctions and illiteracy hinder women's freedom to opt for various choices to assert greater mobility in social interactions. Resulting from these situations, women's contribution to agriculture and other sectors in the economy remain concealed and unaccounted for in monitoring economic performance measurement. Consequently, they are generally invisible in plans and programmes. They were, in fact, discriminated against by stereotypes which restrict them to a reproductive role, and denied access to resources which could eventually enhance their social and economic contribution to the society.

In developing countries, among the poor, rural women are the poorest and more vulnerable. Empirical evidences suggest that women in rural areas are more adversely affected by poverty than men. The incidence of poverty among rural women is on the rise in most of the developing countries. The issues of gender bias and equity point to the double burden women have to bear—that on being poor and being a woman. Further strategies and programmes for development had largely overlooked the question of gender equity. Projects aiming to reduce poverty view the poor rural women as the recipient of benefits of development, instead of active participant and still poor rural women have the least access to basic needs such as food, health and education.

Hunger and Poverty

Hunger, which usually follows food shortages, is caused by a complex set of events and circumstances (social, economic and political factors) that differ depending on the place and time. Although hunger has been a part of human experience for centuries and a dominant feature of life in many low-income countries, the causes of hunger and starvation are not very well understood. Our understanding of the main causes of hunger and starvation has been hampered by myths and misconceptions about the interplay between hunger and population growth, land use, farm size, technology, trade, environment and other factors.

Poverty cannot be defined simply in terms of lacking access to sufficient food. It is also closely associated with a person's lack of access to productive assets, services and markets. Without access to these, it is unlikely that production and income-earning capacities can be improved on a sustainable basis. Rural poverty is related to food insecurity, access to assets, services and markets: income-earning opportunities; and the organisational and institutional means for achieving those ends.

Throughout the history and in many societies, inequalities of women and men were part and parcel of an accepted male-dominated culture. It is a complex historical process, which requires detailed study before one can conceive of a viable strategy to improve and sustain the status of women in society. One of the basic factors causing unequal share of women in development relates to the division of labour between the sexes. This division of labour has been justified on the basis of the childbearing function of women and this is biologically important for survival. Consequently, distribution of tasks and responsibilities between men and women in a given society has mainly restricted women to the domestic sphere. Mass poverty and general backwardness has further aggravated the inequalities.

While the women's childbearing and child-rearing functions are respected in many countries, there has been very little recognition of women's actual or potential contribution to the economic, social and cultural states. The role of women within the family combined with high level of unemployment and under-employment of the population in general, has led to the unequal state of priority to men in matters of employment. It is understandable that women cannot be expected to join the army, for instance, as foot soldiers but Israel's well-known and rightfully feared *sabrahs* or women commandos have shattered the myth of man's physical superiority and thus priority for most jobs.

Discrimination and Underdevelopment

It is relevant to consider some aspects of the marginalisation of the status of women in the world by having a look at the figures which are based on the documents of the United Nations. Some of the findings are:

Unemployment Rate: Male unemployment rate decreased by 11 per cent from 1984 to 1988, while that of women, unemployment rate increased by 0.5 per cent during the same period;

Women in the Informal Sector: Without legal protection or security, women depend on informal trade for their survival. In Third World countries, a high percentage of food vendors were women: in Nigeria 94 per cent, Thailand 80 per cent, 63 per cent in the Philippines;

Inequality in Pay: All over the world women earn only two-thirds of men's pay and earn less than three-quarters of the wages of men doing similar jobs. Women form one-third of the world's official labour force, but are concentrated in the lowest-paid jobs and are more vulnerable to unemployment than men;

Domestic Work: Women do almost all the world's domestic work and coupled with their additional work in the productive spheres—this means most women work a double day. Unpaid domestic work is regarded as women's work. Though it is vital work, it is invisible work, unpaid, undervalued and unrecognised. Yet, the women's contribution to society in this regard is enormous;

Agriculture: Women grow about half of the world's food, but own hardly any land, have difficulty in obtaining credit and are overlooked by agricultural advisors and projects. In Africa, three-quarters of the agricultural work is done by women while in Asia, Latin America and the Middle-East, women comprise half of the agricultural labour force;

Health: Women provide more health care than all health services combined and have been major beneficiaries of a new global shift in priorities towards prevention of disease and promotion of good health;

Education: Women continue to outnumber men among the world's illiterates by about 3:2 ratio, but school enrollment boom is closing the education gap between boys and girls;

Political Affairs: Due to poorer education, lack of confidence and greater workload, women are still under-represented in the decision-making bodies of their countries.

The effects of the long-term cumulative process of discrimination against women have been accentuated by underdevelopment. Graphically, while women represent nearly 50 per cent of the world's adult population and one-third of the total labour force, they labour nearly two-thirds of the total working hours but receive only one-tenth of world income and own less than one per cent of property. The story of overworked women in the rural areas of the developing and underdeveloped countries of the world is too well known.

The type of agricultural activities generally expected of women is highly labour-intensive and the rural women generally do not enjoy the benefits of new technologies. Their wages are generally less because it is assumed that the efficiency of women's labour is poor compared to that of men. Regarding ownership of land, women do not enjoy equal rights, particularly in the developing countries where most of the production, processing, storage and preparation of food is carried out by the women. These account for 50 per cent of the total labour required for food production. Many of these tasks are performed by children, especially the girls. Besides helping the menfolk in many farm operations, women have to shoulder the entire responsibilities for household chores. Bringing water from far-off wells and rivers and gathering fuel wood from forests are also part of their daily duties. Such enormous waste of human energy is unnecessary in this technological age.

Gender Division of Labour in Agriculture

The particular tasks done on farms by men and women have certain common patterns. In general, men undertake the heavy physical labour of land preparation and jobs which are specific to distant locations, such as livestock herding, while women carry out the repetitious, time-consuming tasks like weeding and those which are located close to home, such as care of the kitchen garden. In most cultures, the application of pesticides is considered a male task, as women are aware of the danger to their unborn children of exposure to chemicals. Women do a major part of the planting and weeding of crops. Care of livestock is shared, with men looking after the larger animals and women the smaller ones. Marketing is often seen as a female task, although men are most likely to negotiate the sale of crops. Some jobs are gender neutral. The introduction of a new tool may cause a particular job to be reassigned to the opposite sex and men tend to assume tasks that become mechanised.

The impact on women of the modernisation of agriculture is both complex and contradictory. Women have often been excluded from agrarian reform and training programmes in new agricultural methods. Where both men and women have equal access to modern methods and inputs there is no evidence that either sex is more efficient than the other. Technological changes in post-harvest processing may even deprive women of a traditional income-earning task.

Women and Food Security Issues

Not only do women produce and process agricultural products but they are also responsible for much of the trade in these and other goods in many parts of the third world. In many parts of the world, women continue to play an important role as rural information sources and providers of food to urban areas. This may involve food from the sea as well as from the land. Although women rarely work as fisherpeople they are often involved in net-making and the preparation and sale of the catch.

Women's roles and status all over the world are generally determined by social institutions and norms, religious ideologies, eco-systems and by class positions. The Indian social systems exhibit such grave disparities. Indian women are not a homogeneous group. Their traditional roles are not identical in all strata of society. Norms and taboos governing their roles and behaviours within and outside the family, the structure of family organisations and social practices and the positions accorded to women in a community differ considerably across regions, cultures and levels of socio-economic development.

It is needless to emphasise on the significant contribution of women to agricultural production and household food security. In the process of production, handling and preparation of food, women play a multiple role throughout the sequence. They are said to be "feeding the world". Do women really feed the world? Let us consider the evidence. On a global scale, women produce more than half of all the food that is grown. In sub-Sahara Africa and the Caribbean, they produce up to 80 per cent of basic foodstuffs. In Asia, they provide from 50 to 90 per cent of the labour for rice cultivation. And in Southeast Asia and the Pacific as well as Latin America, women's home gardens represent some of the most complex agricultural systems known. In countries in transition, the percentage of rural women working in agriculture ranges from about a third in Bosnia and Herzegovina to more than half in Poland. Across much of the developing world, rural women provide most of the labour for farming, from soil preparation to harvest. After the harvest, they are almost entirely responsible for operations such as storage, handling, stocking, marketing and processing.

Women in rural areas generally bear primary responsibility for the nutrition of their children, from gestation through weaning and throughout the critical period of growth. In addition, they are the principal food producers and preparers for the rest of the family.

Despite their contributions to food security, women tend to be invisible actors in development. All too often, their work is not recorded in statistics or mentioned in reports. As a result, their contribution is poorly understood and often underestimated. There are many reasons for this. Work in the household is often considered to be part of a woman's duties as wife and mother, rather than an occupation to be accounted for in both the household and the national economy. Outside the household, a great deal of rural women labour—whether regular or seasonal—goes unpaid and is, therefore, rarely taken into account in official statistics.

In most countries, women do not own the land they cultivate. Discriminatory laws and practices for inheritance of and access and ownership to land are still widespread. Land that women do own tends to consist of smaller, less valuable plots that are also frequently overlooked in statistics. Furthermore, women are usually responsible for the food crops destined for immediate consumption by the household, that is, for subsistence crops rather than cash crops. Also, when data is collected for national statistics, gender is often ignored or the data is biased in the sense that it is collected only from males, who are assumed to be the heads of households.

These handicaps have contributed to an increasing "faminisation" of poverty. Since the 1970s, the number of women living below the poverty line has increased by 50 per cent, in comparison with 30 per cent for their male counterparts. Women may feed the world today, but, given this formidable lists of obstacles placed in their path, will they be able to produce the additional food needed for a world population expected to grow by three billion in 2030?

During the FAO-sponsored World Food Summit of 1996, world leaders from 186 countries adopted the Rome Declaration on World Food Security and a Plan of Action. These international agreements specified that the role of women in agriculture and food security must be emphasised, in order to create the enabling political, social and economic environment required for the eradication of hunger ad poverty.

Under Commitment-I of the World Food Summit Plan of Action agenda, governments committed themselves to:

Support and implement commitments made at the 4th World Conference on Women that a gender perspective is mainstreamed in all policies;

Promote women's full and equal participation in the economy including secure and equal access to and control over credit, land and water;

Ensure that institutions provide equal access for women;

Provide equal gender opportunities for education and training in food production, processing and marketing;

Tailor extension and technical services to women producers and increase the number of women advisors and agents;

Improve the collection, dissemination and use of gender-disaggregated data (which distinguishes between males and females);

Focus research efforts on the division of labour and on income access and control within the household; and Gather information on women's traditional knowledge and skills in agriculture, fisheries, forestry and natural resources management.

FAO's Plan of Action for Women in Development (1996-2001) ensures that gender issues are considered in its development work. Objectives include giving women equal access to and control of land and other productive resources, increasing their participation in decision-making and policy-making, reducing the workloads of women and enhancing their opportunities for paid employment and income.

Gender Equality and Sharing of Opportunities

The Universal Declaration of Human Rights recognised several dimensions of human rights for all people. Some are tangible and quantifiable, such as access to education, health and a decent standard of living and ability to take part in the government of the country. Others are intangible, such as freedom, dignity, and security of person and participation in the cultural life of the community.

The goals of gender equality differ from one country to another, depending on the social, cultural and economic contexts. So, in the struggle for equality, different countries may set different priorities, ranging from more education for girls, to better maternal health, to equal pay for equal work, to more seats in parliament, to removal of dissemination in employment, to protection against violence in the home, to changes in family law, to having men take more responsibility for family life.

Equality is not a technocratic goal—it is a wholesale political commitment. Achieving it requires a long-term process in which all cultural, social, political and economic norms undergo fundamental change. The UNDP Human Development Report—1995 outlines a vision for the 21st century that should build a world order that:

Embraces full equality of opportunity between women and men as a fundamental concept;

Eliminates the prevailing disparities between men and women and creates an enabling environment for the full flowering of the productive and creative potential of both sexes;

Promotes more sharing of work and experience between women and men in the workplace as well as in the household;

Regarding women as essential agents of change and development and opens many more doors to women to participate more equally in economic and political opportunities;

Values the work and contribution of women in all fields on par with those of men, solely on merit, without making any distinction;

Puts people—both women and men—clearly at the centre of all development processes.

The UNDP Report-1995 also states that the GDI (Gender-related Development Index) ranking can be different in different situations, as is shown by the following conclusions of a recent survey:

> No society treats its women as well as its men. Substantial progress on gender equality has been made in only a few societies;
>
> Gender equality does not depend on the income level of a society. What it requires is a firm political commitment, not enormous financial wealth;

Significant progress has been achieved over the past two decades, though there is still a long way to go. Not a single country has slipped back in the march towards greater gender equality at higher levels of capabilities, though the pace of progress has been extremely uneven and slow.

Much progress remains to be made in gender equality in almost every country. And in equality of choice in economic and political participation, industrial countries are not necessarily taking the lead. The areas showing the least progress are parliamentary representation and percentage share of administrators and managers. The clear policy message from this simple exercise is this: "In most countries, industrial or developing, women are not yet allowed into the corridors of economic and political power. In exercising real power or decision-making authority, women are a distinct minority throughout the world."

Women Role in Agriculture

Women play an indispensable role in farming and in improving the quality of life in rural areas. However, their contributions often remain concealed due to some social barriers and gender bias. Even government programmes often fail to focus on women in agriculture. This undermines the potential benefits from programmes, especially those related to food production, household income improvements, nutrition, literacy, poverty alleviation and population control. Equitable access for rural women to educational facilities would certainly improve their performance and liberate them from their marginalised status in the society. Other areas where women's potential could be effectively harnessed are agricultural extension, farming systems development, land reform and rural welfare. Landmark improvements have been recorded in such cases as the extension of institutional credit and domestic water supplies where women's potential have been consciously tapped.

Socioeconomic goals of productivity, equity and environment stability are closely woven around the agriculture sector policies and new dimensions in programmes implemented are already emerging as new values. Regardless of the level of development achieved by the respective economies, women play a pivotal role in agriculture and in rural development in most countries of the Asia-Pacific Region. Asia-Pacific region had witnessed spectacular development in crop yields which even surpassed the population growth rate in the past decade. However, pockets of hunger remain when landless or small farm rural population lack economic access to food because of a lack of remunerative non-farm employment in rural areas, where 80 per cent of Asia-Pacific's 400 million poor live. It has also been suggested that with the acceleration of crop-diversification programmes and the transformation of agriculture to commercial production levels, women's lot had been even further worsened by the addition of new burdens which they have to shoulder in order to realise profits in farm operations.

Rural women who are obliged to attend to all the household chores, children's welfare, nutrition and family cohesion along with farm work, are desperately driven to adopt a survival strategy to save the family food security from total collapse. Rural poverty has increased in the region particularly for farmers as priority has been accorded to the industrial and service sectors: this is both the cause and an effect of rural-urban migration leading to the "feminisation of farming". Thus, the numbers and the proportion of rural women among the absolutely poor and destitute, currently around 60 per cent, is expected to increase to 65 to 70 per cent by the year 2000.

In spite of social, political and economic constraints, women farmers have proved extremely resourceful and hardworking in their attempt to ensure household food security. Social constraints place barriers around their access to scientific and technological information. Lack of collateral denies them access to agricultural credit. Culture or traditions accord membership of cooperatives only to heads of households—usually a man. Many rural women, even in highly mechanised farming systems such as the Republic of Korea and Japan would have agriculture for work in other sectors if choices were available.

After some decades of development, global problems and issues concerning environment, women in development, and poverty have reappeared. All these have emerged in rural communities and threatening their sustainability. Rural communities with norms developed for managing resources are important for the stability of community life. Gender-oriented rural development programmes which focus on role of women to guarantee the stability of life provide a sound basis for integrated development of the quality of life.

In progressive economies like Japan, rural women have shown anxieties over several concerns affecting their livelihood. Some of the priority items include measures for success in agricultural enterprises, expansion of periodic farming resulting in reduced holidays, the need to reduce agricultural work, changes in awareness of rural societies and reduction in the work connected with caring for elderly people. In order to redress these problems, five tasks have been identified for promotion which will result in making rural living more pleasant and comfortable. These tasks include:

(i) Creating awareness of changes and measures pursued to change the status of women by their active participation in agricultural and fisheries cooperatives;

(ii) Improving working conditions and environment;

(iii) Appreciating the positive aspects of living in rural areas and creating a conducive environment which will contribute towards better rural life;

(iv) Acquiring skills to diversify areas of involvement by women supporting women in entrepreneurial roles; and

(v) Adopt a structured approach to execute the vision to improve rural conditions.

Rural Women in Agricultural Cooperatives

Women are represented in various forms and in various types of cooperatives in the region. In most of the South-Asian countries women membership in mixed membership cooperatives is generally lower as compared with those from other countries in the region. In societies where culture restricts women's membership in cooperatives, women—only cooperatives proliferate. It is in women—only cooperatives that women feel freer and less restricted in their participation in cooperatives. In countries like India, Nepal, Bangladesh, Sri Lanka and Pakistan, women comprise just 7.5 per cent as compared with men (92.5%) of the total membership. In Malaysia, it is around 30.6 per cent. In many of the Asian countries women's membership is low (ranging from 2 to 10.5%) in agricultural cooperatives. This reflects the age-old stereotype that men are the farmers and not the women, and the title of the farm property should be in the name of the man. This situation automatically prohibits women to be the members. Out of a total of 450,000 cooperatives with a total membership of 204.5 million in India, there were 8,171 women—only cooperatives with a total membership of 693,000. It is also known that the women—only cooperatives e.g., cooperative banks, consumer stores, fruits and vegetable vendors, have done exceedingly well and provided a whole range of services to their members. In India, with a view to involve women in the process of decision-making in local self-government bodies including cooperatives, a 33 per cent representation has been instituted and in a number of states all boards of directors have women serving on them. There has also been a discussion to have a similar representation in state and national legislatures as well.

The highest number of women in cooperatives in the region comes from the credit and consumer sectors. In Japan, the membership of women in agricultural cooperatives and in decision-making organs is low. No discriminatory provisions preventing women's participation in agricultural cooperatives are contained in the Agricultural Cooperative Law nor in the bylaws of the agricultural cooperatives. In the majority of the bylaws, membership is based either on land ownership or work on the farm for more than 90 days a year. Despite this, women membership has not increased mainly due to the fact that most cooperatives have a membership policy that allows only one member per household, based on the idea that a household is the minimum unit for production. In addition, it is customary that women follow their husbands in the village life and decision-making. Women themselves do not want to cause troubles by challenging such a tradition. Therefore, men became the majority of directors and delegates and women quietly accepted the situation. However, the concept of plural membership from households is being encouraged.

There are still some prevailing laws which place barriers for women's participation in agricultural cooperatives and/or farmers' associations, like land-ownership and head of the household. In many societies, the very women who need to organise to cooperate and prosper, lack the time for participation due to multiple work demands. Cooperatives being people-centered movement had recognised these limitations place on women by the society and economic institutions. Experiments made in different parts of the world clearly indicate that women's participation in cooperatives and other local government bodies not only provides them an opportunity to articulate their problems but it also helps them to be an active partner in decision-making process.

The relationship between women and their cooperatives in the context of gender integeration can be summarised as under:

A cooperative being a social development agency should play an active role in advocating for gender equality;

Since women have been active in development work, they should play central role in development;

The cooperative can be a venue to improve women's social status and economic conditions; and thus, cooperatives should promote women's empowerment by integrating gender concerns and formulating a strategy that would address gender issues.

In terms of the ratio of membership of women in agricultural cooperatives, the percentage is rather low, but they have a strong influence on them—through the heads of the household. Certain obvious barriers restrict their direct and formal entry in agricultural cooperatives. Agricultural cooperatives, in present times, everywhere have come under dark clouds due to heavy competitions and pressures of open market economy systems. They are now expected to meet the challenges which they had never anticipated before. Their business methods remain traditional and they expect government support in the form of protection and subsidies. These are no longer available and will not be available in the near future. In several countries, agricultural cooperatives have either folded up or are under massive reorganisation. The challenges faced by agricultural cooperatives can be enumerated as under:

Need to improve professional management skills of those who provide advisory or guidance services to cooperatives and of the managers and some key members of primary level cooperatives;

Establishment of a marketing intelligence system within the Cooperative Movement to enable the farmer-producers follow market trends and plan their production and marketing strategies;

Assured supply of farm inputs (quality seeds, chemical fertiliser, farm chemicals, credit and extension services);

Establishment of business federations through cooperative clusters to undertake primary agro-processing marketing of local products and to cover financial requirements;

Beaware of quality controls and standardisation of farm products to be able to compete effectively in the open market;

Participate in efforts to conserve natural resources which directly and indirectly, influence farm production and rural employment;

Need for providing information to the farmers and farmers' organisations on the implications of restructuring, globalisation and WTO agreements.

Constraints faced by Rural Farm Women

Based on the experiences of farm extension workers, field advisors and rural farm women in the Asia-Pacific Region, the following are the general constraints faced by them:

High illiteracy rates and poor living conditions among rural women;

Lack of leadership and inadequate participation in the organisational and economic affairs of their agricultural cooperatives;

Absence of property inheritance rights, restriction on acquiring membership of agricultural cooperatives consequently being deprived of farm credit etc.;

Inadequate health care services in rural areas;

Inadequate water supply for household and farm operations;

Lack of appropriate agricultural technology aimed at reducing the physical burden of farm women;

Inadequate access to credit and agricultural inputs and other services;

Lack of female farm extension workers;

Lack of marketing facilities and opportunities;

Traditional, religious, social and cultural obstacles;

Less participation in decision-making—even within the household;

Male migration/urban drift which increases pressure on women;

Lack of opportunities to improve socioeconomic status of farm women;

Lack of skills and attitudes in leadership and management development; and

Lack of secretariat supporting functions for women's organisations and allocation of funds for them in cooperative organisations.

Facilitation Role of the ICA and its Development Partners

Since the establishment of the ICA Regional Office in New Delhi in 1960, efforts have consistently been made to initiate and promote programmes aimed at emancipation of women and their involvement in the organisational and business activities of cooperatives. This has been done through a long chain of seminars, discussions, conferences and technical assistance programmes which have been carried out with the collaboration of its Member-Organisations and development partners. In the agricultural cooperatives sector, some of the most recent initiatives have been as follows:

A series of technical meetings and conferences were held which had taken note of the recommendations of UN and other international conferences and initiatives on women in cooperative development;

A series of specialised training courses for rural women leaders in agricultural cooperatives, on an yearly basis, with the financial support of the Government of Japan and in collaboration with the JA-Zenchu and the IDACA;

Three top level Asian and African Conferences on Farm Women Leaders in Agriculture and Agricultural Cooperatives during 1997 and 1998 (one more conference is planned in 1999) in collaboration with the JA-Zenchu, AARRO and the IDACA and with the full technical support of the Government of Japan in the Ministry of Agriculture, Forestry and Fisheries-MAFF;

Development of training manuals and other supporting materials for the use of women leaders to develop women's associations and help increase women's participation in agricultural cooperatives.

Issues Involved

In the background of the above discussion and in view of the constraints faced by women with regard to their participation in agricultural cooperatives, the following issues need to be tackled by the concerned authorities and cooperative institutions:

Identification of an appropriate mechanism which could provide development opportunities to women in rural areas;

Encouraging cooperatives to have special programmes and tasks for women to perform in the organisational and business affairs. It has been observed that in many of the countries of the region more women are being taken in to undertake administrative and functional activities—they make very good, reliable and honest cashiers, sales girls, inventory controllers, secretaries, public relations officers and member contact persons;

Review, revision and reformation of cooperative legislation and government policies which facilitate and encourage women to become members of cooperatives and participate in decision-making processes. Cooperative institutions and their federations may take the lead on their own to institute programmes for the participation of women in cooperatives. Voluntary initiatives by cooperatives themselves do not necessarily to be qualified by government approvals. Cooperatives should lobby with their governments to replace or suitably amend the restrictive laws;

Accord due credibility to the achievements of women in agricultural cooperative development through publicity, exchange of visits, participation in meetings and conferences. Women need a platform through which they could justify their participation in cooperative action;

Replication of successful experiences. The work done by the Women's Associations of Japanese agricultural cooperatives and Han Groups has produced good results for the community and business of their cooperatives. Such experiences need a thorough study. They have a lot of good things to offer;

Development of Plans of Action at all levels. Women's cooperative organisations at primary levels should try to federate themselves into higher federations or association so that their 'bargaining power' is strengthened. The cooperatives and women's associations should develop realistic plans of action to be followed for three-five years;

Cooperatives to initiate education, training and extension programmes for women through vocational and literacy programmes (these also include home improvement activities e.g., cooking classes, handcrafts, social interactions, environment related activities etc.);

Creating conditions for women to market their products through outlets established by agricultural cooperatives. (Agricultural cooperatives in Japan set apart a space in their shopping areas exclusively for the Women's Associations and even for the individual farmers to sell their products, including organising Morning Markets etc.).

Summing up

Women have been the focus of attention of all international and national development programmes. Efforts have been directed at empowering them in all fields of activity. Special programmes have been instituted to improve their social and economic status through provision of education, employment, health care and involvement in social and economic institutions, including cooperatives. Cooperative institutions and especially the agricultural cooperatives are the agencies which hold enormous potential for the development of women, and more particularly the rural women. Rural women are actively involved in the process of food production, processing and marketing. They often lack the legal status which prohibits them to have access to credit, education and technology. Cooperative institutions can help accelerate the process of development and participation of women in their organisational and business activities. Institutions like the International Cooperative Alliance (ICA) and the Institute for the Development of Agricultural Cooperation in Asia-Japan (IDACA) together with the support of other international organisations and national level institutions can develop and sponsor programmes which are aimed at improving the lot of rural women. In the past, some efforts have been made through which member-organisations, cooperative and agricultural departments all over Asia and Africa have been requested to make special programmes for rural women and set aside budgets for their implementation. In some cases some good responses have been received.

While it is generally agreed that education is central to women's development, the participation of girls in the national educational system continues to lag well behind that of boys at every level. Among the factors that are believed to contribute to this gap are women's self-perpetuating negative social status, economic constraints and male-oriented biases in the design and delivery of primary and secondary education. These limitations have meant that millions of women have not received formal education and that millions more are deprived of the opportunity for more than token participation. Women, however, retain a strong orientation to self-help and group cooperation. They look to their own resources and to other women when faced with a problem of opportunity. This perhaps is the key factor on which women's development programme could be developed. This is their greatest asset. They have kept folk art, family bonds, religious traditions, cultural heritage alive, thriving and vibrant. They have played significant role in food security efforts and rural and small industrial sectors.

7

WOMEN AND POLITICAL EMPOWERMENT

Introduction

Political under-representation of women has emerged as one of the key concerns for women's movements in the nineties. Arguments relating to it revolve around two broad issues: the representative character of democratic institutions and their public accountability on women's issues. Recent developments in feminist politics in India not only indicate growing concern with under-representation of women in elected and decision-making bodies, but also with arguments for some form of reservation or affirmative action to redress existing gender imbalances. These arguments are advanced precisely because gender balanced representation is expected to alter development priorities, perspectives and concerns and thereby increase accountability.

The notion of affirmative action has always been contested both in terms of its meaning and the goals and practices it encompasses. The term had its genesis in the United States and includes a range of policy measures and programmes (Bacchi, 1996). In India, the term reservation is commonly used to denote similar state sponsored initiative. Reservation policy, therefore, seeks to redress inequalities in labour force representation, in political parties, educational institutions and public committees. The understanding of affirmative action or, in the Indian case, reservation, includes notions such as equality of opportunity, social justice, positive or protective discrimination, compensatory discrimination, and so on. In addition, several other subsidiary questions such as concession versus right and compensatory justice versus meritocracy have also been debated. In the Indian context, the terms 'reservation' or 'quotas' have been used and apply to "socially and educationally backward classes of citizens and scheduled castes and scheduled tribes," ever since the framing of the Indian Constitution in 1950.

It is significant to note that the egalitarian framework of the Constitution had to be altered in order to accommodate non-discrimination. Articles 14 and 15 of the Constitution, prohibiting discrimination on grounds of religion race, caste, sex, and language, had to be amended to give powers to the state to make special provisions for the advancement of socially and educationally backward classes. This followed the judicial verdict in Champakam Dorairajan's case in 1951 that characterised any preferential treatment to socially and economically weaker sections as discriminatory, leading to the first constitutional amendments to Articles 15 and 16 of the Constitution. This empowered the state to make reservation in favour of any disadvantaged group, without being challenged on grounds of discrimination. Thus, as Justice P. S. Poti, in his Foreword to *Dynamics of Reservation Polity* noted, this amendment made reservation a non-issue. Instead, the question that continues to persist in the debate relates to who are the disadvantaged groups? Article 15 (4) brought in by the Constitution (first Amendment) Act in 1951 enabled the state to make special provisions for the advancement of any "socially and educationally backward classes of citizens." Similar provision was made in Article 16

(4) for reservation of posts in favour of any backward class of citizens, who in the opinion of the state, are not adequately represented in the services under the state. Significantly, both these clauses refer to 'classes of citizens' and not to individuals.

The persistent paradox of liberal democracy has been the tension between the notion of political equality and pre-existing social and economic inequalities. Thus, while introducing and justifying the first constitutional amendment, Nehru said:

> We come up against the difficulty that on the one hand, in our Directive Principles of State Policy, we talk of removing inequalities, of raising the people in every way—socially, educationally and economically, of reducing the distances which separate the groups or classes of individuals from one another, on the other hand, we find ourselves handicapped by certain provisions of the Constitution.... We cannot have equality because we cannot have non-discrimination, for if you are thinking of raising those who are down, you are somehow affecting the *status quo*, undoubtedly. You are thus said to be discriminating because you are affecting the *status quo*. If this argument is correct then we cannot make any major changes in the *status quo* whether in the economic or any other sphere. Clearly whatever law you may make you have to make some change somewhere.

Thus, the greatest appeal of liberal democracy was the promise of equality of status and opportunity. However, the biggest challenge to the stated goals has come from the social and political elite and other hegemonic forces in the multicultural and stratified society of India. A strong sentiment was expressed at the time by Ambedkar, the architect of the Indian Constitution, in his address to the Constituent Assembly debates, preceding the framing of the Indian Constitution: he saw Indian society based on privilege and inequality, and at the same time, entering a public life of contradictions. The political system, he noted, would recognise equality, insofar as it would be based on the individual right to vote but in social and economic life, inequality would continue to prevail.

Thereafter, it is seen that the inverted pyramid that became the basis of India's planning and development administration, resulted not only in uneven growth but reinforced the class, caste, and gender hierarchies of an unequal society. The criteria for deciding 'backwardness' or who are the disadvantaged groups, have dogged reservation policies in India. Even during the Constituent Assembly debates, the policies of preferential treatment for the disadvantaged Scheduled Castes (SCs) and Scheduled Tribes (STs) were criticised on the grounds that they placed a premium on backwardness and inefficiency. The Kalelkar Commission, appointed in 1953, submitted its report in 1955 and recommended that the social position of a community in the caste hierarchy should be used as the criterion to determine backwardness. No action was taken on this report as the criterion of caste was viewed as promoting the dangers of separatism.

The second Backward Classes Commission was appointed in 1978 under the chairmanship of B. P. Mandal to determine the criteria and examine the condition of "socially and educationally backward classes." The Commission identified eleven indicators and 3,743 castes as backward, constituting 52 per cent of India's population. The belief that certain sections have suffered historic injustices and need special safeguards and affirmative action to realise their constitutional rights, has formed the basis for reservation policy in India. This, however, has been strongly opposed by entrenched class interests. For example, the V. P. Singh Government that sought to implement the Mandal Commission recommendations in 1990 met with fierce opposition and agitation by the educated middle class, is well-known. A series of writ petitions were also made against it in the Supreme Court, challenging caste as a criterion for determining backwardness.

Several political thinkers, social scientists, and activists are of the view that the issue of reservation should be seen in the wider perspective of social change in a hierarchical caste-ridden society. Arguments in favour of reservation place emphasis on the case for equality of opportunity as well as for social justice. In the case of scheduled castes and scheduled tribes, the Indian Constitution recognises that the unequal status of these sections has to be dealt with on a preferential basis. The programmes envisaged for them are of three types: reservation of seats in legislatures, reserved posts in the public sector, and quotas for seats in educational institutions. The package evolved, thereby, was one of social justice, intended for the advancement of "socially and educationally backward classes of citizens" (Constitution of India: Article 15 (4) and 16 (4)). According to Marc Gallantar, reservation as proactive or compensatory discrimination is envisaged only for the purpose of mitigating inequalities. He sees the role of reservation for its instrumental qualities. According to him, these policies show a sense of connection and shared destiny, while this compensatory discrimination embodied the brave new hopes of India that animated the freedom movement and crystallised in the Indian Constitution. Both arguments, for social justice and for equality of opportunity, assume that systematic inequality and discrimination prevent certain groups, such as women, from playing equal roles.

There is considerable ambiguity, however, over how representation of gender, ethnic, or minority groups can serve the cause of social justice. Accordingly, the Beijing Platform for Action states that "women's equal participation is not only a demand for simple justice or democracy but a necessary condition for women's interest to be taken into account." It further adds that "women in politics and decision-making positions in governments and legislative bodies contribute to redefining political priorities, placing new items on the political agenda that reflect and address women's gender specific concerns, values and experiences and provide new perspectives on mainstream political issues". However, the paradox of reservation is that the claim of certain groups for equality, as a matter of constitutional right, is forgotten and it is mainly viewed as protective or compensatory, whereby discrimination can be reduced through preferential treatment for certain sections of the population.

In a limited sense, the concept of social justice has been carved out from a number of other rights and presupposes protection of the underprivileged sections of society. Equality implies creation of favourable conditions and equal opportunities to all, for transforming the position of those sections that are victims of existing social arrangements and inequality of status, power, and knowledge. The *laissez faire* liberal democratic paradigm propagates that it is the business of the state to provide a level playing field and the state is seen as an agent that promotes equality of opportunity. The notion of equality, which implies competition based on merit, ignores political and social arrangements that invidiously discriminate against certain groups.

The idea of compensatory justice or preferential treatment, through a series of actions by the state, has given impetus to movements for people's rights and the demand for proportionate representation in decision-making structures. People's movements have thus constituted a critical arena for debates on democratisation and representative democracy. However, they have also generated tensions due to conflicting demands being made by different interest groups. Within democracy, there are disagreements over development priorities and goals and whose interests are being served through political and economic processes. These differences go on to arouse mobilisation of group interests around shared ideals and experiences. The principles of the liberal democratic framework are being questioned by the debate on political processes, democracy and the perspectives of different movements engaged in transforming institutions and systems of governance. People's movements—for instance, of civil rights activists, women's groups, and ethnic groups—representing the interests of disadvantaged groups, have tried to forge a unity and collective identity around shared experiences. The current demand by the women's movement in India for reservation of seats in the Parliament and State Assemblies has partly arisen in the wake of the experience of women in panchayati raj institutions (institutions of local self-government), following the 73rd and 74th Constitutional Amendment that provides one-third reservation for women in these bodies.

This chapter is primarily concerned with the debate on political representation of women and reservation of seats in elected bodies. Increasingly, the concern with the under-representation of women in political institutions is seen as a by-product of gendered spaces and opportunity structures. A worldwide comparative survey on parliamentary representation of women also suggests a corollary between the degrees of democratisation in a country and the extent of women's participation in political life (IPU, 1997: 11). Women's participation is seen not only as central to the functioning of democracy but also for their ability in struggling for their rights and challenging the ideologies and hierarchies that keep women in subordinate positions.

In the 1990s, the demand for Indian women's political representation in legislative bodies has been raised with renewed vigor, not only by the women's movement but also by elected women representatives across all party lines. The arguments in defense of political reservation are tied to an understanding of the historical legacy of women's oppression and disadvantage, the nature of gender inequality, male dominance in political institutions, gender insensitivity in systems of governance, the nature of electoral politics, and so on.

Political Reservation for Women: The Pre-Independence Scenario

The current debate on political reservation or quotas for women in parliament and in state assemblies in India has to be seen in its historical context, as it is more than seventy years old. The early phase of the women's movement began with the emergence of three women's organisations: the All India Women's Conference (AIWC) in 1927, Women's India Association (WIA) in 1917, and the National Council of Women in India (NCWI) in 1925. Several local and provincial women's associations had started after 1910 but later merged to form these national organisations. The battle for the vote began in 1917 when Sarojini Naidu led an all India women's deputation to Montague, the Secretary of State for India, who had arrived to discuss India's demands for political representation. The memorandum said that when franchise was extended to the people of India, women must be recognised as "people." When Montague's scheme of reforms for India was published, however, women were completely left out.

The 1919, Government of India Act enfranchised a mere three per cent of Indian adults for the provincial assemblies, based on qualifications of education and property. It excluded women from the vote but allowed provincial assemblies to drop the exclusion clause of property and educational qualification if they wished. Indian nationalist leaders, however, were sympathetic to the cause of women's suffrage, for example, in his Presidential Address delivered at the thirty-fourth Annual Session of the Indian National Congress (INC) on 27 December 1919, Motilal Nehru brought attention to this failure in providing for the political rights of women.

In the light of the demonstrable lessons of the women's suffrage agitation in England, he expressed the hope that Indian men would come to the rescue of their sisters (Pannikar and Parshad, 1961). Subsequently, in 1924, a Reforms Enquiry Committee started recording evidence and views on whether Indian women really desired membership of the Legislatures. With the removal of the ban in 1927, the Madras State Provincial legislature threw open its membership to women, just a few weeks before the elections. Jana Everett has argued that the campaign of the Indian women's movement for political representation had two phases: in the first phase (1917-1928) the issue was female enfranchisement and eligibility for the legislature; in the second phase (1928-1937) its focus was on liberalisation of the terms of enfranchisement and increasing female representation in the legislatures.

In both phases, the extent to which the interests of the women's movement and those of the political authorities coincided, was the main factor determining the outcome of the demands of the women's movement. In 1928, the Simon Commission came to India to discuss the issue of franchise and political representation. At the time, many women leaders, the Congress and other nationalist parties boycotted the Commission.

However, one faction of the women's movement appeared before the Commission and argued for extension of female suffrage and reservation of four seats for women in the legislatures in order to encourage women to take part in political affairs and to represent their interests in education and social welfare. The Simon Commission did not recommend reservation of seats for women in the legislatures, but left it to the provincial governments to nominate women if none were elected. The Commission also rejected the system of separate electorates for minority groups, nonetheless recommended reservation of seats for the depressed classes. Everett has called this group of women representatives the "women's uplift faction." Their approach to encouraging women's enfranchisement was in line with the government's position as they supported the idea of wifehood qualifications and reservation of seats for women in legislatures.

At the first conference, which was boycotted by the Congress, the British Government appointed two women, Radabhai Subbarayan and Begum Shah Nawaz. These representatives supported the idea of wifehood qualifications and seats reserved for women in legislatures, though not on a communal basis. The memorandum they presented was on the lines of the British women's memorandum and was presented on behalf of the three All-India women's organisations. Furthermore, it demanded the principle of equality. Everett argues that a split developed within the women's movement between those who aligned themselves with the Congress and those women who were not involved in nationalist activities.

In 1931, when a new Constitution for India was being discussed in the British Parliament, the three major organisations, i.e., Women's India Association (WIA), All India Women's Conference (AIWC) and National Council for Women in India (NCWI), met and drafted a joint memorandum supporting adult suffrage. They, however, rejected special measures to ensure women's representation in legislatures. The AIWC, along with NCWI, organised a meeting of women representatives in Bombay, where a Drafting Committee of eight women was elected to prepare a Memorandum for submission to the Franchise Committee of the so-called Second Round Table Conference. Their main demands were for universal adult suffrage and mixed general electorates, but not for reservation, nomination, or co-option of women. Thus, while Sarojini Naidu during her Congress Presidential address in 1925, had pleaded for a women's section of the Congress, reservation was rejected by women leaders as a retrograde step after the acceptance of political equality in the Fundamental Rights Resolution of the Indian National Congress in 1931. In her presidential address to the All India Women's Conference (INC), Sarojini Naidu said:

> We are not weak, timid, meek women. We hold the courageous Savitri as our ideal, we know how Sita defied those who entertained suspicion of her ability to keep her chastity. We possess the spirit of creative energy to legislate for the morale of the world. I think this conference is writing the history of women of the world. I will, however, confess to you one thing. I will whisper it into this loudspeaker. I am not a feminist. To be a feminist is to acknowledge that one's life has been repressed. The demand for granting preferential treatment to women is an admission on her part of her inferiority and there has been no need for such a thing in India as the women have always been by the side of men in Council and in the fields of battle.... We must have no mutual conflict in our homes or abroad. We must transcend differences. We must rise above nationalism, above.

In the same session, one of the members, Lady Tata, lamented the absence of women members in the Legislative Assembly as a great drawback as women could have voiced the feelings of their sisters with greater directness and force than men. In their letter to the Premier and Chairman of the Minorities Committee, the three organisations (AIWC, WIA and NCWI) jointly issued a memorandum on the status of Indian women in the proposed new Constitution and demanded immediate and complete recognition of women's equal political status in theory and practice. They further stated that they did not wish to seek any form of preferential treatment as that would violate the integrity of the universal demand of Indian women for absolute equality of political status (AIWC, 1931a).

In 1932, the AIWC and WIA met to draft a declaration and send representatives before the India Franchise Committee (1932), also known as the Lothian Committee.

Nine members gave evidence before this Committee and they opposed the reservation of seats for women as it may have created "a spirit of communalism against women." The Lothian Committee's Report stated that women should be treated as one of the main sections of the community and be represented in a manner similar to the Muslims, Sikhs and depressed classes. It recommended that 2 to 5 per cent of the seats in provincial legislatures be reserved for women for the first ten years, but did not elaborate on any particular method of selection.

The India Franchise Committee took the view that unless special provision is made for women, it was improbable that many women would be able to fight or win elections, considering the existing prejudice against women entering public life in India. Recognising the fact that the AIWC was opposed to the granting of any special facilities, as they wished to be returned by the open door of competition, the Committee pointed out that a very large number of witnesses, both men and women, who gave evidence individually or as representatives of associations, felt strongly that some minimum representation should be secured for the first ten years. The report further stated that under a system of responsible government, nomination is ruled out. The Communal Award specifically mentioned that in the provincial legislatures, all seats, including those reserved for women, would be allocated to members of specific communities and the electorate for each seat would consist of members of a single community. The Congress and the women's organisations continued to oppose communal electorates first established in the so-called Morley-Minto reforms of 1909.

In the seventh session of the AIWC at Lucknow (AIWC, 1932-1933), a resolution was moved and unanimously adopted to reiterate the demand for "universal franchise in all its bearings." One of the members pointed out that women do not want favours, but wish to resist reservation of seats or anything that may tend to perpetuate their inferiority. It was Rajkumari Amrit Kaur, an important woman leader of the Congress Party, who, while supporting the resolution, stated that I want you to fully understand the importance of these words 'franchise in all its bearings'—for there have been one or two persons who have put forward the view-point that though the Conference can give its opinion on Franchise, as far as women are concerned, it cannot discuss the issues of either 'joint electorates' or 'the Communal Award'—for these bring us into politics. All India Women's Conference is pledged not to take part in 'party poEtics' and I am quite certain that we have never broken this pledge.... But if we are to eschew politics altogether we might as well as give up all our work in connection with vital questions for us— for we want our status to be fully recognised on an equal basis with men from the very beginning in the new Constitution. But the mere obtaining of the power of the vote is not enough. We must consider the basis of franchise, secondly the methods employed for the exercise of the vote and thirdly the manner in which women are to be represented, in the future councils of the country.

The manner in which women are to be represented never became part of the political debate in the post-Independence period. Another leader, Aruna Asaf Ali, seconded the resolution but thought reservation of seats for women to be meaningless and absurd if the demand for equality was genuine (AIWC, 1932-33). In the pre-Independence period, several women's organisations made a distinction between political participation and or politics. Politics was a taboo word, while education and legislative measures were considered necessary for the improvement of women's status. It is seen that the dilemma of women's organisations as to what constitutes politics and political participation continued into the post-Independence period.

In 1933, when the new Constitution was under consider-ation of the Joint Select Committee, the premier women's organisations sent three representatives to place the women's case before it. The memorandum presented to the Committee demanded a democratic Constitution, conferring full self-governing rights on India; fundamental rights granting equal rights to women; no communal electorates; and no reservation of seats for women and no special women's constituencies of wife-hood and literacy qualification for franchise.

The report of the Joint Select Committee on Indian Constitutional Reform (1933-34) made proposals for women's representation and the Government of India Act that followed in 1935 incorporated these with minor changes. Despite opposition from women's organisations, wifehood qualifications were the main instrument for women's enfranchisement and 41 seats allocated among the minority communities were reserved for women. Under the 1935 Act, as finally adopted, 6 million women and 29 million men became eligible to vote. Seats were reserved for women on a communal basis though women could contest any of the general seats. The three major women's organisations issued a joint statement on 22 January 1935, expressing their disapproval of the wifehood qualifications, the indirect election, the absence of a declaration of fundamental rights and communal electorates.

Furthermore, the women's movement, in the 1930s could not remain unaffected by the growing tensions between the Congress and the Muslim League in the political arena and separate all India organisations of Muslim women were formed in the late thirties. Everett also comments on the inadequate role of women's organisations in the electoral mobilisation of women. The integral links between the nationalist movement and the women's movement have always been reaffirmed by political activists and analysts, but large scale mobilisation of women during the freedom struggle did not resolve the question of equal representation of women in the political decision-making process. In this context she points out that

> AIWC leaders appeared to hold a naive view of electoral politics and the influence of their organisation on mass politics before the 1937 elections...When the parties selected their candidates, women leaders discovered that very few women were nominated from general seats and once they entered the legislatures, they considered party affiliation to be more important than sex in voting on legislation.

The attitudes of politicians, policy makers and women leaders in the pre-Independence period thus display an ambivalence and failure to understand the varied nature of women's constraints within the complex system of structural inequalities. Instead, patterns of marginalisation of underprivileged groups, who lack access to power, authority and decision-making, were reinforced, as these did not automatically disappear with Independence. The ideology of national liberation incorporated a vision of society with a liberal political agenda. Within the nationalist discourse and during the initial phase of nation-building, women received support from men for equal political rights, but the policies and programmes of Independent India hardly reflected the recognition of women's contribution and potentialities. However, the ambivalence and at times contradictory approaches to the women's question has also been noted by commentators such as Joanna Liddle and Joshi who mention that:

> the two issues central to the women's question in Independent India were—women's suffrage and the reform of Hindu Personal Law. Votes for women united the nationalist movement with the women's movement but the nationalists were bitterly divided over personal law reform which

included issues like marriage and inheritance which were of special concern to women.

Male chauvinism came to the fore on the issue of family laws. Whenever patriarchal control in the family was questioned during the debate over the Hindu Code Bill, it met with opposition. While a kind of liberal ideology —of equal rights in education, the right to vote, women's welfare and so on — was promoted, it is not surprising that patriotic, cultural and nationalistic arguments were used to reject or oppose other proposals. Demands for change in family law and property rights for women were also said to be the result of western education and influence.

The perceived threat of the colonial regime to indigenous tradition and values, influenced the debate on women's roles during the pre-Independence period. India's colonial experience and the manner in which men played an important role in the social reform movement, and later in the nationalist movement, in focussing on the women's question, influenced the logic and strategies of the women's movement to a considerable extent. The right to representation symbolised to many at the time an entry point into the all male-world of decision-making. Omvedt accordingly suggests that Gandhi recognised the power of the women and the lower castes and used it for the cause of Independence and the freedom struggle, at the expense of caste, class and gender relations (Omvedt cited in Iiddle and Joshi, 1986).

The Post-Independence Debates

It was women's large scale participation in the civil disobedience movement, rather than any radical notion of gender equality, that tilted the balance in favor of political equality in the Constituent Assembly debates. In the first Lok Sabha of independent India, only 43 women contested and 14 were elected. Of the 216 women, who contested about 3000 assembly seats, only 82 were elected. During the fifties and sixties, several laws were passed, promising a better deal to women. Nonetheless, as an indication of how little is known about this period, some scholars have called it the "silent years" of the women's movement.

The question of political reservation in favor of women died out or at least became dormant till the early seventies, when the report of the Committee on the Status of Women in India (CSWI, 1974) again debated the issue. The All India Panchayat Parishad at its Sixth National Conference held at New Delhi in 1973 also passed a resolution recommending a fuller representation of women and a reserved percentage of not less than one-third to start with (All India Panchayat Parishad, 1995). This resolution was not followed up in any of its subsequent meetings till 1990.

At the Panchayati Raj Sammelans or conferences of the Northern and Western states in January 1989, delegates expressed different views about the reservation of seats for women. The report of the CSWI pointed out that "the rights guaranteed by the Constitution have helped to build an illusion of equality and power which is frequently used as an argument to resist protective and accelerating measures to enable women to achieve their just and equal position in society". The demand for a system of reservation came from several groups of women during the Committee's tour to different parts of the country. While the CSWI rejected, by majority voice, the proposal for statutory reservation of seats for women in legislative bodies, it recommended statutory women's *panchayats* at the village level because of the neglect hitherto of women in rural development programmes. It also called upon political parties to adopt a definite policy regarding the percentage of women candidates for contesting elections. The dissenting minority of two members who advocated reservation, criticised

> ...the policy of 'tokenism' by having few women in the legislative and executive wings of government whose minority

and dependent status offered serious obstacles to their acting as spokespersons for women's rights and opportunities. Their greater representation may also increase the women legislators' concern for problems affecting women, ensuring a body of spokespersons of the women's cause in representative bodies. This will also help political mobilisation of women.

The Committee also argued that the process of marginalisation of women will result in their losing faith in the political process to change their conditions of life. They may opt out of the political system and become either passive partners or rebels. In this view, a political system cannot be based on ideology alone but must keep in touch with the actualities of the social situation

> .... The continuing under-representation of women prevents their proper participation in the decision making process in the country.... When one applies the principles of democracy to a society characterised by tremendous inequalities such special protections are only spear heads to pierce through the barriers of inequality. An unattainable goal is as meaningless as a right that cannot be exercised.

In these arguments, women's representation was seen as an instrument for change and women were seen as an interest group who would take up the cause of other disadvantaged women. It was also anticipated that once they became part of the decision-making process, they would demand participation in development decisions and a reorientation of public policies. Several of these arguments have since been thrown back and forth in the current debate on reservation for women in Parliament and in the State Assemblies.

Support for reservation thus came from a group of scholars who examined women's role in the political process, as part of the CSWI exercise. Thereby, they came to the conclusion that the process of Indian women coming into their own in politics has been slow because Indian culture is apolitical and the force of tradition has been pitted against their political participation. Improving the political status of women is an integral aspect of the overall problem of socioeconomic change and of broadening the political elite structure. They noted that the failure of Indian society to "look upon women's participation with sympathy and understanding is an exceedingly retarding factor in political socialisation of men and women.' It was argued that 30 per cent reservation of seats in the legislative bodies for women cannot lead to their becoming "isolated pockets in the nation" because women are not marginal to society as a minority group might be. Such a transitional measure to break-through the existing structure of inequalities will not be retrogression "from the doctrine of equality and the principle of democratic representation".

Significantly, opposition at the time came from political parties and most women legislators, the very sections who are today advocating political quotas for women. Some of these arguments were still couched in the language and discourse adopted during the nationalist struggle. Rejecting the suggestion for reservation as a retrograde step, the CSWI put forward the following views:

- the women's cause in India has always been championed by all progressive elements, men and women; separate constituencies for women will narrow their outlook; women's interests cannot be isolated from the economic, social and political interests of groups, strata and classes in society.
- it may precipitate similar demands from various other interest groups.
- the privilege once granted will be difficult to withdraw.
- women are not a community and a category and hence there is no rational basis for reservation.

The emergence of autonomous women's groups (or non-party women's organisations) in the seventies, raised radical questions about the relationship between the feminist movement, formal political institutions and power structures, and the need to organise as women. Disillusioned with party politics, many of the groups preferred to mobilise outside formal political structures. These new women's groups achieved a fair degree of success in getting amendments to laws pertaining to rape and dowry; in questioning development concepts, policies and their gender-neutrality; and pressing for a reorientation of the state.

The derailment of constitutional democracy, with the declaration of the National Emergency in 1975, activated a variety of people's organisations, partly because issues such as the safeguarding of civil liberties and democratic rights and ensuring the greater participation of women and other deprived groups in the political process, took centre stage. Several of these grassroots initiatives and people's movements, which resisted state power, are part of the dynamics of democracy in India and have their origins in unequal social and economic relationships. Their struggles started as the economic and social bases of various groups were threatened and were a direct consequence of public policies that protected the interests of the power elite. Class, caste and gender identities provided the socio-political context for popular struggles. By partially addressing the popular demands through public policies, the state tried to co-opt dissent. For example, today, much of the terminology of the women's movement has been co-opted by the government and other agencies.

Nonetheless, the experiences of leadership and collective action by women's groups on a variety of issues such as land, credit, literacy, and so on have made a significant contribution in enlarging the definition of 'politics,' even though a majority of women remain excluded and under represented in formal politics. Feminists challenging the liberal models of politics argue that the present conception of politics is a male one and women's concerns cannot be accommodated within such a framework. Thus, in 1983, a meeting of experts on the participation of women in political life, felt the need to redefine women's participation in politics and what constitutes the sphere of politics. The report pointed out that "the sphere of politics includes the social relations which create and institutionalise power relations and use them to foster, control or manipulate people's behaviour, attitudes and beliefs in order to supervise and regulate the distribution of resources" Accordingly, political participation is involvement (commitment) in respect of a deliberate and organised activity which seeks to influence (modify) the character (functioning, structure, policies, statement, behaviour) of one or more of these institutions or the mechanisms of power within one of these spheres. Attempts to overcome the obstacles and to produce new (alternative) channels of power in places where access to established channels is blocked, inadequate or ineffective should be regarded as a form of political participation. Most people's movement fall in this category.

Political participation is an exercise of power. The women's movement has to grapple with the issues of representation, governance, and the nature of politics and political institutions in a multi-party democratic system. Debates on women's representation in India are, therefore, a classic example of how politics contested around different identities can push the concern for representation on or off the political agenda. Since the 1980s, most mainstream political parties have begun viewing women as a constituency and they have introduced women's issues in their party manifestos. Political parties' heightened awareness of the importance of women's votes; the participation of women in popular movements; the pressures of the women's movement; the dynamics of grassroots organisations; judicial interventions; and executive action, all taken together, have forced varied political groups to address women's issues and revive the demand for reservation.

Some policy statements on reservation for women have been made in the last two decades, for example, the draft National Perspective Plan for Women (NPP) recommended reservation of 30 per cent.seats at panchajat and zilla or district level and local municipal bodies through nomination and co-option (Government of India, 1988). National women's organisations, however, rejected this as subversive of the Constitution and emphasised the need for elections at all levels to ensure the emergence of grassroots leadership (CWDS, 1989). The NPP, therefore, did not take the debate on political representation raised in the CSWI any further, though the final version did recommend 30 per cent reservation of seats at the district and lower levels, to be filled by election. But reservation in Parliament and the State Assemblies was not raised at all. It is interesting to note that the demand for reservation of seats for women in Municipalities, District and Boards was endorsed earlier as well in the pre-Independence period. In the post-CSWI period, women have definitely emerged as a distinct category in development planning, but women's experience of collective action and mobilisation did not result in the greater representation of women in elected bodies.

The critique of the NPP draft from the women's movement argued that the under-representation of women in elected bodies is a manifestation of their subordinate position in the family, community, and society. As such, it undermines the democratic process. The women's groups reiterated the demand for one-third reservation for women in Panchayati Raj institutions and municipal bodies (CWDS, 1989). Subsequently, a National Conference on Panchayati Raj and Women (1989) was addressed by the late Rajiv Gandhi who announced that 30 per cent of seats in Panchayati Raj Institutions would be reserved for women. He, however, claimed that this was only the beginning and that his government would extend it to fifty per cent in two years time. It is seen that those arguing in favour of reservation for women, support it on grounds of both the historic injustice and inequalities suffered by women, as well as of women's moral superiority in providing clean politics. Echoes of these arguments have been heard at various points of time during the parliamentary debates on representation of women. Those against the quotas called it inherently undemocratic and against the principle of equality, while those supporting it argued that the continued under representation of women is a failure of liberal democracy and the promise of equality of status and opportunity. During the debate on the 64th and 65th Constitution (Amendment) Bill, 1989 it was hailed as a 'historic measure,' 'a revolutionary approach' and an old dream of Mahatma Gandhi. It was opposed on the grounds that it was an attempt to usurp the powers of the state. Doubts were also raised over whether Parliament had the power to amend the Constitution, which would change the nature of the federal polity. Others said it was an election gimmick.

The patronising attitude of the male MPs during the debate on the 64th and 65th Amendments was quite obvious. A veteran MP said that they wanted to break away all these shackles and liberate their women; they should be brought to the fore in an important manner into villages, panchayats, and councils and enthroned wherever possible. In a magnanimous vein, he also said that they had done much for women earlier as well by preventing them from committing suicide and sati *(Parliamentary Debates,* 1989). An MP, Syed Shahabuddin called the two Bills "children of political compulsion" as he saw reservation for women as nothing more than a tactical manoeuver by the higher castes, the elite groups and by vested interests. The Bills could not be passed in the Rajya Sabha (the upper house of Parliament) for want of the requisite majority. Panchayati Raj thus became an election issue and when the Congress party took over the reins of government, the Constitution (72nd Amendment) Bill 1991 was again introduced in the Lok Sabha, with suggestions for insertion of new elements. The 73rd and 74th

Constitutional Amendment Bills, providing for one-third reservation for women in Panchayati Raj Institutions, were finally passed in December 1992 and were ratified by all the state governments by April 1993.

These two historic constitutional amendments could mark a shift from the politics of protest to pro-active politics and an opportunity for women to shape the agenda at the local level. The overwhelming response by women to these measures and the entry of nearly one million women in the Panchayati Raj Institutions encouraged the women's movement to make a similar demand for reservation of one-third seats in Parliament and the State Assemblies before the general election in 1996. The experiences and effectiveness of the first generation of elected women representatives in the panchayats have generated further debate on the issue of political quotas. However, all major political parties supported the demand and incorporated it in their election manifestos. It was also included in the Common Minimum Programme of a previous ruling coalition government at the national level. The United Front government introduced the 81st Constitution Amendment Bill that proposes reservation for women in 1996 and the debate in Parliament on it reflected stiff opposition from several quarters. The political threat to the position, power, and privileges of a male dominated Parliament brought to the fore serious divisions within political parties and various interest groups. Despite assuming a brave public posture, many party leaders conceded dissension within their ranks.

The ruling party's pretence was unmasked when the champions of social justice shouted down their own Prime Minister within the Parliament. Not many were convinced that it would achieve social justice for women, as argued by the women's movement. Even the beleaguered Prime Minister relented, saying that legislation of such social importance cannot be enacted without a consensus as it requires persuasion and accommodation. The Bill was referred to the Joint Select Committee of the Parliament, composed of members from both the Houses of Parliament. Seven national women's organisations submitted a memorandum to the Committee, expressing deep concern over the demand for a separate quota for minority and other backward classes (OBCs) within the one-third reservation for women, seen as diversionary tactics being used by certain political parties to sabotage the bill (Memorandum by Seven Women's Organisations, 1996). Under the chaipersonship of Geeta Mukherjee, a woman MP from the Communist Party (Marxist), the Committee submitted its report in December to the two Houses of Parliament and suggested several amendments (Mukherjee, 1997). However, it did not make any recommendations as to how reserved constituencies would be determined and left it to the Government and the Election Commission. It did not accept the amendment regarding the provision of reservation for women belonging to the other backward castes and the issue of quotas for backward castes and religious minorities has dogged the Bill ever since its introduction in Parliament.

The Bill for women's reservation was twice stalled in the Lok Sabha. Thus, the current political scenario, characterised by compulsions of coalition politics and the need to assuage the feelings of various interest groups within the ruling coalition, may seal the fate of the Bill. It is interesting to note that there was near unanimity on the 73rd and 74th Constitutional Amendments, which were hailed by all political parties as historic steps and as instruments for democratic decentralisation.

In contrast, the reactions of the intellectual elite, politicians, and the media to the 81st Constitutional Amendment are sharply divided. The women's movement has managed to keep a united front, however fragile, and despite some dissonant voices. Is there a gender divide on the reservation issue? No, says a country-wide survey conducted by the Centre for the Study of Developing Societies. Seventy five per cent men and seventy nine per cent women favoured reservations in legislative bodies *(India Today,* August 31, 1996). The fate of the 81st Amendment tells a different story as the predominantly male Parliament developed cold feet and did not pass it, because opposing a move towards women's political empowerment is regarded as politically incorrect, while supporting the Bill is seen as politically suicidal. Therefore, consensus continues to elude the Bill. Behind-the-door lobbying to reduce the proposed one-third quota to a lower one, which may be more acceptable to all parties, has also not yielded any results. The women's movement, however, has taken a firm stand in that they will not accept any dilution, even if the Bill is defeated in Parliament (IAWS, 1996). Clearly, in the era of coalition politics and the continuous battle for political survival, political agendas are determined by other considerations.

Paying lip service to women's causes on public platforms never gets translated into concrete strategies. The number of women parliamentarians has never exceeded more than seven per cent. The protagonists of reservation for women argue that the male-dominated political system refuses to provide space for women, and reservation of seats will help in creating such political space and also lead to their social mobilisation. Women are arguing for parity, not charity, and they see reservation as a vehicle for social justice.

The antagonists, in contrast, are apprehensive about the whole rationale of reservation at the parliamentary and assembly levels. They not only consider it a retrograde step and a violation of the principle of equality, but are also opposed to the idea of reservation *per se.* As one commentator put it: "It is a horrible method of dismembering India.... The Amendment would be judged by history as one of the most important factors in destroying social cohesion in India" *(Hindustan Times,* November 30, 1994).

Such a viewpoint ignores the challenges posed by other forces such as caste, ethnicity, and identity politics. Some believe that such a step promises to resurrect the Mandal ghost, although it is not perceived to be divisive enough to subvert society. Some add a note of caution that the proponents of women's reservation ought to be more concerned about the speedy acceptance and endorsement of their demand, rather than a fear of possible backlash, as it conceals the hypocrisy of neo-converts to reservation (*The Pioneer*, July 28, 1996). The realisation that one-third reservation for women in Parliament and State Assemblies is going to gradually erode male power, has led to violent scenes within Parliament. The bitter hostility to the women's quota Bill, both by casteist and fundamentalist forces, demonstrates entrenched vested interests and also warns against easy optimism.

The attempt at redressing the gender balance in Parliament and the State Assemblies has evoked animated discussion on the quantity and quality of women's participation and whether or not reservation will empower women and reduce disparities. The debate has been proceeding at different levels. Some question the basic premise that a change in the gender composition will bring something distinctive to these bodies, inspire more women to enter politics, and represent and articulate women's interests better. These persons do not agree that securing greater representation is a matter of social justice. Others argue that it will introduce tensions in the social system and ask on what criteria will constituencies be designated as reserved? In this context, a suggestion has also been made to introduce multi-member constituencies so that each constit-uency will have the choice to elect both men and women. The Shetkari Mahila Aghadi, the women's front of the Shetkari Sangathan (a peasant organisation in Maharashtra), suggested a system of three seat constituencies combined to form a single constituency.

The print media's responses were equally interesting, sometimes dramatic. The *Indian Express* called it "the mandalisation of gender, yet another manifestation of social engineering perfected to the divisive best". The same newspaper called it "wrong headed affirmative action which is ruthlessly self-aggrandising." In this item entitled, "Hypocrisy Unlimited," *Hindustan Times* called it "competitive populism at its basest with no commitment or concern for the status and welfare of women in society". Yet another newspaper said:

> strangely enough, on the issue of women's right to equality with men and their representation in legislature, there appears to be a close similarity of prejudice between the orthodox Hindu Pandit [Brahmin] and the anti-Hindu non-conformist. Gender justice is virtually unknown to either.

It is evident here that group interests are central to the democratic process and, currently, attacks on reservation are emerging from class interests. The oft repeated clich that women have less interest in politics is another expression of the male resistance to women in politics and public life. Similarly, in the context of the U.S., Katzenstein (1984) says that the politics of mobilisation and the politics of electoral representation are not identical and that since the defeat of the Equal Rights Amendment in 1982, feminists have turned from the strategy of mobilisation to the politics of representation. She describes three paradigms that seek to capture the meaning of electoral politics: elections as an instrument of social control and co-optation; elections as a means for the representation of group interests; and elections as a means of mobilisation. It is significant that while elected women representatives often act collectively on controversial issues, party affiliation affects their responses.

The opposition from male politicians has also been commented upon, as there is growing realisation that reser-vations could change power equations forever. Jayanthi

Natarajan, a Rajya Sabha Member, counters the argument that the framers of the Constitution never intended reservations for women, by noting that it was women members of the Constituent Assembly who did not want a crutch of reservation, but fifty years down the road and the percentage of women members in Parliament has not even crossed the double digit. An eighty-four old ex-member of the Constituent Assembly in a recent interview admitted that her initial perception was wrong and she now believed in reservation. The reactions have thus varied from excitement and high expectation, to guarded optimism and even cynicism about reservations and their impact on the formal political process, institutions, and for sharing of power and responsibilities. The biggest hurdles to transformative politics are the party system, electoral politics, and the polarisation between ideological positions and the reality of women's oppression. The ardent advocates of political reservation usually downplay the nature of electoral politics and group interests and solidarities.

The populist rhetoric of the political discourse on representative democracy, egalitarianism and popular participation disguises the conflict of interests. In India, the 73rd and 74th Constitutional Amendments, providing for one-third representation of women in Panchayati Raj institutions, gave impetus to the demand for similar reservation in Parliament and State Assemblies. It thus reopened the debate on the role of women in political parties, structures and processes.

Electoral Politics, Political Parties, Democracy and Political Representation of Women

Despite the historical ambivalence of the women's movement and the well-entrenched opposition to the reservation issue, the inequalities that characterise Indian social structure and qualify the notion of political equality are important concerns for the women's movement. The agenda of the women's movement spans issues ranging from the redistribution of resources, time and responsibilities at home, changes in electoral process, parliamentary democracy, representation, and women's political engagement with democratic institutions. Activists within the women's movement, however, believe that women's participation in the political process is crucial for women's struggle to access resources. Political parties today are more aware of women's votes, but this has not been matched numerically in their participation in decision-making or in parties nominating more women candidates in the elections. The elections to the 13th Lok Sabha in 1999 clearly indicated the general apathy of most political parties in giving greater representation to women.

A regional consultation on the women's movement in India noted that:

> ... today a large number of activists see the women's movement as a political movement, however, its link with wider political processes has emerged as a major problem area. At one level, the social perception of the movement is of an apolitical struggle by various women's organisations, to improve women's status within the family. Even when sympathetic to women's resistance against familial oppression, this view questions the validity and rationale of the movement's effort to intervene in the political process. The autonomous women's groups, which had distanced themselves from political 'parties,' do not view themselves as apolitical. Many organisations and independent groups, however, see the struggle for gender equality as part of die process of wider participation of women in the political process. In the process over the years there has been an attempt to redefine popular notions of 'politics' and 'political participation from a gender perspective'.

The absence of women in the internal party hierarchy and the lack of necessary means of facilitating women's participation in party activities, have led to a great deal of reluctance about accepting the idea of parity and partnership between men and women in politics. This, in turn, is reflected in the small numbers of women in parliament and the state assemblies. Women's units within political parties, established in the seventies, are regarded as subsidiary or peripheral to the party structures and their activities are largely confined to social events, campaign work, and mobilising women to support and defend the agenda of the party in power. But, without logistic, financial, and strategic support from the parties, women cannot succeed as candidates in the multi-party democratic system.

A worldwide comparative survey conducted by the Inter-Parliamentary Union (IPU) examines three main factors in explaining the under-representation of women. These are: women in political parties, women's participation in the electoral process, and women in national parliaments. The study, based on replies from 115 countries, confirms a major discrepancy between the two sexes. With the relative exception of the Nordic countries, all countries conduct politics in a way that excludes nearly half their people. It suggests establishing of a new social contract to secure the common good. The report clearly states that "part of the answer to the limited parliamentary representation of women should be sought within political parties, especially in their hierarchy and political practices. Women are often numerous among the grassroots and are increasingly becoming aware of their electoral clout. They are now beginning to react against the very narrow space in which they remain confined when it comes to power structures".

The IPU has adopted a Plan of Action for correcting existing imbalances in the participation of men and women in political life. It is thus seen that political parties in Nordic countries introduced gender quotas for the selection of parliamentary candidates from the mid-seventies onwards.

Other countries have also made some headway in this direction, for example, the African National Congress in the first election in South Africa introduced a quota system for women; the British Labour Party adopted a target of 50 per cent women to be elected in the next three general elections; and the proportion of women in legislative assemblies has reached 38 per cent in Denmark, 21.3 per cent in Netherlands and 15 per cent in Germany. Does this perception about political parties being effective instruments for integrating women in the political process, alter their attitude towards women? In this context, the response from Denmark in the IPU survey report, is worth quoting:

> The interplay between 'from above' and 'from below' is often highlighted as a fundamental characteristic of the integration of women in politics in the Nordic countries. This interplay, between the integration of women's issues in the state and the spread of women's movement activities, provides one of the explanations of the comprehensive mobilisation and notable progress made in the Nordic countries is a combination of pressure from below, especially from the social movements and the system's comparatively high degree of responsiveness towards new groups and demands (the political opportunity structure) that are among the decisive factors with respect to the integration of women into politics. It is also important to point out an understanding of the political significance of gender focus both on changes in political culture and on changes in relation to gender.

Issues of women's representation in India, as debated in the nineties, clearly demonstrate how social and economic inequalities combine with cultural values and political compulsions, making it harder for women to challenge dominant ideologies and structures. Added to this perspective are the issues of caste, class, ethnic, and religious identity, and the tension of differing ideologies and positions. The nature of Indian party politics in a multi-party democratic system, given the kind of political institutions that consolidate vote banks along caste, religious and ethnic bases, have fostered new political divides, not always along conventional ideological grounds. Coalition politics has further demonstrated its own contradictions, as electoral arithmetic cannot always accommodate legitimate concerns in their political agenda because of their own concerns about survival. In a multi-party democracy, where the "numbers game" has significant impact on the formation of governments, the logic of selecting so-called "winning candidates" often works against women, despite lip service being paid to them in party manifestos. For example, the Congress Party President Sonia Gandhi's attempt to introduce a 33 per cent gender quota in fielding candidates for the recent parliamentary election in 1999 was scuttled, thanks to the dominant male group of the party. The final election results showed that only 48 of the 543 women were elected to the Lok Sabha (Lower House of Parliament). This is despite the agitation by women's organisations over the 84th Constitutional Amendment Bill relating to reservation of seats for women.

Caste mobilisation, however, cannot be ignored and needs to be understood from the women's viewpoint to expose the patriarchal overtones of casteist rhetoric. Communal divisions and the violence stemming from identity politics pose yet another serious challenge to the women's movement, wherein gender identities are enmeshed with caste and communal identities and place women, in a peculiar position (CWDS, 1995). Violence and the criminalisation of politics also tend to push women out of politics. The failure of the women's movement to forge links with mass based organisations and the initiatives taken by casteist and communal forces to mobilise women has thrown yet another challenge to the women's movement. As Agnihotri and Mazumdar point out:

> The wave of fundamentalist xenophobic upsurges sweeping across the world threatens the international women's

movement as a whole. In India, the complex social structures, economic constraints and political opportunism have provided ample breeding ground for the growth of revivalist ideologies and identity politics.

It is obvious that, as a socially and economically disadvantaged section, women have begun to understand the ways in which power is shared and why greater representation is needed to influence the redistribution of power and resources. Can policies of reservation redress the imbalance? Or, is reservation an attempt to co-opt women's growing militancy? Undoubtedly, the women's movement is faced with a dilemma regarding the need to engage in politics and at the same time ask the state to intervene. Women activists believe that political representation will equip women with power to change and redefine the political agenda and articulate women's interests. The women's movement also emphasises the need for transforming the standards of politics and governance, which remain male-dominated and can begin with the process of progressive political representation of women. Furthermore, the movement has to address issues surrounding caste, ethnicity, and religion, which, again, raise questions about politics contested around excluded identities. This is particularly important in a context where identity-based politics is a potential threat to society, wherein competing and exclusionary groups promote factionalism.

Summing up

In conclusion, the current demand for parliamentary representation of women is built around several arguments and equal opportunity for participation in decision-making is one of them. The relationship between representation and social justice is a problematic one, even though several arguments have been made in favour of women's political representation. For instance, it is said that women's interests and priorities are neglected in a male-dominated parliament and women's presence will make a qualitative difference in increasing the level of empathy for their concerns. It is also said that women's representation will have a civilising effect by removing barriers to institutionalised discrimination against women and so on. These arguments are quickly countered by those who do not see women as a collectivity or who consider it is not only women who can best represent women's interests. Sawyer thus argues that the emphasis on under representation of women has blurred the distinctions between representation of interests, the representativeness of the legislature, and the equal right to act as a representative. She is of the view that the presence of women may be used as an alibi for policies with a disproportionate impact on women.

Incorporation of women without questioning the nature of the political institutions, undoubtedly, is a way of co-opting women rather than challenging the *status quo*. Accordingly, eminent political scientist, Rajni Kothari argues that "unless the three issues—the demand for representation, the demand for a role in governance and the movement for basic transformation— are taken together, the larger game being played by the highly entrenched power structure will co-opt these new social movements. We are living in a period when the best of terminology of the grassroots movement is co-opted by the canopies, including GOI and World Bank" (CWDS, 1998: 2). For transforming political structure, power relations and processes, organised pressure and vigorous advocacy on behalf of women is needed. The real issue is that group interest, based politics, which stresses a shared sense of marginalisation and exclusion, should focus on institutional mechanisms rather than on political fixes for short term gains.

The conceptualisation of women as a category, forging unity around the historical sense of neglect and political marginalisation, despite the promise of equality, has not only created political space for women, but has also altered the terms of the debate. It also means submerging or denying differences among women. The political conceptualisation of women as a disadvantaged group is also turned upside down by emphasising that not all women are disadvantaged, indicating that a false universalism is always problematic. Such ambivalence reflects conflicts between competing interest groups and women's multiple identities.

The anti-discrimination discourse was central to affirmative action programmes. Linking reservation questions to equal opportunity and social justice for women as a disadvantaged group has given rise *to* an inconclusive debate on the criteria for determining backwardness. Does it open the door to equal opportunity; does it realise social justice, and does it alter power relations? Many of these dilemmas apparent in the reservation debate have profound implications for political theory and practice and for the attempts by the women's movement to give a new meaning and dimension to the slogan "political empowerment of women." The contradictions seem to be inherent in the process. On the one hand, decline in the accountability and credibility of democratic institutions and institutions of governance lead to cynicism; on the other, there is a strong feeling that a larger participation of women in the political process can reverse the process of deterioration in public life. This, in turn, spurs women to demand political representation, while expectations of gain from representational politics, definitely marks a shift in the strategy of the women's movement.

REFERENCES

Agnihotri, Indu and Vina Mazumdar (1995), "Changing Terms of Political Discourse: Women's Movement in India, 1970-1990," *Economic and Political Weekly,* Vol. XXX, No. 29, July 22: 1869-1878.

AIWC (All-India Women's Conference) (1930), "Proceedings of the Fourth Session of the AIWC," unpublished, Bombay: Author.

– (1931a), "Letter to the Premier and Chairman of the Minorities Committee," 16 November, unpublished, New Delhi: Author

– (1931b), "Proceedings of the Sixth Session of the AIWC," 16 November, unpublished, Madras: Author.

– (1932), "Statement Issued on the Report of the India Franchise Committee," unpublished, Delhi: Author.

– (1932-1933), "Proceedings of the Seventh Session of the AIWC," unpublished, Lucknow: Author.

All India Panchayat Parishad (1995), "Panchayat Sandesh," New Delhi: Author.

AVARD (Association of Voluntary Agencies for Rural Development) (1962), "Panchayati Raj as the Basis of Indian Polity: An Exploration into the Proceedings of the Constituent Assembly," Delhi: Author.

Bacchi, Carol Lee (1996), *The Politics of Affirmative Action: Women, Equality and Category Politics,* London: Sage Publications.

Backward Classes Commission (1955), Report of the Backward Classes Commission, New Delhi: Government of India.

Chattopadhyaya, K. (et al.) (1939), *Awakening of Indian Women,* Madras: Everyman's Press.

CWDS (Centre for Women's development Studies) (1989), "The National Perspective Plan for Women: A Critique from die Women's Movement," New Delhi: Unpublished.

– (1995), "Confronting Myriad Oppressions: Voices from the Women's Movement in India: Report of a Consultation, Bombay, 7-9 January 1994.

– (1998), "Symposium on 'Gender, Democracy, and Governance,'" September, New Delhi: Audior.

CSWI (1974), *Towards Equality: Report of the Committee on the Status of Women in India,* New Delhi: Department of Social Welfare, Ministry of Education and Social Welfare, Government of India.

Everett, Jana (1981), *Women and Social Change in India,* New Delhi: Heritage Publishers.

Gallantar, Marc (1984), *Competing Equalities,* New Delhi: Oxford University Press.

Government of India (1988), *National Perspective Plan for Women,* New Delhi: Government of India. *Hindustan Times* (1994), November 30, New Delhi.

— (1996), 14 September, New Delhi.

India Franchise Committee (1932), "Report of the Indian Franchise Committee, Vol. 1" ("Lothian Committee Report"), Delhi: Government of India.

India Today (1996), "The Maturing of a Democracy," August 31. IAWS (Indian Association of Women's Studies) (1996), *The Eighty-first Amendment Hill: A Report,* New Delhi: Author.

Indian Express (1996), 18 July, New Delhi.

— (1996), "India Genderised," 20 July, New Delhi.

IPU (Inter-Parliamentary Union) (1997), "Men and Women in Politics: Democracy still in the making—A World Comparative Study," Inter-Parliamentary Union Series "Reports and Documents," No. 28, Geneva: Author.

Joint Committee on Indian Constitutional Reform (1933-1934), "Report of the Joint Committee on Indian Constitutional Reform, Session 1933-34, Vol. I, Part I," New Delhi: Government of India.

Katzenstein, M.F. (1984), "Feminism and the Meaning of the Vote," *Signs: Journal of Women in Culture and Society,* Vol. 10, No. 1, Autumn.

Keer, D. (1983/1994), *Ambedkar. Life and Mission,* Tokyo: Sen-Ichi shobo & Bombay: Popular Prakashan.

Liddle, Joanna and Rama Joshi (1986), *Daughters of Independence: Gender, Caste and Class in India,* New Delhi: *Kali for Women,* Sed Books Ltd.

Mehta, Haroobhai and Hasmukh Patel (eds.) (1985), *Dynamics of Reservation Policy,* "Foreword" by Justice P. S. Poti, New Delhi: Patriot Publisher.

Memorandum by Seven Women's Organisations (1996), "Memo-randum Presented by Seven Women's Organisations to Parliamentary Select Committee," November 5, New Delhi, unpublished.

Mukherjee, G. (1997), *United in Support of One-Third Reservation of Women,* New Delhi: National Federation of Indian Women.

Pannikar, K.M. and A. Parshad (eds.) (1961), *The Voice of Freedom: Selected Speeches of Pandit Motilal Nehru,* Delhi: Asia Publishing House.

Parliamentary Debates (1989), New Delhi: Government of India.

PFA (Platform for Action) (1995), "Platform for Action and the Beijing Declaration," Fourth World Conference on Women, 4-15 September, Beijing: UN Department of Public Information.

Reddy, Muthulakshmi (1930), *My Experience as a Legislator,* Madras: Light and Life Publishers.

Sawyer, Marian (1999), "A Matter of Simple Justice? Arguments about the Parliamentary Representation of Women," Paper presented at Women's World 99: 7th Interdisciplinary Congress on Women, Tromso, 20-26 June.

Second Backward Classes Commission (1980), "Report of the Second Backward Classes Commission" ("Mandal Commission Report"), New Delhi: Author.

The Hindu (1996), "Reservation and Gender Justice," Madras: 31 December.

Times of India (1996), "Gender Mender," 21 November, New Delhi. *The Pioneer* (1996), July 28, New Delhi.

UNESCO (1983), "Report of the Meeting of Experts on the Participation of Women in Political life and the Means to Increase the Participation," 13-16th December, Lisbon: Author.

8

WOMEN IN PRIS

The Millennium Development Goals (2000) also highlighted the above concern. The goals included the eradication of extreme hunger and poverty, universal primary education, gender equality, empowerment for women, reduction of child mortality, improvement of maternal health, combating HIV/AIDS, malaria and other diseases as well as ensuring environmental sustainability and developing a global partnership for development. All these goals assume additional significance once it is realised that women suffer a lot of deprivation due to lack of achieving the above goals.

As for example, it is well known that majority of the poor in the world are found among women, the percentage of illiteracy among the women is higher than those of men, and access to primary health care is always denied to large percentage of women so on so forth. Realising the above picture, various governments have been taking various measures to improve the conditions of women. Indian government is no exception. Along with various measures such as providing micro-credit to women, the government has also amended the Constitution in 1993 in which the local government institutions have been given a new lease of life to plan and execute the local development planning in which not less than one-third seats have been reserved for women.

The local government institutions are known as panchayats or village councils in India. According to 73rd Constitution Amendment Act, 1993, the panchayats have been given tenure of five years, an election and a finance commission, 29 subjects to plan and execute and a wide based participation at the grassroots level. Interestingly, the 29 subjects given to panchayats include eradicating the poverty, providing primary education as well as the other aspects of well-being of the villagers. In other words, the panchayats have been involved in the task of fulfilling the MDG in a participatory manner. It is our contention that being in the panchayats the women themselves have been involved in the task of the local development (in turn fulfilling the MDG) in a big way and have assumed the role of leadership in Asia in spite of being the beginners in the political process.

In order to test the above hypothesis, the following steps will be followed. First some of the government initiatives including that of panchayats and the structure of those institutions will be discussed followed by a discussion on the impact of the panchayats on the lives of villagers. After that the impact of panchayats on women such as social mobilisation etc. as well as the quality of participation will be taken up. After that some of the factors affecting the quality of participation will be high lighted. A summing up will follow in the last section.

Government Initiatives and Pancahayati Raj Institutions

After Independence, the government of India did take various initiatives to improve the status of women in India. The government initiatives can be characterised as 'Women in Development' 'Gender and Development' and finally 'Rights-based development'. The details of these approaches have been discussed by many.

Suffice to say here that the government of India passed a piece of progressive legislation in 1993 to enable the presence of a 'critical mass' of women in the decentralised decision making process. The above enabling measure can be characterised as the facilitator of 'rights based approach' to women's empowerment. These would address some of the deprivations which face Asian women in general and Indian women in particular. In the next section, some of the features of the panchayats will be discussed.

The Constitution (Seventy-third Amendment Act) was originally initiated by the late Rajiv Gandhi as Sixty-fourth Amendment but got defeated in the Parliament. It was passed after the death of Rajiv Gandhi during the tenure of Narasimha Rao. Since the Act was a landmark in the history of the local government or Panchayati Raj system, it is worthwhile to narrate some of the salient features of the above Act. First of all, the new Panchayati Raj system has a three tier system namely, village panchayat, block panchayat and district panchayat. The size of population in an area determines the size of each tier. In each tenure about 600 District panchayats, 5912 Block panchayats and 2, 31630 *gram* panchayats are formed in which around three million elected representatives interact (Mathew 2000).

The most important feature of the Act from the women's perspective is the reservation of at least one-third of total seats for women both at the functionaries and membership level. Another landmark of the above Act is the importance given to the *gram sabha* or the village assembly, having adults of the panchayat as its members. The panchayats act as an executive body and the *gram sabha* acts as the watchdog to which the panchayats would be accountable. Panchayats have a separate Finance Commission as well as an Election Commission (Mathew 2000). Twenty-nine subjects ranging from agriculture access to primary education, and poverty alleviation have been devolved to the panchayats. Needless to say that the panchayats have been given the tasks of planning, implementing and monitoring those subjects which form the core of millennium development goals. Almost all the schemes meant for poverty alleviation directly such as *Swarnajayanti Gram Swarozgar Yojana* (SGSY), *Gram Samridhi Yojana* etc. are routed through the panchayats, though money is subject to sanction from the Central Government. At present the Employment Guarantee Scheme(EGS) providing 100 days of work to whoever seeks for it has been routed through the panchayats. The main chunk of the panchayat income is utilised on infrastructure(construction of small irrigation structures, source of drinking water, roads, repairing of community buildings etc.), and implementing the welfare schemes (old age and widow pension and maternity benefits). In principle, the panchayat has complete flexibility in allocating these funds.

For the first time, incidentally, the Eleventh Finance Commission (meant for allocating finances to local bodies in different states) has devoted one complete chapter for panchayat's finance. It has recommended an amount of 80,000 million rupees ($1=45 Rupees) for all the panchayats in the country. This amount is meant for five years! Even though it is highly inadequate and fulfills only a fraction of the requirements, it is worthwhile to note that the Commission gives due emphasis on the index of decentralisation. Incidentally, the amount of money given to each village panchayat varies from state to state. For example, in West Bengal a *gram panchayat* gets on an average 1.5 million rupees per year but in a state like Rajasthan it used to get only 60 thousand rupees in the first tenure. In Kerala on the other hand, panchayats were given 35 to 40 per cent of the plan funds to work with. In terms of the financial resources, it amounted to 1025,000 rupees excluding the grant from the central government in one year only (Isaac 2000). Interestingly, the new government at the centre has been reiterating the importance of *panchayati raj* institutions in furthering the rural development *(The Economic Times,* 2004).The government has set up a separate panchayati raj ministry and so far eight consultative meetings have been organised by the ministry to discuss various aspects of the system with a view to make it more efficient than before.

At the same time, it is worth mentioning that the real fiscal decentralisation in terms of deciding to spend money their own way and augmenting local revenue is yet to be with the *panchayati raj* institutions. (The study conducted by the World Bank showed that none but only two states in Kerala and to some extent, Karnataka have devolved the financial and administrative power to the panchayats.)

Impact of the Panchayats on the Lives of Villagers

The first and foremost impact of the above Act has been the widening and strengthening the base of participatory democracy. Because of reservation a large number of women has been elected particularly from the lower socio economic strata. Further, at least 90 per cent of the ward members are from low socio-economic background and those of higher categories are from the high caste/class. Almost all the states have conducted elections at the panchayat level. Some states have conducted the elections for the second time. About three million elected representatives have been elected to these political institutions of which about one million are women as mentioned above. The most significant impact of the legislation has been to bring five million women to active politics within a span of ten years. We are interested to know the impact of the large number of women emerging at the level of grass roots politics which will be taken up at a later stage. (The arithmetic of the five million women can be explained in the following manner. First of all, in each tenure one million women get elected. Secondly for each seat two to three women on an average contest the election. Thus all together five to six million women participate in the political process.)

Yet another impact of the PRIs is the reduction of poverty ratio from 38 per cent to 26 per cent and a slight increase in the rate of urbanisation by 2 per cent between 1991 and 2001. At least a major part of these results can be explained by the implementation of schemes meant for poverty alleviation through panchayats. It is interesting to note that within a span of two years, between 1999 and 2001, about 35793 million rupees were allocated, out of which 72 per cent was utilised. About 2.4 million *Swarozgaries* (self-earners) were assisted of which 44 per cent are women. (By the way, the government has a policy to allocate at least 30 per cent of the total amount of money available for any scheme for women). This forms a significant portion of a total sum of 97650 million rupees, which were allocated for rural development, rural employment and poverty alleviation programmes for the financial year 2001-02.

Unfortunately, the total allocation of financial resources to rural development is not restricted through panchayats, but the schemes routed through these institutions are better targeted, as is pointed out a little later. There are debates regarding the role of decentralisation in reducing the incidence of poverty in a particular area. Johnson (2002), who has reviewed the existing literature on the subject, is of the opinion that there is a weak relationship between decentralisation and the reduction in poverty. Johnson also cites other studies to show that the panchayats provide space for marginalised sections of the people to articulate their needs. Further, it is also observed that the panchayats decisions are not restricted to class.

On the other hand, other experts have shown that the panchayats were responsible for reducing the poverty ratio in India by targeting the delivery of services in a more focused manner.. The authors have done extensive empirical research in West Bengal. They have pointed out that panchayats in West Bengal have targeted land reforms, delivery of agricultural mini-kits, initiating employment programmes and access to credit - all of which have led to poverty alleviation. They have analysed the performance of 89 villages and the time period extends to twenty years. Of course, they agree with the above author in so far as inequality of assets and lack decentralisation is concerned but they also conclude that if the political party in power feels vulnerable at the state level then the anti-poverty programmes are targeted in an efficient manner. The literature on decentralisation and development outcomes is more or less silent regarding the gender. However, if one clubs women with the poor the same analysis as above will be applicable.

Impact of Panchayats on Women

The impact of panchayats on women's lives have been tremendous and varied. In fact, the entry to the panchayats has been described by some as a beginning of a 'silent revolution'. These institutions have influenced social, political and economic lives of the village women in more than one ways as will be seen below.

The sources of data are: (a) A longitudinal study of 235 elected women representatives in panchayats in 22 panchayats spread over three districts of Orissa–an eastern state of India keeping different locales in mind, with an objective of monitoring and capacity building for leadership roles. (The study was conducted for four years. Close monitoring of their performance in the panchayats, and capacity building and other related activities were taken up at the village level.) The project spanned for five years. It was taken up by the Institute of Social Sciences, New Delhi. A survey was conducted among more than 800 elected women representatives (EWRs) from fourteen states who had come to attend an annual programme to celebrate the Women's Political Empowerment Day to New Delhi.

According to various micro-studies including our own observations from the field, about 80-90 per cent women attend the panchayat meetings regularly. (Buch 2000, EKATRA 2003). Given their sheer numbers, one might conclude that democracy has become more participatory than before, at least at the grassroots level. This argument is strengthened by the fact that the socio economic background of these women showed that majority of them come from the lower income group, particularly in the case of membership at the village panchayat level. As for example about eighty five per cent of the EWRs who came to the above programme were from village panchayats and most of them belonged either to Scheduled Caste or Scheduled Tribes or Other Backward Castes—all three castes are at the bottom of the caste hierarchy. So far they have been excluded from the decision-making process. Asked about whether they attended gram sabha or village assembly or not—which is mandatory for the panchayats members—about seventy per cent of them said that they participated the meeting regularly.

In so far as the effective participation of these women is concerned, it is noticed that if they get outside support in terms of NGO intervention, women's groups, or any other social or political movement, the women become relatively more vocal. Their knowledge about the functioning of the panchayats increases (Kumud Sharma nd.). Again the EWRs were asked as to what kind of activities they have taken up during their tenure, they pointed out that ensuring safe drinking water, air distribution of ration, looking after the village sanitation, etc. have been their main priority. Related to the above issue (the impact on the institutional standards) is the question of the 'proxy women'. Let us define the term called proxy women. It is alleged that since many of the women are first timers and are illiterate they depend on their men folk for conducting the panchayat activities. In other words, the women follow their men folk without understanding the implications. Hence they are termed as 'proxy' women.

There are several issues involved here. First of all, the husbands or other male relatives shield them from the panchayat Secretary, and block development officers if they try to harass the women. In fact, some of the state governments have passed a rule that the women elected representatives should be accompanied by their male relatives to the panchayats. This is because in some cases, the secretaries of the panchayats, and male colleagues tried to implicate inexperienced women by asking them to sign blank cheques. Some of the women chiefs went to jails because of their ignorance. In many cases, no-confidence motions were passed in the panchayats, against the women chiefs on false charges.

Again, even if they depend on their husbands, the power relation between husband and wife has already changed because of reservations, particularly because the husband gets a chance to come to the public sphere because of the wife, and in the process the character of patriarchy gets altered. As a result, in many low-income families the husband-wife relationship has not soured. On the other hand, the husband supports the wife and also helps her in her domestic work. Even the other members of the family including the mother-in-law and sister-in-law help her to complete domestic chores. The community leaders of the same caste also support the women candidates.

Besides, those who argue that the women coming to panchayats are all 'proxy' women forget to analyse their socio economic background. Many of the women, even in places like Northern India, are recruited from the white-collar background. Since they are educated and know about the working of the official system they will not remain silent in the panchayat meetings. The same critics assume that all the men who work on behalf of women are corrupt and want to grab power. But in reality, it may not be true.

Finally, the 'proxy' women syndrome is seen only in the first one or two years of the tenure. Gradually, the women become independent, as studies conducted in Karnataka show (Mathew 2002). In the process, they come to know about many modern institutions like courts, block development office, agriculture and other offices, the existence of various officials and some times about the Prime Minister, Chief Ministers and other ministers. Women not only take up issues relating to basic needs, such as, drinking water, availability of doctors and teachers in the villages, which are dear to them, but also general developmental activities, for example, augmenting the income of the panchayats and generating irrigation facilities for the paddy field. The micro-study conducted by the Institute of Social Sciences referred to earlier also shows that not only are the schemes better targeted but also the knowledge about different largesse such as widow and old age pensions, availability of free rice spreads fast among the women because of the presence of women in the panchayats. The women of the neighbourhood act as the 'watchdog' in compelling the elected women to deliver at least some goods. Women of the villages can easily approach the women elected members and can get subsidised rice at any time.

Micro-studies conducted in various parts of the country (Datta 1998, Chattopadhayay and Duflo 2004, Buch 2000) reveal that given a chance the elected women representatives try to engender the developmental activities. For example, in her study on twelve all women panchayats, Datta pointed out that elected women representatives gave more priority to such programmes, which were 'need based' and 'sustainable'.

Thus, we see that, contrary to the popular criticism, the standard of the political institutions at the grassroots level has not been lowered as a result of women's reservations and on the other hand the development process has been engendered to some extent.

Social Mobilisation

Involvement of three million women in grass roots politics by itself has created an expansion of public space as well as that of private space for the women. In the public space they have been allowed to attend the panchayat meetings along with other male colleagues, address gram sabha(village assembly),go to government offices to meet the Block Development Officer and other Line Department personnel. In addition, women get opportunity to network and facilitate conditions for creating the 'social capital'. These conditions get reinforced with another set of forces which also involve a large number of women through micro-credit programme. In the private sphere, their working relations change. The area of cooperation increases at the family level also.

At this point a reference can be made to the implementation of an important scheme, namely, SGSY through the panchayats and its impact on the poor in general, and poor women, in particular. The main features of the scheme are that it lays stress on a few select activities in each developmental block and attends to all aspects of these activities ranging from availability of raw materials, upgrading skills to marketing. The main objective of the scheme is to augment a sustainable income of the *Swarozgaries* (Self-earners) through the above investment. A major component of the scheme was in operation since the eighties in the form of Development of Women and Child in Rural Areas (DWCRA) and had created some successful groups in one of the states of India i.e. Andhra Pradesh.

The scheme was initiated by the government being encouraged by the women's conference in Nairobi. (Of course, the government is not sole agency in initiating the micro finance programme. It is not always routed through the panchayats. World Bank, NABARD and other funding agencies have taken up the micro-credit programme in a big way). The revised scheme has borrowed a few innovative concepts from the Grameen bank, Bangladesh such as flexibility in payment. In addition, the above scheme emphasises social mobilisation of poor in the rural areas.

Several women entrepreneurs have emerged as a result (Government of India, (nd) SGSY: Guidelines). In order gauze the magnitude of women's involvement in micro-credit programme, it would be sufficient to mention here that in Dhaka Declaration of the South Asian Coalition for the Micro-credit Summit1996 articulated the collective consensus among 21 networks which deliver financial services to 4.5 million poor people in Nepal, India, Bangladesh and Pakistan.

Studies conducted on the impact of Self Help groups (SHGs) show that women's group formation, new knowledge and moreover, group mobilisation is capable of creating an alternative to women's traditional status in the family. Group mobilisation also enables women to speak out in the village meetings.The micro-credit scheme has also caught the imagination of various funding agencies as has been referred to earlier. Several studies have been conducted to assess the impact of micro-credit on the status of women. (Kabeer2005). It is agreed that even though it doesn't lead to 'virtuous spiral of economic, social, and political empowerment of women' (Mayoux, 1999), it does lead to empowering some women. In economic terms, it also reduce the vulnerability at the time of natural calamity so that extent the power relation at the family level changes. It is also noticed that if men are involved in the programme women's 'practical needs' are met. In addition, the programme helps in creating the 'social capital' in a community since it encourages collective action. The social mobilisation created by the SGSY/SHGs gets reinforced by another factor namely, women's participation in the political process through campaigning, addressing the meetings and going to cast their votes.

Sen (1983) has mentioned that the family is an arena of cooperation and conflict. It is observed that the reservation of seats in the local governments has increased the areas of cooperation at the family level. The in-laws help the EWRs in finishing the household chores and look after the small children to allow them for attending the panchayat meetings. Some times the husbands take them on bicycles if the panchayat office is far away from their own villages. The results of the Census of India, 2001 shows that the female life expectancy at birth has exceeded that of males marginally. It indicates that women's self-perception has changed and they look after their health and nutritional status.

Similarly the female literacy rate has jumped from being 39 per cent to 53 per cent within a decade. A part of this quantum jump could be explained in terms of the women's excitement to become literate after getting elected. Because it was noticed that women came to National Literacy Mission camp in large number at night to get them selves educated (Saldanaha 1995). Same kind of enthusiasm was noticed when they were asked about getting educated and sending their daughters to schools.

Constraints

The constraints are many. The most important constraint of women's empowerment through panchayat is that they are not a homogenous category. They represent different interest group depending on their class and caste, which get perpetuated through patriarchy. However, one redeeming factor in uniting the women is the access to the basic services such as drinking water, health care facility and education—the practical needs. Secondly predominant trend of Indian culture is still very patriarchal and the women are looked down upon. The EWRs are not taken seriously by their male colleagues and the bureaucrats and they get very scant information about the functioning of the panchayats. In some places, EWRs get over burdened because of household chores as well as that of panchayats. Even though theoretically one may dismiss the notion of 'proxy women' in the real world husbands do take advantage of the ignorant women and work on behalf of them without giving any space.

Again, in many places the women are not immune to systemic corruption though as beginners they are relatively more cautious. Joining politics is still considered 'dirty' and is frowned upon. The community leaders of the village try to choose candidates who are non-performers or would toe their line. The women themselves do not come forward. It is always the family members, or party leaders who push them to contest. The selection of seats for reservations—which are done on a lottery basis and only for one term—does not provide much scope for nurturing a constituency. Even if the women perform well during the first term, the men do not allow them to contest from the same seat again. The panchayat institutions are used as an implementing agency. So the bureaucrats feel that they are the bosses and the first timer leaders are there to obey them.

Violence against women has also increased. A woman chief of the panchayat was killed in one of the states because she defied her husband and called the meeting of the village assembly to discuss the agenda of the budget. In some cases, women representatives do not know that they have been elected from certain constituencies (Rai et. al. 2001). The inter-caste violence has become more acute and so much so that a woman member of a *nagar palika* (township government) in an urban part of Tamil Nadu was murdered because she wanted to bring piped water to her ward. She belonged to a low caste community. In yet another case another woman was forced by the villagers to quit her menial job because it did not suit her status as elected representative.

In a nutshell, men support women in panchayats so long as women do not challenge them to fulfil the 'practical needs'. But men feel threatened as and when the women try to fulfil the 'strategic needs'.

Apart from the specific constraints, the PRIs system as a whole face several structural constraints such as limited power and resources, the absence of appointed cadre and hence, dependence on the state level functionaries and so on. Again the panchayats are given 29 subjects which are included in different departments. But the policy matters are not conveyed to the elected representatives at all. So the elected representatives can not take decisions on their own regarding any subject, such as, agriculture, irrigation, family welfare etc. except only in implementing schemes or acting as the spokespersons of the state governments.

Besides, there are a number of parallel structures such as Janmabhumi programme in Andhra Pradesh, Vana panchayat (Joint Forest Management), Uttar Pradesh and Water Harvesting Management, etc. which try to ignore the involvement of the PRIs. All these systemic constraints also affect the functioning of the women in panchayats.

On the whole, however, it can be argued that reservation of seats in the local council has provided a critical mass of women with an opportunity to empower themselves by being partners in decision making process.

Summing up

The MDG has set various goals such as eradication of poverty which includes access to primary education, sanitation, drinking water, reduction of maternal mortality, empowerment of women etc. to be achieved within a span of a decade. In India, a bold experiment has been taken up in the form of giving more power to the village councils or panchayats which in turn will be responsible to local level of development by involving the entire village. Not less than one-third seats have been reserved for the women in all three tiers of panchayats. In the process, three million elected representatives have been elected per term of five years out of which one million are women. In other words, women and men at the grassroots level are the planners for realising the MDG on their own terms.Debates on decentralisation and poverty are not conclusive but it is agreed that the delivery of basic services become more targeted if they are routed through the panchayats.

The impact of panchayats in the lives of women has been quite significant because it affected women's lives socially, politically and economically since they got enough space to negotiate at the private and public space. They could cross the four boundaries of the hearth which has been assigned to them traditionally. The presence of a large number of women in panchayats as well in the micro-credit programme has led to social mobilisation and created conditions for social capital. The patriarchal values which permeate all the institutions of India also affect the panchayati raj institutions. Women who get elected to the panchayats become subjected to the caste, class and patriarchal values. Domestic violence has increased against women since some of them try challenge the male bastion by entering into politics. The panchayats also suffer from systemic constraints such as lack of financial and administrative power. Corruptions is also rampant among the elected representatives.

Nonetheless a space has been created for Indian women to emerge as a formidable force to fight for social justice and human rights.

REFERENCES

Bardhan, P. and Dilip Mukherjee. 2004. 'Poverty Alleviation efforts of Panchayats in West Bengal', *Economic and Political Weekly*, 39 (9).

Bose, Ashish. 2001. 'Promoting Health and Family Planning through Panchayats', in Bidyut Mohanty (ed.), *Women and Political Empowerment* 1999, Women's Political Empowerment Day Celebrations on Panchayats, Women and Family Welfare, ISS, New Delhi.

Buch, Nirmala. 2000. 'Panchayats and Women', in George Mathew (ed.), *Status of Panchati Raj in the States of India. Concept, New Delhi,* Chattopadhyay, R. and Esther Duflo. 2004. 'Impact of

Reservation in Panchayati Raj: Evidence from a Nationwide Randomised Experiment', *Economic and Political Weekly.*

Datta, Bishakha. 1998. *And Who will make Chapatis? A Case Study of All Women Panchayats in Maharashtra,* Calcutta: Stree Publications.

Dreze, J. and Mamta Murthy. 2001. 'Fertility, Education and Development: Evidence from India', *Population and Development Review,* 27 (1).

EKATRA. 2003. *Women and Governance, Reimagining the State,* New Delhi: EKATRA.

Government of India. 2001. *Provisional Population Totals,* India Registrar General, New Delhi.

Government of India. 2001-02. *Economic Survey,* Ministry of Finance, New Delhi.

Government of India. 2002-03. *Annual Report* Ministry of Rural Development, New Delhi.

Government of India (nd) SGRY: Guidelines.

Haq, M., Human Development Report. 1997. *Human Development Report,* United Nations Development Programme, New York: Oxford University Press.

Issac, T.M. Thomas. 2003. 'Women Elected Representatives in Kerela (1995-2000): From Symbolism to Empowerment', Paper presented at the workshop on 'Women's Empowerment through Seventy-third Constitution Amendment Act', Institute of Social Sciences, 20-21, October, New Delhi.

Johnson, Craig. 2002. 'Decentralisation and Poverty: Exploring the Contradictions', *The Indian Journal of Political Science,* 63 (1).

Kaushal, Avdhash and Bindu Kalia. 2003. 'Uttaranchal: Betrayal of grassroots democracy', *Panchayati Raj Update* (March).

Mathew, George. 2000 (ed.) *The Status of Panchayati Raj in India,* New Delhi: Concept Publishing House.

Mathew, George. 2002. *Panchayati Raj: From Legislation to Movement,* New Delhi: Concept Publishing House.

Mohanty, Bidyut. 1998? 'Women and Family', in Tan Chung (ed.) *Across the Himalayan Gap, India's Quest for Understanding China,* New Delhi: Gyan Publishing House.

Mohanty, Bidyut and Vandana Mohajan. 2004. 'Women's Empowerment in the Context of the Constitution (73rd and 74th Amendments) Acts 1992: An Assessment', Background paper in ISS and SAP Canada (2003) (ed.) *A Decades of Women 's Empowerment through Local Government in India Workshop Report,* New Delhi: ISS.

Mohanty, Manoranjan and Mark Seldon. 2003. 'Reconceptualising Local Democracy: I and II Preliminary reflections on democracy, power and resistance', *Panchayati Raj Update* (April and May).

Mohbub Haq, Human Development Centre. 2000. *Human Development in South Asia 2000: The Gender Question,* Karachi: Oxford University Press.

Pal Mahi. 2002. *Swarnajayanti Gram Swarozgar Yojana, Evolution, Assessment and Future Prospects,* Kurukshetra (June). Government of India.

Rai, Manoj et al. (eds). 2001. *The State of Panchayats: A Participatory Perspective,* New Delhi: Sanskriti.

Rai, Sirin. 1994. 'Gender Issues in China: A Survey', *China Report,* 30(4)

Saldanha, Denzil. 1995. 'Literacy Campaigns in Maharashtra and Goa, Issues, Trends and Direction', *Economic and Political Weekly* (20 May).

Sen, A.K. 1983. 'Conflict in Access to Food', *Mainstream,* 21 (8).

Sethi, Geeta. 2004. (ed.) *Fiscal Decentralisation to Rural Governments in India,* The World Bank, New Delhi: Oxford Univ. Press.

Sharma, Kumud (ND). 'From Representation to Presence, The Paradox of Power and Powerlessness of Women in PRIS', Occasional Paper, CWDS, New Delhi.

Vijayanthi, K. N. 2002. 'Women's Empowerment through Self-Help Groups: A Participatory Approach', *Indian Journal of Gender Studies,* 9(2).

BIBLIOGRAPHY

Agrawal, Bina (1997). Bargaining and Gender Relations within and beyond the Household, *Feminist Economics,* 3 (1), pp. 454-87.

Agnihotri, I. and Mazumdar, V. 1995. Changing Terms of Political Discourse: Women's Movement in India. 1970s-1990s. *Economic and Political Weekly* 30(29): 1869-1878.

Banerjee, N.K. 1995. "Grassroot Empowerment (1975-1990): A Discussion Paper", Occasional Paper No. 22. New Delhi: Centre for Women's Development Studies.

Batliwala, S. 1993. *Empowerment of Women in South Asia: Concepts and Practices.* Delhi: Asian South Pacific Bureau of Adult Education.

Berry, K. (2003) 'Developing Women: The Traffic in Ideas about Women and their Needs in Kangra, India' in Sivaramakrishnan, K. & Agarwal, Arun (ed.) *Regional Modernities: The Cultural Politics of Development in India.* Stanford University Press, Stanford, California, pp.75-98.

Bhasin, K. 1984. The Why and How of Literacy for Women: Some Thoughts in the Indian Context. *Convergence* 27(4): 37-43.

Bhasin, K. and Agarwal, B., eds. 1984. *Women and Media: Analysis, Alternatives and Action.* New Delhi: *Kali for Women.*

Boserup, Ester (1990). "Economic Change and the role of women" in *Persistent Inequalities: Women and World development,* (ed) Eren Tinker, Chapter-2, Oxford U. press, New York.

Burkey, S. (1993) *People First: A Guide to Self-Reliant Participatory Rural Development.* Sed Books, London.

Burra, N., Deshmukh-Ranadive, J. & Murthy, R. (2005) (ed.) *Micro-Credit, Poverty and Empowerment: Linking the Triad.* Sage Publications, New Delhi.

Byrne, Eileen M1993, Women and Science: The Snark Syndrome, Falmer Press, Bristol.

Calmen, L. 1992. *Toward Empowerment: Women and Movement Politics in India.* Boulder: Westview Press.

Chakravarty, R. 1980. *Communist in the Indian Women's Movement.* New Delhi: People's Publishing House.

Desai, N. 1977. *Women in Modern India.* Second Edition. Bombay: Vora and Company.

Dighe, Anita, Ila Patel, Sadhna Saxena, Probha Krishnan, Azra Razzack and Ilina Sen. 1996. *Deconstructing Literacy Primers.* New Delhi: National Institute of Adult Education.

Edwards, Paul N. (1996). The closed world: Computers and the politics of discourse in cold war America, Cambridge, Mass: MIT Press.: 167-72.

Everett, J. M. 1979. *Women and Social Change in India.* New York: St. Martin's Press.

Faulkner, Wendy. (2000). The power *and* the pleasure? A research agenda for "making gender stick" to engineers. *Science, Technology, & Human Values, 25(1),* 88-120.

Fernandez, A. P. (1994) *The Myrada Experience: Alternate Management Systems for Savings and Credit of the Rural Poor.* MYRADA, Bangalore, India.

Fernando, J. L. (2006) *Microfinance: Perils and Prospects.* Routledge, London.

Fisher, T. & Sriram. M.S. (2002) (ed.) *Beyond Micro-Credit: Putting Development Back into Micro-Finance.* Vistaar Publications, New Delhi.

Friedmann, J. (1992) *Empowerment: The Politics of Alternative Development.* Blackwell, Cambridge, USA.

Gandhi, N. and Shah, N. 1991. *The Issues at Stake: Theory and Practice in the Contemporary Women's Movement in India.* New Delhi: *Kali for Women.*

Gladstone, M. 1994. Feminist Research Methodology from Women's Movement Experiences. *Bulletin of Madras Development Seminar Series* 24(11): 470-479.

Government of India. 1964. *Committee on Differentiation of Curricula for Boys and Girls.* New Delhi: Ministry of Education and Social Welfare.

Government of India. 1974. *Towards Equality.* Report of the Committee on the Status of Women in India. New Delhi: Department of Social Welfare, Ministry of Education and Social Welfare.

Government of India. 1986. *National Policy on Education - 1986.* New Delhi: Department of Education, Ministry of Human Resource Development.

Government of India. 1988a. *Shramshakti.* A Report of the National Commission on Self Employed Women and Women in the Informal Sector. New Delhi.

Government of India. 1988b. *Mahila Samakhya* (Education for Women's Equality). New Delhi: Department of Education, Ministry of Human Resource Development.

Hassan, S. 1992. Muslim Women's Struggle for Education, Social and Political Equality: A Historical Perspective. *Man and Development* 14(2): 27-33.

Karlekar, M. 1986. Kadambini and the Bhadralok: Early Debates over Women's Education in Bengal. *Economic and Political Weekly* 21(17): WS9-WS24.

Kishwar, M. 1985a. Gandhi on Women. *Economic and Political Weekly* 20(40): 1691-1702.

Kishwar, M. 1985b. Gandhi on Women. *Economic and Political Weekly* 20(41): 1753-58.

Kishwar, M. 1986. Arya Samaj and Women's Education: Kanya Mahavidyalaya Jalandhar. *Economic and Political Weekly* 21(17): WS25-WS32.

Krishna Raj, M. 1988. Women's Studies: Case for a New Paradigm. *Economic and Political Weekly* 23(18): 892-94.

Liddle, J. and Joshi, R. 1985. Gender and Imperialism in British India. *Economic and Political Weekly* 20(43): WS72-WS78.

Mazumdar, V. 1976. Social Reform Movement in India from Ranade to Nehru. *Indian Women: From Purdah to Modernity.* Delhi: Vikas Publishing House.

Mazumdar, V. 1987. Education, Development and Women's Liberation: Contemporary Debates in India. In: R. Ghosh and M. Zachariah, eds., *Education and the Process of Change.* New Delhi: Sage Publications.

Mazumdar, V. 1989. Research and Women's Development: Seeds of Change, A Case Study of the ICSSR Programmes of Women's Studies. *Prashasnika* 18(1-4): 21-44.

Mazumdar, V. and Sharma, K. 1979. Women Studies: New Perceptions and the Challenges. *Economic and Political Weekly* 14(3): 113-120.

Pandhe, S. 1988. Women's Studies and Women's Movement. *Economic and Political Weekly* 23(40): 2049-50.

Patel, I. and Dighe, A. 1997. *Gender Issues in Literacy Education.* Working paper 108. Anand: Institute of Rural Management.

Patel, S. 1988. Construction and Reconstruction of Women in Gandhi. *Economic and Political Weekly* 23(8): 377-87.

Poonacha, V. 1994. Gendered Stp: Review of Two Decades of Women's Movement and Women's Studies. *Economic and Political Weekly* 29(13): 725-28.

Ramdas, L. 1990. Women and Literacy: A Quest for Justice *Convergence* 23(1): 27-40.

Shah, K. 1984. Historical Antecedents. In: *Women's Liberation and Voluntary Action.* Delhi: Ajanta Publications.

Shah, N., Lokhandwala, S. and Pathak, I. 1987. *An Assessment of the School Text-Books Published by Gujarat State School Text-Book Board under NPE.* Ahmedabad: Ahmedabad Women's Action Group.

Sharma, K. 1991-1992. Grassroots Organisations and Women's Empowerment: Some Issues in the Contemporary Debate. *Samya Shakti: A Journal of Women's Studies* 6: 26.

Sharma, K. 1992. Contemporary Women's Movement in India: Its Dialectics and Dilemmas. *Indian Journal of Social Sciences* 5(1): 1-31.

Thomas, B. (1985) *Politics, Participation, and Poverty: Development through Self-Help in Kenya.* Westview Press, Boulder, USA.

Titus (2002) 'Costs in Micro-finance: What do Urban Self-help Groups Tell Us?' in Fisher, T. & Sriram. M.S. *Beyond Micro-Credit: Putting Development Back into Micro-Finance.* Vistaar Publications, New Delhi, pp. 199.

Uphoff, N.T. & Esman, M. J. (1984) *Local Organisations: Intermediaries in Rural Development.* Cornell University Press, Ithaca, USA.

Usha Devi, M. D. 1992. Research Perspective for Understanding Women's Education. *Economic and Political Weekly* 27(24-25) 1279-1282.

Vyas, A. and Singh, S. (compiled). 1993. *Women's Studies in India: Information Sources, Services and Programmes.* New Delhi: Sage Publications.

Walby, S. (1990) *Theorising Patriarchy.* Blackwell, Oxford.

Wilson, K. (2002) 'The New Microfinance: An Essay on the Self-Help Group Movement in India'. *Journal of Microfinance,* Vol. 4, No. 2, pp. 217-45.

INDEX

D

E

F

G

H

I

J

K

L

M

N

O

P

R

S

T

U

V

W